William P. Treacy

Irish Scholars of Penal Days

Glimpses of Their Labors on the Continent of Europe

William P. Treacy

Irish Scholars of Penal Days
Glimpses of Their Labors on the Continent of Europe

ISBN/EAN: 9783337126131

Printed in Europe, USA, Canada, Australia, Japan

Cover: Foto ©ninafisch / pixelio.de

More available books at **www.hansebooks.com**

IRISH SCHOLARS

OF

The Penal Days:

GLIMPSES OF THEIR LABORS

ON

THE CONTINENT OF EUROPE.

BY

Rev. William P. Treacy.

"As gold in the furnace He hath proved them, and as a victim of a holocaust He hath received them, and in time there shall be respect had to them."
Wisd. III., 6.

FR. PUSTET,
Printer to the Holy Apostolic See and the S. Congregation of Rites.

FR. PUSTET & CO.,

50 & 52 BARCLAY ST., | 204 VINE STREET
NEW YORK. | CINCINNATI.

H. BARTSCH,
PRINTER & ELECTROTYPER,
51 Beekman Street,
New York.

RIGHT REV. MICHAEL J. O'FARRELL, D.D.,

BISHOP OF TRENTON,

Who so admirably represents in his own person the Virtues, Learning, Eloquence, and Patriotism of the Irish Prelates, Priests and Students of the Penal Days, this Work is respectfully and affectionately inscribed by the author.

CONTENTS.

	PAGE.
INTRODUCTION	
THE PENAL DAYS IN IRELAND	1
PATRIOTISM OF IRISH PRIESTS IN PENAL TIMES	16
IRISH PROFESSORS IN PENAL DAYS	37
IRISH CHAPLAINS WITH THE IRISH BRIGADES	50
IRISH CHAPLAINS IN EUROPEAN COURTS	56
IRISH HAGIOLOGY	62
IRISH COLLEGES FOUNDED ABROAD	71
ST. ISIDORE'S COLLEGE, ROME	80
THE IRISH DOMINICAN CONVENT, ON MONT-CESAR, LOUVAIN	93
THE IRISH DOMINICAN CONVENT, LISBON	104
THE CONVENT OF SAINT ANTHONY OF PADUA, LOUVAIN	109
THE IRISH COLLEGE AT PARIS	134
THE PASTORAL COLLEGE, LOUVAIN	147
PONT-A-MOUSSON, LORRAINE	161
SOME IRISH AUTHORS OF THE PENAL DAYS	168
IRISH GENIUS ABROAD	182
GRAVES OF IRISH EXILES ON THE CONTINENT OF EUROPE	205
A PROTESTANT CRITIC IN CATHOLIC COUNTRIES	213
IRISH MONKS IN CORNWALL	226
THE LAST VICTIM OF ELIZABETH'S REIGN IN IRELAND	260
DOMINICUS DE ROSARIO	275
OUR LADY OF MONTAIGU	294
PILGRIMS AT MONTAIGU	303

CONTENTS. (POETRY.)

	PAGE.
A Hymn to Faith	47
Lines to Irish Students	48
The Homes of Old Tipperary	49
The Sword Alone	55
The Cross	60
When Night Comes On	61
The Patriot's Address	69
Erin, Dear!	79
Her Rosary of Wells	91
Good Night	92
Erin's Prayer	103
The Irish Peasant's Song	107
Refuge of the Wretched	108
Lines on the Death of Maurice Eustace, S. J.	130
Our Crosses and Shamrocks	132
Memories of the Continent	146
There is Hope for Erin	160
The Isle of the Living	166
The Monks of Erin	180
Ave Maria!	204
Shadows	209
To a Singing Bird by the Sea	223
The Fishermen's Song	224
Lines on Finding a Singing Bird Dead in the Snow	252
Kind Hearts	253
An Ode to St. Isidore	254
I Roam a Land of Golden Dreams	256
I'll Tell my Beads	257
Be not Afraid	258
Holy Spirit, Come and Guide Me	259
Rome	266
The Holy Viaticum	267
Our Lady of Sorrow	269

The World	270
Come, and See the Capitol	271
To Aubrey De Vere	272
A Soul in Sin	273
The Bard	274
Sweet Night	284
Up, Up, and Mount for Evermore	285
I am weary of the City	286
In the Country	287
Mater Inviolata	288
Oh, thus the Bards	289
On Smiles	290
What is Love?	291
Yea, Lord, Thou knowest that I Love Thee	292
World-Music	310
The Beauty of Childhood	311
Ocean Waves	312
Apostles Love the Race of Man	313
On Seeing the Capitol	314
No Unalloyed Happiness on Earth	315
To a Priest	316
No More We'll Sail O'er a Troubled Sea	317
The Old Year is not Dying	318
Mother's Beads	319
If Thou wert not my Love, O! God	320
There is always Light in Heaven	321
St. Mary Magdalen	322
Fair Spouse of Christ	323
To the Queen of May	324
Dark of Eye, and Dark of Skin	325
A People's Prayer	326
Faith, Hope, and Love	327
My Soul is like yon Glowing Fire	328
Lines to Sister Angeline	329
A Hymn to the Queen of May	330
Sacred is the Glorious Banner	331
The Bell is the Voice of God	332

On Dust, on Clay, We Daily Tread	333
A Voice in the Soul	334
Lines on the Death of an Irish Maiden in Exile	334
My Last Hymn	335
Rome, the Mother of all Churches	336
My Secrets	337
Hope On	338
To a Beach Bird	339
My God, I'm Tired of Worldly Thoughts	340
The Bird at Steinberg Chapel	341
Weary Pilgrims	343
'Gainst Winds and Tides	344
The Dying Child to his Mother	345
Poetic Inspiration	346
To the Rev. Abram J. Ryan	347
To America	348
Love of Ireland	350
Irish Bards	351
A Home Rule Song	352
This is my Native Land	353
Sweet Lyre, Adieu	354

PREFATORY.

WHILE the author of these pages was a student at Louvain, he spent a great part of his recreation time in gathering up historical points connected with the history of the Irish Students and Schools of the Penal Days. He then had no idea of writing a book on the subject. He merely wished for some information for his own private satisfaction. It was a real pleasure for him to learn how many of his dear countrymen, in evil times, rose and shone in "the land of the stranger." It was with no little enthusiasm that he entered the chapel of St. Anthony's Convent, where Ward, Colgan, Fleming, O'Cleary, Conry and Mooney were wont to pray for the Island of their love. With uncovered head he entered the ruins of the Irish Dominican House, on Mont-Cesar. Great, too, was his joy when he discovered the site of the Pastoral College—that College which for so many years had been the asylum of the brave secular priests of Ireland.

In the pursuit of his pleasing and, he hopes, useful pastime, he received every encouragement from some of the distinguished archeologists then at Louvain. Some of these gentlemen lent him rare books and documents in which references to his favorite study could be found. In the course of time he had amassed a great pile of notes. These, for convenience sake, he tried to embody in a series of articles.

Some time ago a few of his literary friends, gentlemen for whose judgment he had a high regard, urged him to send several of his papers on the Irish Students and Colleges to some of the Catholic journals or magazines. He did so, and found that they were well received by the public and praised by able literary men. Most of those printed in this country were copied by the Catholic Press of London and that of the leading cities in Ireland. The encouragement thus generously given on all sides makes him bold to think that the collection he now prints in this volume is not wholly devoid of merit. If love and reverence for the sacerdotal heroes of the Penal Times; if sympathy with his subject; if a desire to glorify Old Catholic Ireland; if a longing to do something for the scattered sons of St. Patrick could enable him to write well, then indeed he ought to have succeeded beyond measure.

It is a sad fact that full justice has never been done the Irish continental students. The story of the Irish Brigade at the defense of Cremona, and their large share in the battles of Blenheim, Ramillies and "loved Fontenoy" are familiar to all; but, alas, how few know anything about the devoted and pale-faced students who, in foreign lands, within cloistered walls and silent cells, wept and spoke and wrote and prayed for bleeding Ireland. The names of Sarsfield, O'Brien and Dillon rise "like a litany to our lips," while even those of Conry, French, Wadding, Talbot and Colgan sound strange and meaningless in our ears. Yet Conry was drawn from his cherished solitude and favorite studies through love for Ireland and its creed, and was tossed about in the tempest-lashed waves that destroyed King Phillip's friendly flotilla, while as yet the Irish soldier-chiefs were in the court of Elizabeth or were feasted by the national enemy at Dublin Castle; yet French left peace and friends and honorable station behind him to become the soul of the great confederacy, and to partake of all its risks and toils and dangers; yet Colgan worked hard day and night, and wasted his life in old, dusty libraries in France and Belgium in order to preserve, or increase ever so little, the glory of the Island of Saints; yet Wadding and Talbot created a great interest in the Irish Confederation at Madrid, Paris and Rome. Talbot procured money at Madrid and "great guns" at Paris; Wadding obtained at Rome, money, muskets, a nuncio to Ireland, and the Papal benediction for the war.

As a student I am happy and proud to be able to say that while Erin's exiled warriors were cutting their way to fame, rank and glory upon the reddest battle-fields of Spain, France, Italy, Austria and the Netherlands, her scholars were bravely climbing the steep, rough hills of science and sanctity in classic halls at Antwerp and Louvain, at Lisle, Douay, Bordeaux, Rouen and St. Omer, at Salamanca and Alcala, at Coimbra and Prague, and at St. Isidore's at Rome.

The penal days are gone, and gone, we trust, forever. The noble Irish students who devoted their time and energies, their talent and their lives, to the service of God and fatherland, have long since been crowned at the gates of Paradise and may now be seen in that vast multitude whom no man can count; still this is an age of historic justice, an age in which honor is given where honor is due. So old Ireland cannot allow the names or the memory of her dearest, holiest, grandest sons— her continental students of the penal days—to pass away into the dark, cold sea of oblivion, "unwept, un- honored and unsung." She bids her bards strike the saddest chords in her mournful lyre above their graves; she bids her orators rise into the loftiest regions of their art when they name their names or refer to their deeds; she encourages her pilgrim-sons to seek in old European libraries and churchyards for everything that can add one ray to the glory that surrounds them. Ireland is a grateful land, a land with a great heart and a wonderful memory. A cup of cold water given to one of her children will be remembered with feelings of deep and lasting gratitude. She never ceases to bless the hand that is raised in defence of her, however weak that hand may be. How then can she ever forget the noble and generous and gifted army of students who with voice and potent pen defended her rights, proclaimed her ancient glory, aroused the sympathy of the nations for her, and made peoples alien to her in tongue, though not in creed or feeling, weep over the sad, sad story of her wrongs?

The memory of the just man is eternal. Though he has to carry his cross and bear his heavy load of sorrow during life, after death an impartial posterity will love and revere his name, and recount with pride the glories of his works and pains. Tyrants may have crushed him beneath their heels, vile tongues may have slandered him, still, when his white bones are slumbering in the gloom of the grave, good men and true will be found to do him right and to keep his memory ever fresh and green. The Irish Students of the Penal Days were just men, who suffered persecution for justice' sake. Their only crime was fidelity to their consciences and an ardent love of the land of their birth. Though many of them died in strange lands, still their epitaphs have not been left unwritten. Slabs and marble crosses, commemorating their virtues and learning, may be found at Paris and Madrid, at Lisbon, Alcala, Louvain and Rome. When will the Irish People raise a National Monument in grateful remembrance of them? Has Glasnevin no spot for a pillar bearing the great names of FRENCH, WADDING, WARD, LOMBARD, FITZSIMON, COLGAN, ARCHER, CONRY, STANIHURST, WHITE, O'CLERY and O'DALY? From the depths of Ireland's generous soul, from the love of Ireland's great heart; from the lips of all "the sea-divided Gaels," I hear one loud, triumphant— "YES!"

THE PENAL DAYS IN IRELAND.

> "Oh, Holy Cross, dear symbol of the dread
>   Death of our Lord,
> Around thee long have slept our Martyr-dead,
>   Sward over sward,
> An hundred Bishops I myself can count
>   Among the slain;
> Chiefs, Captains, rank and file, a shining mount
>   Of God's ripe grain."

THE history of the Penal Time is one long psalm, full of sad pathos and mournful music. It is like the wail of Rachel, or the loud cry of Israel by the waters of Babylon. It is truly the "blackest picture" in the history of a generous and faithful people. It is no wonder that our Davis was inspired by it to sing the saddest of his songs. Yet to us, who possess the true Faith, that pearl without price, there is something in the sound, in the echo of its sorrowful strains that causes our hearts to beat with joy, that tempts our lips to pour forth the glad, triumphant notes of the old *Te Deum* of Ambrose and Augustine:

> "We praise Thee, God,
> And we acknowledge Thee to be the Lord;
>   All the earth
> Doth worship Thee, the Father Everlasting."

It is too true that it recalls to our minds the sufferings of the Catacombs; the martyrdom of Agnes and Cecilia, of Sebastian and Theodore, of Ignatius, Polycarp and Callistus ; but it is also true, oh, how gloriously true ! that it recalls the fervor, the constancy, the heroism, the victories of the first ages of Christianity. Though it be sad to us as the "Conquest of Alhama" to the Moors, it touches us like the stirring words of Riga, it fires us and incites us like the war-song of the Swiss. It is something more to us than a mere martyrology, than the dark and hapless annals of injustice, persecution and wrong. It is the story of heroic and saintly lives, it is the *Vexilla Regis* of our country. It brings before us the deeds of some of Ireland's most devoted and most patriotic sons ; it places before us the bright picture of Ireland's most glorious martyrs and confessors, of Ireland's most laborious and gifted students and scholars.

It shows us what sacrifices our fathers were ready and willing to make for the sake of knowledge and religion. It tells us how they kept alive in caverns and on solitary cliffs the torches of Science and Sanctity. It shows us what the Irish priesthood did and suffered for love of of their country and religion. It teaches us to prize and cherish the Holy Faith, handed down to us at the cost of toil and blood and tears. It incites us to purity of life and nobility of action. It points out to us what we may become, for

"Lives of great men all remind us
We can make our lives sublime."

Whether we consider the Irish student as a youth sitting beneath the vines of Italy reading Virgil or Homer, or as a professor of theology or philosophy in some celebrated school, or whether we consider him as a missionary on one of his native hills, with a price set on his head and spies and blood-hounds on his track, or as a lonely prisoner in Birmingham Tower, or the Tower of London, his story is a grand, strange story. The diary of the Irish student in foreign halls and monasteries; the diary of the Irish student crossing dangerous seas in order to enter on his mission of death ; his wanderings in wolf-infested woods and on barren moors : his hours of solitude in gloomy caves and ruined cabins; his arrest, conviction and glorious martyrdom, should afford subjects for the poet's pen and the painter's brush, and should be treated with love and reverence by the simple historian, by the narrator of cold, dry and common facts.

The life of every true missionary is hard, perilous and laborious. He must be ready to work and travel as well during the night as during the day. He can never think of himself or his own convenience while there is a duty to perform, while there is a soul to save. He must be willing to suffer from fatigue, from hunger, from cold. He must hourly take up his cross and follow closely in the footsteps of his Divine Master. But when his mission is beset with dangers and difficulties; when the great ones of the land hunt him down ; when he is considered as an enemy of the State, and his labors and sacrifices condemned as treasons; then is his life filled with sorrow and affliction, though his every act becomes an act of heroism. The Irish priests and Prelates all through the Penal days had such a mission. Neither in China nor Japan, nor in the wilds of Africa, had missionaries of Christianity more to suffer, nor more difficulties to encounter, than the Irish priests had during the gloomy hours of sectarian persecution. They led lives of poverty and suffering, and died in most cases either in loathsome prisons or on the shameful scaffold. Kings and queens were their enemies, law was no protection for them, justice was no shield for them, judges were their accusers, exile and death were their heirlooms. Their altars were cast down, their churches were burned, their people impoverished, the Cross they loved was hated, their Faith was proscribed. Whole armies with naked swords were sent to cut them down, ships were built to carry them off to penal settlements, they were deprived of all civil rights, they were outlaws in the land that gave them birth, they were forced to hide in caverns by the seaside, to sleep in woods with the fox and wolf, to beg a crumb to eat from a robbed and down-trodden peasantry. No one could with impunity assist or harbor them. In secret they said Mass, in secret they attended the sick and dying, in secret they blessed the marriage, and in secret they baptized or blessed the grave. Terrors of every description surrounded them; they lived in disguise, and continually walked in the shadow of death. But nothing could chill their fervor, nor daunt their courage. They feared neither fire, nor persecution, nor the sword. "Their conscience was their crown." They loved suffering and they sighed for martyrdom. They knew that Stephen had been stoned, Paul beheaded, and Peter crucified. If they were the true followers of Christ they knew well that the servant is not greater than his master, and that, as Jesus had to suffer so that He might enter into His glory, so they, too, would have to pass through many tribulations before they could enter the Kingdom of Heaven. They knew that their cause was just and holy, and that triumph it would in the end, for the gates of hell can never prevail against Christ's Spouse.

"Your Religion, noble countrymen," wrote the patriotic Bishop French, in his exile home, "your Religion is the sole cryme for which you suffer (blessed forever be the name of God for this). Your Religion hath stirred up this tempest, which ought not to terrifye you over much, seeing the Apostles, our first Captains and Leaders in the holy cause, those darlings of God, endured hard things for Religion: prisons, whippings, contumelies, and all sorts of vexations were to them delights and consolations. They, after 'being scurged, went from the sight of the councell rejoycing, because they were accounted worthy to suffer reproach for the name of Jesus.' Doe not therefore feare all that men can doe against you, while with teares and patience you march under the purple Standart of Crucify'd Jesus, for in the end the day and victory will be yours; feare not the power of men in this glorious tryall: there be more with you then against you (Legions of Angells, though you see them not). Those heavenly hostes are pitching theire tents round about you. Hee that led the children of Israel out of Egypt in wonders through the Redd Sea, never wants power to deliver you; waite for his good tyme, for hee will come."

These noble words, written in Ireland's darkest hour, written by a venerable Prelate, far from his people and his country, in our day have been verified. The God who led the Israelites through the Red Sea; who gave them pure waters from flinty rocks; who gave them manna white from heaven; who consoled them while their harps were hung on the willows and they wept by the waters of the Babylon; who sent them mighty men; who sent them angels to fight their battles, to mow down their enemies; who gave them prophets, wonder-working prophets, with fingers of light, to point out to them the Promised Land, has graciously conducted Ireland out of the darkness and misery of religious persecution and oppression, out of chains and bondage, into the glorious light, and peace, and joy, and freedom of conscience. Now, as in the days of yore, in the days of Ireland's saints and doctors, of Ireland's heroes and sages, vast and beautiful cathedrals are found in every Irish city; chapels with golden crosses stand on every hill-top; monasteries are hidden away in all Ireland's valleys; and colleges and schools are opened in every town and village. Old abbeys have arisen from their ruins "with pomp such as glows round a sunrise in summer." Again the gemmed-chalices are lifted by ten thousand hands immaculate; again the virgin-daughters of Erin are free to dwell in peaceful convent homes, to follow in the footsteps of Bridget of Kildare; again the hymn of love and praise to God Most High is heard ringing from shore to shore.

The illustrious Father Thomas Burke, the eloquent son of St. Dominick, thus speaks in his lecture on "The History of Ireland, as Told in Her Ruins," of the conduct of Irish priests during the three centuries preceding the fifteenth: "During these three hundred years, the combat for Ireland's nationality was still continued. The O'Neill, the O'Brien, the O'Donnell, the McGuire, the O'More, kept the national sword waving in the air. The Franciscans and the Dominicans cheered them, entered into their feelings, and they could not be said to be more Irish than the Irish themselves, because they were the heart's blood of Ireland. They were the light of the national councils of the chieftains of Ireland, as their historians were the faithful annalists of the glories of these days of combat. They saw the trouble; and yet, for three hundred years the Franciscan and Dominican had not discovered what his real mission to Ireland was. But at the end of the three hundred years came the fifteenth century. Then came the cloud of religious persecution over the land. All the hatred that divided the Saxon and the Celt, on the principle of nationality, was now heightened by the additional hatred of religious discord and division; and Irishmen, if they hated the Saxon before, as the enemy of Ireland's nationality from the fifteenth century, hated him with an additional hatred, as the enemy of Ireland's faith and Ireland's religion."

Father Burke, after some remarks, which though eloquent, are not pertinent to the subject of this article, continues: "Well, my friends, then came the hour of the ruin of the dear old convents of the Franciscans and Dominicans. Their inmates were driven out at the point of the sword; they were scattered like sheep over the land. Five pounds was the price set upon the head of the friar or priest—the same price that was set upon the head of a wolf. They were hunted throughout the land; and when they fled for their lives from their convent homes, the Irish people opened their hearts and said: 'Come to us, Soggarth Aroon.' Throughout the length and breadth of the land they were scattered, with no shelter but the canopy of Heaven; with no Sunday sacrifice to remind the people of God; no Mass celebrated in public, and no Gospel preached; and yet they succeeded for three hundred years in preserving the glorious Catholic Faith, that is as strong in Ireland to-day as ever it was. These venerable ruins tell the tale of the nation's woe, of the nation's sorrow. As long as it was merely a question of destroying a Cistercian or a Benedictine Abbey, there were so few of these in the land that the people did not feel it much. But when the persecution came upon the *Bhreahir*, as the friar was called—the men whom everybody knew—the men whom everybody came to look up to for consolation in affliction or in sorrow; when it came upon him—then it brought sorrow and affliction to every village, to every little town—to every man in Ireland. There were, at this time, upwards of eighty convents of religious—Franciscans and Dominicans—in Ireland, that numbered very close upon a thousand priests of each order. There were nearly a thousand Irish Franciscans, and nearly a thousand Irish Dominican priests, when Henry began his persecution. He was succeeded, after a brief interval of thirty years, by his daughter Elizabeth. How many Dominicans, do you think, were then left in Ireland? There were a thousand, you say? Oh! God of Heaven, there were only four of them left—only four. And all the rest of these heroic men had stained their white habit with the blood that they shed for God and for their country. Twenty thousand men it took Elizabeth, for as many years as there were thousands of them, to try to plant the seedling of Protestantism on Irish soil. The ground was dug as for a grave; the seed of Protestantism was cast into that soil; and the blood of the nation was poured in, to warm it and bring it forth. It never grew—it never came forth; it never bloomed. Ireland was as Catholic the day that Elizabeth died at Hampton Court, gnawing the flesh off her hands in despair, and blaspheming God—Ireland was as Catholic that day as she was the day that Henry VIII. vainly commanded her first to become Protestant.

"Then came a little breathing-time—a very short time—and in fifty years there were six hundred Irish Dominican priests in Ireland again. They studied in Spain, in France, in Italy. These were the youth, the children of Irish fathers and mothers, who cheerfully gave them up, though they knew, almost to a certainty, that they were devoting them to a martyr's death ; but they gave them up for God. Smuggled out of the country, they studied in these foreign lands; and they came back again by night, and by stealth, and they landed upon the shores of Ireland ; and when Cromwell came he found six hundred Irish Dominicans upon the Irish land. Ten years after—only ten years passed—and again the Irish Dominican preachers assembled to count their numbers, and to tell how many survived and how many had fallen. How many do you think were left out of the six hundred? But one hundred and fifty were left; four hundred and fifty had perished—had shed their blood for their country, or had been shipped away to Barbadoes as slaves. These are the tales their ruins tell. I need not speak of their noble martyrs. Oh, if these moss-grown stones of the Irish Franciscan and Dominican ruins could speak, they would tell how the people gave up everything they had, for years and years, as wave after wave of persecutions and confiscations and robbery rolled over them, rather than renounce their glorious Faith or their glorious priesthood."

The sufferings of the Jesuits, and of the members of other religious bodies, of secular priests and Prelates, for Ireland and Ireland's Faith, fully equalled the sufferings of the devoted Irish Dominicans and Franciscans. The heroic Dominick Collins, the faithful son of St. Ignatius, taken by the heretics, in the fort of Beerhaven, and hanged by order of cruel Mountjoy, at Cork ;

Maurice Eustace, young, generous and brave, executed at Dublin, on pretence of treason against Elizabeth ; Father James Boyton, slain by the followers of the renegade and savage Inchiquin at the siege of Cashel of the Kings, while he administered the sacrament of Penance to the dying defenders of the Holy Rock ;—Collins—Eustace—Boyton—these, and hundreds of others of their Order, remind us of what the Jesuits did and suffered for Ireland during the penal days. The fate of Thaddeus O'Connell recalls the heroism of the canons of St. Augustine; Mulcahy of Clonmel, O'Kelly of Connaught, Fitzpatrick, descended from the noble barons of Ossory, and Ormily of Clare, vividly recall to our minds the patriotism and self-sacrifice of the secular clergy. If the members of religious Orders ; if the secular clergy were faithful to Ireland ; if they freely poured out their blood for the cause of Religion and Freedom ; if the people of Ireland suffered, and fought, and died, like true martyrs ; faithful above all, we are tempted to say, and we are proud to say it, were the noble Prelates of the Irish Church. Bishop after Bishop, Archbishop after Archbishop, in all the Sees of Ireland, died gloriously for the Faith and the liberty of the Church of St. Patrick. Well did the purple become them in those days of blood and slaughter.

In 1521, rather late in the year, the devastating monster, so ironically called the "Reformation," was brought forth in Germany of the pride and lust of an apostate monk. The Immaculate Bride of Christ, the Church without spot or wrinkle, was declared unclean, and the doctrines she had received from the Son of God, and which she had preserved by the special aid of the Paraclete, were condemned as degrading, superstitious, and revolting to reason. Her sacrifices were regarded as shadows, empty types; her power was considered null and void; many of her sacraments were laughed at and rejected as worthless. Bold, bad men rose up and spoke loudly to vitiated and thoughtless crowds against the teaching which had been held by the apostles, explained and revered by saints and doctors, and for which thousands of martyrs had shed their blood. The success of the "Reformation" is the strongest proof that history affords of the corruption of the human heart and the weakness and darkness of human reason. The fall of Germany from the true faith, in its unreasonableness and evil effects, finds no parallel except in the fall of Lucifer and that of Adam. If the "Reformation" was not an accomplished fact, all reasonable men would place it among the things impossible.

In 1538, Henry's vical-general, Cromwell, undertook the massive and vain task of changing the faith of the Irish people. Monasteries that had been the safe retreats of science and virtue, were suppressed; the Scriptures were translated into the vulgar tòngues; the psalms were distributed by the cart-load to those who frequented the public-house more often than the church. The Irish people are world-renowned for their wit and and their keen sense of the ridiculous. When Henry first declared himself "supreme over ecclesiastical matters as well spiritual as temporal, and head of the Church, even of both isles, England and Ireland," they langhed and enjoyed it as a huge joke. The mere thought of "the new Pope," with his corpulency and pride, his avarice and tyranny was enough to make the gravest of them smile. But when he showed that he was terribly in earnest, when his Parliament passed laws worthy of Nero, when his minions began to enforce them, their mirth was turned to sadness, and their smiles gave way to frowns and tears. Then the Irish people rose to their feet and declared with determination and courage that their island was the "Island of Saints," and that it owned no authority in spiritual matters, that it acknowledged no Pope, except the Pope of Rome. Then began the long and heroic struggle of the Irish clergy and laity against the supremacy of the English sovereigns and the polluted doctrines of Luther's heresy. The history of this struggle is written in the best, the purest, the holiest blood of Ireland. From that black day in the year 1540, when the gray monastery of Monaghan was destroyed and its guardian beheaded, down to the fatal day when Father Nicholas Sheehy was hanged at Clonmel and his head hoisted on a pole over the arched porch of the old jail, what a host of martyrs was born to Ireland. God alone knows how many priests and noble laymen were slain for His love and Church during the bloody reigns of Henry and Elizabeth and James I. and Charles I., during the Commonwealth and the reigns of Charles II.

and Anne, and George II. The martyrs of the early Church died in the arena with thousands of spectators looking upon their glorious combat; but angels alone saw the Irish heroes who were butchered in lonely woods and in deep, dim caves. On All-Saints' Day our Holy Mother the Church honors them in her sacrifices and sings their praises. How glorious is the story of of those about whom we find detailed accounts! What Catholic heart is not moved to feelings of pity and admiration at the thought of Dermod O'Hurly, Archbishop of Cashel, with his tin boots filled with blazing oil; of Oliver Plunket, having his legs and arms broken on an anvil in the forge of a Calvinistic ironsmith; of the Franciscan, Eugene O'Teman, being flogged to death; of O'Gorman being beaten with heavy clubs; of Boetius Egan, Bishop of Ross, being hacked to pieces by a cruel and infuriated soldiery, and finally expiring with the reins of his own horse around his neck?

It is not necessary for us to dwell upon the great sufferings of Most Rev. Archbishop Malachy O'Queely, who being found with the Connaught army after its defeat by Sir Charles Coote, had his right arm cut off and his body cut up into small pieces by the Puritans; nor is it necessary to speak of the trials of De Burgo, of Peter Talbot, of Richard Creagh, of Murtagh O'Brien, all of whom, distinguished prelates, were confined for years in loathsome prisons; their histories are well known; their wrongs are still recounted on many a winter's night by the firesides of Ireland, recounted by the people for whose faith they suffered;—

If tears could fertilize the field,
   Or Celtic blood make roses blow,
What harvests would fair Erin yield,
   What blushes would her valleys know!

Ah! Sorrow's tears are not for earth,
   They dew the gardens of the sky;
A martyr's blood will ne'er give birth
   To fruits or flowers that swiftly die.

The lilies round the Virgin's head,—
   The palm the martyr holds in hand,—
The tree that shades the Blessed Dead,
   Are nourished by my suffering Land.

PATRIOTISM OF IRISH PRIESTS IN PENAL TIMES.

Against the enemy of his country every man is a soldier.
—TERTULLIAN.

DURING the Penal Days every Irish college on the Continent was a stronghold for Ireland. The founding of a college at Douay, at Lisbon, at Paris, at Salamanca, or at Rome, was of more importance, and more pregnant with happy and lasting services to poor Erin, than the capture of Dublin Castle or the possession of the Fort of Duncannon. Books and pamphlets, private letters and glorious pastorals, came forth from the schools of Louvain, Rome, Seville and Antwerp, condemning and exposing the cruelties and errors of English Protestant tyranny, and calling upon Catholic Europe to look with pity and compassion upon poor, persecuted, bleeding Ireland. Every Irish student in foreign lands became a Peter, the Hermit, a St. Bernard, and his voice thundered, and his face shone, as he preached in strange tongues and before different races, a new and sublime Crusade for Ireland. Beautiful queens wept when they heard from the pale student the sad, sad story of his little "Island of Sorrows;" kings heard him in their cabinets, and swore by their sceptres and their crowns that they would aid the princes of Ireland in freeing themselves from injustice; the leading soldiers of France, and Spain, and Italy, offered their swords and their lives for the defence of the Church of St. Patrick; the Sovereign Pontiffs listened with tenderness to the Irish students, whom they loved to keep near them at the Vatican, when they told them of the destruction of religion in the Island of Saints, and one of the Popes, Clement VIII., who sent a crown of peacock's feathers—the symbol of Glory—to O'Neill, offered the Irish "the same indulgences granted to those who fought in Palestine for the ransom of the Holy Sepulchre, provided they furnished no recruits to the queen's army, and incorporated themselves in that of 'the magnanimous Prince O'Neill.'" When, in 1642, the Confederates met in Kilkenny, in the old Church of St. Canice, the noble Pontiff, Urban VIII., who cherished Ireland in his heart of hearts, knelt "at the tomb of the Apostles, and invoked blessings on the arms of his faithful Irish children." The good Pope, Innocent XII., wrote a letter of condolence to the Prelates and people of Ireland. In this epistle, after glancing over the past trials and sufferings of the Church of Ireland, and after referring to the fierce storms that threatened it in the future, the glorious Pontiff exhorted the Prelates and people to look up to Heaven and fear not the tyrant nor his rod. "Nor," writes the Vicar of Christ, "are your sufferings like those of yesterday; they are the sufferings of centuries; your nation, renowned for sanctity, has preserved for ages the glory of the Faith, to your eternal honor and the salvation of your souls. Therefore, suffer all things with Christian patience, knowing that the Lord will not permit any being to be tried beyond his strength ; as to us, our prayers shall be unceasing before the throne of mercy." The same venerable Pontiff immediately after, by apostolical letters, enjoined processions to be made and public prayers to be offered in behalf of the suffering Church of Ireland, throughout the several dioceses of Italy and all the adjacent islands.

Distinguished Irish soldiers in the service of France, Austria, and Spain, heard of Ireland's wrongs from Jesuit, Franciscan, and Dominican students, and they vowed in their hearts to renounce wealth, station, and glory in foreign armies, and to return to Ireland to lift her trambled banner from the dust, and make it wave in pride over a free, prosperous, and happy people. If the Irish people could sing with one of their great poets, Aubrey de Vere,

> Owen Roe, our own O'Neill,
> He treads once more our land ;
> The sword in his hand is of Spanish steel,
> But the hand is an Irish hand,

they have to thank the Irish students of Rome and Madrid. If the Flag of "God and our Lady," of the "Red Hand of Ulster"—if "the Banner of Tyrconnel" were often cast to the free breezes of heaven, and often floated over a risen people, over victor-fields, the glory, for the greater part, is due to patriotic students in the halls and courts of Europe, or hidden away in the woods and glens of Ireland.

As the encouragement given Ireland in her present heroic struggle by her exiled sons scattered throughout the world gives her heart, and emboldens her to demand with no faltering voice her just rights, so did the encouragement given her by her Bishops, and priests, and students, on the Continent during the Penal Days, nerve her arm and cheer her heart in her deadly fight for freedom and liberty of conscience. During the Penal Days Ireland was ground down to the very earth beneath the blood-stained heel of oppression, her princes and chiefs were plundered and rendered almost spiritless, her disbanded kerns were deprived of arms and ammunition, all that human and diabolical ingenuity could do to rob her of her ancient Faith and kill her as a nation, was done. But often did she look up with hope, often did she unsheathe her rusting swords, often did she rise with the proud light of defiance in her eyes, when students on the far Continent wrote her letters with promises of aid from France, and Spain, and Italy, and the Netherlands; when they wrote her letters bidding her to cast away her fears, to trust in a kind Providence, and to look for deliverance from the God of Battles, the God of Victory. Of old, they told her, God raised up a Moses to his people, and "nerved the arm of a Jewish maiden to smite a drunken tyrant in his tent." Ireland heard them, and she kept her lamp well trimmed, and she did not die as a Nation, though she suffered and bled like a true martyr.

The Irish students on the Continent were the true and faithful friends of the Celtic princes and chiefs who had to fly from English tyranny. They obtained for them high positions in the armies and courts of Europe. They befriended them at Rome, and obtained for many who were too old for active service, and who had grown tired of all earthly warfare, pensions from kings and Popes. They were faithful to them in life, they were faithful to them in death. The Franciscans of Louvain sheltered many a young exiled Irish lord. Under their hospitable and renowned roof the sons of Hugh O'Neill were protected and instructed. Florence Conry closed the eyes of Hugh Roe O'Donel at Simancas, in Spain, and watched by the death-beds of the Earls of Tyrone and Tyrconnel, at Rome. The Spanish steel that flashed so brightly, and cut so truly, in the hand of the hero of Benburb, was presented to him by a student in a brown Franciscan habit—Luke Wadding.* When the gallant Lord Clare, so famous in the songs of Davis, was laid to rest in the village of Ramillies, and while the English banners taken by him were being hung in the Irish Convent of Ypres, a monument was raised to his memory by the patriotic Dominicans of Louvain, in their College of the Holy Cross, with a touching and appropriate epitaph. This monument, like the Dominican

---

* While the Papal Nuncio, Renuccini, "was in Ireland, the sword of Aodh O'Neill came into the possession of Father Wadding ; he transmitted it by the Dean of Fermo to the Nuncio, who presented it to Owen Roe O'Neill. The blade that rifted the field like lightening at Beal-an-atha-buidhe, was to shed glory once more over the same Irish ground in the battle of Benburb." See "Irish Writers" p 98, by Mc.Gee.

house itself, has mouldered into dust, but it must not be forgotten by the Irish historian or antiquarian.

"When the exiled princes of Tyrone and Tyrconnel were driven from Ireland, they found their best friends and warmest supporters among the Irish students on the Continent. In Douay, Father Conry met the nobles, and embraced them while tears of joy trickled down his cheeks. Thither also came Dr. Eugene McMahon, a most erudite and elegant scholar, to give them greeting. Happy were the exiles when they met this eminent ecclesiastic." Father Meehan, from whom we have just quoted, again says: "Antwerp, Malines, and other great towns received them with all the consideration due to their rank and misfortunes. In the former city there was a college for the education of Irish aspirants to the priesthood, and the fugitive nobles were welcomed there with formalities like those shown them in Douay. Indeed, wherever there was an Irish seminary or conventual establishment, alumni and superiors vied with each other in congratulating the 'illustrious princes,' for such was the designation by which they were recognized in Belgium, Italy, and all over the Continent."

At Louvain the exiled chiefs were received with enthusiasm by the Irish professors among the Jesuits, Franciscans and Dominicans, and by the students of the University. The great Peter Lombard wrote one letter to Hugh O'Neill and another to Rory O'Donel, the worthy brother of young Red Hugh, who was then sleeping, free from persecution and wrong, in the quiet cloister of the Franciscan convent of Vallodolid, inviting them to the Eternal City.

O'Neill and O'Donel, on their pilgrimage to Rome, were feasted by the greatest princes and warriors of Europe. Many of the cities received them with the firing of guns and the ringing of cathedral bells. Everywhere they showed their devotion and truly Catholic spirit by visiting famous shrines and the tombs of saints and martyrs.

"It was not until the spring following that the Ulster princes arrived at Rome. The day of their arrival had long been anticipated, and Peter Lombard, with several Cardinals, awaited them on the left bank of the Tiber, with sumptuous carriages and a long train of servitors in gala liveries. On passing the Flaminian gate they proceeded to the palace which the Pope had appointed for them, in that region of the city known as Borgo Vecchio. Here they were visited by the chief nobility of Rome and by the Cardinal Borghese, brother to Paul V., who bade them welcome in His Holiness' name, and stated that the latter was desirous of seeing them at their earliest convenience. His Holiness, who was deeply affected at the story of their misfortunes, congratulated them on their escape from their merciless foes, and amply provided them with every requirement befitting their condition."

Archbishop Lombard did all he could to honor the illustrious exiles and to prove his love and admiration for them. He was truly their guide, their spiritual father, their friend. Often did his eyes well with tears as he thought of the noble fight they had fought for the holiest of causes. Often did he pray in the "Holy of Holies" that the God of Battles, the God of Justice, would avenge their wrongs and restore them to their rightful possessions, restore them to their bleeding country, give them back the crown and sceptre of Ireland.

The last hours of the great Hugh O'Neill were cheered by the presence of Archbishop Lombard and Florence Conry, Archbishop of Armagh. "O'Neill!" "Conry!" "Lombard!" with uncovered head and reverential, loving breath, I speak your glorious trinity of names. Oh, fragments of Ireland's scattered glory! "Oh, shamrock from the Irish shore!" may your memory forever flourish in Irish hearts! may your picture remain forever before Erin's eyes, as a symbol of the unity and love that should ever exist among Irish exiles, as a symbol of the friendship that should ever reign among Irish chiefs and Irish Prelates! * "O'Neill!" "Conry!" "Lombard!" patriots, true heroes, noble champions of Ireland's Faith and Ireland's freedom, if ever I forget the land you loved, the creed you cherished, let my right hand forget its cunning; if ever I do not speak kindly and respectfully and lovingly of the altars at which you knelt, of the shrines and temples in which you adored and received strength and consolation, may the heavens grow dark above my

---

* When will some great Irish artist give the world a picture of these renowned men?

head, may the flowers at my feet perish, may my tongue cleave to the roof of my mouth!

Father Meehan, when referring to the deaths of the O'Donels, the Baron of Duncannon, MacMahon, Cuconnaught Maguire, Maurice O'Multully, O'Donel's secretary, and O'Carroll, their physician, says: "We can easily imagine how bitterly O'Neill was afflicted by the loss of those who were so dear to him, and above all, by that of the Baron of Duncannon, whom he regarded as the staff of his declining years, and his successor to the ancient Gaelic title. Often and often would the grand old prince—for he was then in his sixty-eighth year—toil up the steep ascent that leads to the church Montorio; and no day passed that did not see him there, kneeling on the tombs of his son and kinsmen, praying for their everlasting peace. Happily, as God would have it, he lacked not men who were able and willing to console him; for under the same roof with him lived Peter Lombard, Archbishop of Armagh, and in the convent of Montorio, Florence Conry, then Archbishop-designate of Tuam, both of whom spared no pains to reconcile him to his terrible bereavement. Both were eminent for piety and learning; and the portrait of the latter, evidencing, as it does, unmistakable traits of firmness, penetration and profound thought, shows that he was the person to whom O'Neill would have turned for counsel at such a crisis."

Sir William Drury, writing to "Lord President of Munster, the Queen's principal Secretary of State," thus expresses himself in the month of April, 1577, with regard to the students of Louvain: "The students of Louvain, and come from thence. They are the meerest traitors and breeders of treachery that liveth."

No doubt but this same slander was repeated ten thousand times over during the Penal Days with regard to the Irish students who studied at Madrid, Naples, Bordeaux, Toulouse and Nantes.

No native chief was more zealous in the cause of the "great Rebellion of 1641" than Father Henry Fitzsimon. He knew the state that his country ought to hold among the free nations of the earth, and he saw her crushed beneath the iron heel of a foreign despotism. He knew that she was blessed in her rich soil, in her favorable station, and in her virtuous and strongbodied people, yet he beheld her poor and almost starving. New shackles were daily forged for the Irish national rights, new dangers were prepared for the national faith. The patriotic priest, the zealous missionary, the devoted son of the Church, saw with pain that the leaders in the English Parliament were determined to rob the Catholic Irish of their land, to level their altars, and to abolish their holy religion. He, therefore, thought with all the other devoted ecclesiastics of the Church of St. Patrick that his country should fling the standard of revolt to the breezes that swept from ocean, and sea, and lake, and river. In this feeling he exerted his oratory to rouse his people to arms. He infused into all who heard him his own noble and patriotic sentiments. The Catholic lords of the pale, the chiefs of the old race, the fiery-eyed clan, idolized the eloquent

and venerable priest who thrilled them through and
through as he called upon them to draw the sword in
defence of their altars, their homes, their freedom, their
lives. A glorious band rose up for the defence of Faith
and Country. Among them stand in the front rank
Roger Moore, of Ballynagh; Cornelius Macguire, of Inniskillen; Sir Phelim O'Niel, Lord Gormanstown, Macmahon, O'Quin, O'Hanlon, Macginnis, O'Reilly, Byrne,
Owen Roe O'Niel, General Preston, Barry Garrett,
Burke and O'Donnel. Blessed and praised forever be
the Catholic prelates and divines who met at Kilkenny
in convention on May 10th, 1642. Their conduct is the
best answer ever given to those who accuse the clergy
of Ireland of want of love for the fair land that bore
them.

Father Fitzsimon, on account of the encouragement
he gave the insurgents, was an object of particular
hatred to the victorious oppressors of his country. They
marked him out for destruction. He, therefore, fled for
shelter to the loneliest places. Woods and mountains
now became his dwelling, and he was frequently obliged
to change them through fear of the heartless English
soldiers. At length, in the beginning of 1643, worn out
with the fatigues his advanced age was so ill able to
bear, he retired for refuge to a shepherd's cot, no better
than a hovel, situated in a bog. His only bed was a pad
of straw, which was frequently wet with the rain, which
the shattered and imperfect state of the walls freely admitted, and the damp which rose from the morass. Yet
amid this scene of misery, with no one comfort around

him, he preserved his cheerfulness unimpaired, and was always ready to console others in their misery, continuing still to instruct them and their children. He who had forsaken the world and its vanities to walk the royal way of the cross could not but be happy in the midst of his sufferings; he who had made the vow of poverty in Louvain and Rome could not but feel contented when he found himself badly housed, poorly clad, and without sufficient food to supply the wants of nature. Yet it is sad to think that a learned, holy and venerable priest should be so situated.

Father Fitzsimon, however, was unable long to support such extremes of misery. His constitution had been injured by fastings, long journeys by land and sea, dreary toils and vigils, and incarcerations. Nature at length giving way, he was conveyed with some difficulty by his faithful and loving flock to a more comfortable situation. Amid the tears and sighs and blessings of his loved and loving people, this worthy son of St. Ignatius, this true apostle, this lover and able defender of his race and creed, this genuine Irish priest passed from earth to heaven. From his throne in joy he denies the charges brought against the most devoted, the most faithful, the most patriotic body on earth—the Irish clergy. Shame upon the ignorance that would doubt the patriotism of the living successors of Collins, of Bishop French, of Fitzsimon, of Wadding, of Columbkille, and St. Laurence O'Toole!

An informer wrote to a Captain Stanley as follows: "I am deceived or I told you by mouth, about one *Mar-*

cio, and his speech unto a Jesuit of our nation, now in Flanders, named Henry Fitzsimons, to wit, this Jesuit, discussing with the aforesaid Marcio of the facility to conquer Ireland, and the commodity therein to extend fame and fortunes this nobleman, moved with such interest, gave to understand unto said Jesuit that he most willingly would engage himself and his fortunes for the like enterprise, so that he could have the concurrence of some in the country, or see possibility for him to prevail by any other means."

"On board the Spanish fleet, in company with Oviedo," writes Cardinal Moran, "two remarkable men had sailed for the shores of Ireland. One was F. James Archer, an Irish Jesuit, and the other was Dominick Collins, a lay-brother of the same order. Father Archer had already labored for some years on the Irish mission; and a letter addressed to an agent of the Roman court in England, about 1598, thus sketched his character :— 'Father Archer, alone, is a greater comfort to his Irish countrymen than even a considerable reinforcement of troops. I am a witness that his presence was almost more serviceable to the cause than anything else; for, at his nod, the hearts of men were united and bound together, not only in the district of Berehaven and Munster, but in the greater part of the whole kingdom.'" The spirit that fired the Irish Franciscans may be understood from the following extract from a letter of their Provincial, Very Rev. Father Antony Geoghegan, addressed to Father Wadding :—"Such alacrity do I find in our brethren for the holy cause, that instead of spurring I must hold them hard with bit and bridle; since, instead of being satisfied with the spiritual combat, they gird themselves with carnal weapons and do battle for God and country. Another benefit has been bestowed on Ireland by our order; for it was on the feast of St. John Capristrano * that our nob'e Irish heroes made their first attempt to liberate their country from worse than Egyptian bondage. Hence many have chosen that saint as their tutelar in this holy war; and I believe that the Catholic cause would be greatly advantaged by placing the whole country under his special invocation, and inducing our apostolic father to grant us the indulgences formerly given to the Crusaders. Dispensations in cases of irregularity should also be obtained, so that our friars may have no reason to dread censures for enrolling themselves in those holy battalions. I would also suggest that excommunication shall be pronounced on those who abet our adversaries, and do not act to the best of their ability in forwarding the Catholic cause. As for the actual state of this country, nothing can be worse. Nevertheless, we deem it an honorable duty to perform heroic actions and endure every manner of hardship for love of Christ. We have to deal with implacable enemies, the false Scots and the factious and cruel English Puritans, who do not spare age or sex. There is no chance of peace, so that we must fight to the end for our religion and homes. We have no alternative but to conquer or be conquered.

---

* A Franciscan who, crucifix in hand, marched with the army of Corvin against the Turks, and helped to defeat them on the Danube, A. D. 1456.

Either we or our enemies must be driven out of this land, which is not large enough to hold Irish and Englishmen. So long as Babylonian England and perfidious Scotland have the upper hand, so long will they continue to crush the Irish. This is the reason why we must urge foreign princes to sustain us; and for this object two agents will shortly be sent hence—father Peter Darcy to the French court, and our father Everard to the Vatican, with letters sealed with the new seal, whose legend is, 'For God, king, and country, the Irish United.' Said agents are as yet detained by order of the supreme council. Good father, relax not your well-known efforts to procure us arms and munitions, as our wants are great."

"Hugh O'Neil, Earl of Tyrone," wrote Father Moran, now Cardinal, "was engaged in his last great struggle in defence of his hereditary rights. This chieftain had learned the merits of Peter Lombard, and wished to avail himself of his presence in Rome to entrust to his charge the interests of Ireland, commissioning him to plead the cause of the Confederate Princes at the court of the Sovereign Pontiff. Thus it became his pleasing duty to announce to his Holiness the many successes of the Irish arms which marked the close of the sixteenth century. The victories of the Yellow Ford and the Curlew mountains were hailed with acclamations in the Eternal City; the guns of St. Angelo conveyed the joyous intelligence to the citizens, and the *Te Deum* was solemnly chanted in St. Peter's. More than once, aid in arms and money was forwarded to Ireland through the

Spanish nuncio; pontifical letters, too, were addressed to the Irish people exhorting them to join the Catholic army, and conferring the same privileges, blessings, and indulgences, as had been enjoyed by the crusaders of old, on all those who would assist O'Neil and his army, the champions, and assertors of the Catholic faith.'"—Brief, 18th April, 1600.

The success that attended the efforts of the Earl of Tyrone caused such gratification at Rome, that the Holy Father wrote a letter of congratulation to him. The letter begins thus:

"*To our beloved son, the noble Prince Hugh O'Neil, Commander and Captain-General of the Catholic Army in Ireland.*

"BELOVED SON AND NOBLE LORD, HEALTH AND APOSTOLIC BLESSING.

"We have learned from the letter of your Excellency, as well as from the information orally communicated to us by our beloved son, Peter Lombard, Provost of Cambray, that the holy league which you and many other princes and chieftains and leading noblemen of that kingdom have, in the goodness of God, been led to establish among yourselves, still continues in the cement of charity and goes on increasing; and that, by the aid and might of the same Lord of Hosts, you have on divers occasions been successful in battle against the English—those apostates from the Church and from the Faith. Great pleasure in the Lord have we received from this intelligence, and offered up our thanks to that God, the Father of mercies, who has still left to Himself in that kingdom many thousands that have not bent the knee to Baal. For these have never gone after impious heresies and profane novelties, but, on the contrary, fight bravely in detestation of them, for the inheritance of their fathers, for the preservation of the faith, for the maintenance of integrity and unity with the Church, which is One, Catholic and Apostolic, out of which there is no salvation. We praise, dear son, the excellent spirit of piety and bravery manifested by yourself and by the princes and all others who, having engaged in this league and confederacy with you, shrink not from any dangers whatsoever for the glory of God, and prove and openly profess themselves worthy descendants and proper successors of their ancestors—men eminently famous for their warlike bravery, zeal for the Catholic religion and glorious renown. Preserve, children, such a spirit—preserve your unanimity and concord ; and God Almighty, the God of harmony and peace shall be with you, and fight for you, and will prostrate, as He hath done before, His enemies before your face.

"And as for ourselves, loving and cherishing as we do, in the bowels of Jesus Christ, your Excellency, and all of you who imitate the faith and glory of your forefathers we cease not to beseech our God for your prosperity and welfare, and we are and ever will be, interested in you and for you, so far as God will enable us to be thus minded. And when there shall be occasion we will write effective letters to the Catholic kings and princes, our children, that they may support you and your cause with all the aid in their power."

The Holy Father then promises to send a special Nuncio from Himself and the Holy See. He also imparts an Apostolic Benediction to O'Neill and his devoted companions and followers. "Finally," the Pontiff says: "We pray that He may send His angels to be around your path, direct your pious efforts with His heavenly grace, and evermore defend you with the right hand of His power."

"Together with this Brief," says Cardinal Moran, in his Memoir of Most Rev. Peter Lombard, "was despatched a letter from Cardinal Cinzio Aldobrandini, whose words give abundant proof of the warm sympathy which was cherished by the authorities in Rome, for the Irish princes. He not only congratulates O'Neil on his victories and on the fame which he had acquired throughout all Christendom, but even adds: 'Would to God it were in my power to have a part in your merit and your glory. How readily would I share your perils, and offer my life and my blood in so holy and so just a cause!'"

We have in this book more than once alluded to the Indulgences granted by Sovereign Pontiffs to those who were fighting for the liberties of Ireland; we therefore think it right to insert the following letter, which ought to be printed in characters of gold:

"*Gregory XIII., to the archbishops, bishops, and other prelates, as also to the Catholic princes, earls, barons, clergy, nobles and people of Ireland, health and apostolic benediction:*

"A few years ago we exhorted you by our letters, when you took up arms to defend your liberties and rights, under the leadership of James Geraldine, of happy memory, to be all of one mind, and to give a ready and strenuous aid to the chieftain who, with inexpressible ardor, desired to free you from that yoke which is imposed on you by the English heretics; and that you might the more promptly and efficaciously join with him in this enterprise, we conceded to all those who, with due contrition, had confessed their sins, full pardon and remission, and the same indulgence as was imparted by the Roman Pontiffs to those who fought against the Turks for the recovery of the Holy Land, provided they should enrol themselves under the banners of the aforesaid James, the champion and defender of the Catholic faith, or aid him by counsel, provisions, arms, or other things necessary for the sustenance of his troops. Lately, however, we have learned, with most profound sorrow, that James fell in battle, bravely fighting for the faith, and that our beloved son, John Geraldine, has succeeded him, who has already given heroic proofs of his devotion to the Catholic religion. We, therefore, with all possible affection, exhort, urge, and solicit each and every one of you to unite with the said John, your commander, and aid him and his army against the aforesaid heretics, as you would have aided the aforesaid James, if he were living. We therefore impart the above plenary indulgence to each and every one of you, provided you shall first have confessed and communicated, and given aid, by every means in your power, to the general-in-chief, John, and, in case of his demise, which God avert, to James, his brother, which concession shall continue as long as the brothers John and James shall live and carry on this war against the heretics, etc. Given at Rome the 13th day of May, 1580, the eight of our pontificate."

Thomas Davis wrote in the anguish of his generous soul,—

> "Oh! weep those days, the penal days,
> When Ireland hopelessly complained."

For our part, looking on the bright side of the picture, looking upon the glory of the heroes of that "dark time of cruel wrong," we feel rather inclined to sing in the following, prouder, happier strain :—

> WEEP not beside a martyr's grave,
>   Weep not o'er hunted virtue true;
> Weep not the hour that proved man brave—
>   Though blood lent hill and dale its hue.
> Why should we weep the penal times
>   That showed our country's love of Right?
> Let us forget the tyrants' crimes,
>   And sing the stars of Erin's night.

> When peaceful bloomed our garden land,
>   The hermit and the monk arose,
> And every vale heard virgin-band
>   Sing love of God, at evening's close;

But when our air with war was red,
   From cells and caves Truth's soldiers came,
And every rock a glory shed
   Around some Irish martyr's name.

We must not weep the penal days
   That sanctified our hills and plains ;
We must not shudder when we gaze
   At men that feared nor death nor chains.
In blood and tears, 'neath penal laws,
   Saint Erin's heart was purified ;
For holy Faith and Freedom's cause,
   Our martyred nation grandly died.

IRISH PROFESSORS IN PENAL DAYS.

TALENT, I was going to say *genius*, seems very often to be the birthright of Irishmen. The sons of Ireland may be robbed of every material thing—of land, of money, of home—but of kingly brains, of poetry, of wit, of eloquence, not even the powers of darkness can plunder them. The storms may cloud the skies above their heads, but the lightning-flash of their genius will be all the brighter for the gloom that surrounds them. All through the Penal Days, that blackest epoch in Ireland's history, we find the lamp of Irish learning burning in every school in Europe ; we find Irish students filling distinguished chairs of philosophy and theology in every famous university on the Old Continent. Those who sneer at Irish ignorance, those who feel ashamed of their Irish lineage, would do well to read the following roll of honor.

Dominick Lynch, a native of Galway, of the "marble gates," was professor of Divinity in the University of Seville for over twenty years. He deserved to be ranked by Nicholas Antonio, in his *Biblioteca Española*, among the great authors of a land that produced a Cervantes, a Caldron, a Lopez de Vega, and a Fray Luis de Leon. Michael Moore, a Dublin student, was a distinguished professor in his day. He taught philosophy and rhetoric in the Grassan College, and was made by Rome a Censor of Books—an honor he well deserved by his learning, and love of religion. For some years he acted as rector of the college at Montefiascone, and was twice chosen as rector of the renowned University of Paris. The French *savants* never wearied of conferring honors on him. By them he was appointed Principal of the College of Navarre, and *Regius Professor* of philosophy and Hebrew. Among "les Recteurs Magnifiques" of the University of Louvain, which at one time numbered thousands of the most gifted students of Europe, and had over forty colleges connected with it, we note John Sinnich, a Corkman, and Thomas Stapleton, a true-hearted son of the little town of Fethard, in gallant Tipperary. Waterford, "the most Catholic city" of Catholic Ireland, furnished more than its share of talent during the long night of persecution. But among the most brilliant, the most faithful, the most patriotic of Waterford families, was that of the Waddings.

Father Luke Wadding, one of the grandest characters in Irish history, was renowned as a writer, and was well-known as a great and accomplished professor in the colleges of his Order at Liria, Lisbon, Coimbra, Salamanca and Rome. Father Peter Wadding was highly esteemed as a lecturer in Louvain, and was honored by being chosen as chancellor of the Universities of Prague and Gratz. Richard Wadding, of the Austin Eremites, professed theology at Coimbra. Several other members of the Wadding family were distinguished on the Continent, but for the sake of brevity, I pass over them in silence. John Baptist Hackett, whose early days were passed in obscurity "at the foot of Slievenamon"—so dear to poor Charles J. Kickham—rose to eminence as a theological professor at Milan, Naples, and Rome—"the City of the Soul." Father Stephen White, who imbibed his love of the sublime and beautiful, whose patriotic fires were fanned into a white heat on the banks of the Suir, not far from "rare Clonmel," was a learned writer, and taught with marked success at a Jesuit college at Salamanca, as also at Dillingen, Pont-a-Mousson, and the new University of Ingoldstadt. He was one of the greatest of Irish hagiologists, and helped very much both Colgan and the other Franciscans of Louvain who devoted themselves to the collecting and arranging of the scattered and mouldy fragments of Celtic history. White was undoubtedly a great man—a *savant* of whom any country might well be proud. In some old books in Louvain I found mention made of Professor O'Halloran. This student had a strange, a romantic career. He reminds one of some of the Irish war-correspondents of our own time. He followed literature as a profession, and could tell stranger things about his travels than even Oliver Goldsmith himself. His proficiency in languages was extraordinary. He wrote good poetry in English, and, on the authority of Father Victor De Buck, the great Bollandist, I state that he composed remarkably creditable Flemish verses. He was in Belgium about the time of the invasion of the French revolutionists. O'Halloran taught literature in the college of the Holy Trinity, Louvain.

This was the college in which Daniel O'Connell studied before going to St. Omer's. It is now in the possession of the Josephites. On one of the doors is scratched the name of Daniel O'Connell. Though I was assured that young O'Connell himself inscribed his name on the door, still I feel a little skeptical on this point.

But to go on. Patrick Comerford, of the city of "Meagher of the Sword," taught rhetoric for four years in the Austin Hermit's Convent of Angra, the capital of Terceira, in the Azores. He occupied a chair of theology at Brussels, and on passing through Florence, the far-famed Academy *della Crusca* enrolled him among its members, and conferred on him the degree of Doctor of Philosophy. Dominick McGuire, of the princely house of Fermanagh, obtained by *Public Concursus* the professorship of theology in the Convent of St. Mary Sanitatis at Naples, and continued for twenty-two years to lecture with great success and applause. Hugh McCaghwell, the friend of "the O'Neils," and a very fine Gælic scholar, taught theology at Salamanca, at which place he earned the character of a ripe student, "acute, grave, modest, and sublime." Peter Lombard—not "the Master of Sentences"—Archbishop of Armagh, became not only a renowned professor in the old University of Louvain, when that school was at the summit of its glory, but was appointed by Pope Paul V. as President of the famous Congregation "De Auxiliis." So important did the Sovereign Pontiff consider the discussions of this Congregation, that he himself was frequently present at them, accompanied by no less than seven Cardinals. "I cannot be ignorant of our illustrious Primate, Peter Lombard, so clearly shining even in the theatre of the world," wrote Fitzsimon, "if not above, yet among the brightest Prelates, for rare learning, episcopal mildness and integrity of life."

Father Henry Fitzsimon, "the pillar of the Irish Church" during years of darkness and sorrow, the bold champion of Ireland's ancient Faith and Altars, sat at Louvain in the professorial chair of his holy and illustrious master, Leonard Lessius—one of the brightest and fairest ornaments of the Jesuit Order. Father Hugh Ward, of the Franciscan Order, the noblest of Irish hagiologists, was considered on the European Continent the best skilled of his time in the subtleties of Scotus, while Florence Conry, another Franciscan, the Founder of St. Anthony's Convent, Louvain, the personal friend of Philip III. of Spain, was generally regarded as more conversant in the writings of St. Augustine than any of his contemporaries. James Arthur, a fervent son of St. Dominick, distinguished himself in Spain and Portugal.

Father Richard Stanihurst, uncle of James Usher and kinsman of the martyred Jesuit poet, Robert Southwell, became famous for his learning in France and through the Low Countries. He was, after the death of his wife, chaplain to Albert, Archduke of Austria, and Isabella, the Infanta of Spain. Camden styles him: "*Eruditissimus ille nobilis Richardus Stanihurst.*" "Robert Turner, a first-rate orator," says Dr. Lynch, "thus addresses Stanihurst: 'The two goddesses have lent you their hues: Juno, sweetness; Minerva, eloquence. You have alighted upon this orb with such beauty, or rather favor, in the eyes and ears of men, that you are pronounced a Demosthenes, not by the old woman of Athens merely, but by those to whom art has given eloquence, and nature the keenest perception. You have taken your place among the crowned votaries of the pleasant and the more recondite muse; you walk with the Scaligers"' etc., etc. Two of his sons, William and Peter, both of whom made their novitiate as Jesuit novices with Blessed John Berchmans at Mechlin, were men of great ability. Peter died young in Spain. William had, for over thirty years, charge of the great Sodality at Louvain. He was much admired as a spiritual Father, and was esteemed the best Flemish preacher of his time. He died a martyr of charity in attending to the plague-stricken in Louvain. The present writer paid a visit, some years ago, to the Mechlin Novitiate, the religious home of Blessed Berchmans, the Stanihursts, and other devoted youths, and found that Belgian *Liberalism* had changed it into a *theatre*. The generous reader may imagine his disappointment and indignation.

Bishop Dermot O'Hurley, who was arrested at Cashel, and who subsequently suffered so much for the Faith, was at one time a loved and esteemed professor of Canon Law at the University of Louvain. Edmond O'Dwyer, a native of "the City of the Broken Treaty," made a brilliant collegiate course at Rouen, and won a name for profundity at the great Sorbonne, where he studied theology. Rheims, always jealous of its honors, conferred on him the degree of Doctor of Divinity. Thomas Fleming, one of the sons of William, the sixteenth Baron of Slane, taught theology in the school of Aix-la-Chapelle. Archbishop Talbot, who was so long confined in Dublin Castle, that cesspool of English corruption in Ireland, was highly rated as a professor of Moral Theology at the Jesuit College of Antwerp. Joseph II., Emperor of Germany, frequently attended the classes of Dr. Lanigan, the Irish historian. Not a few of the Hanoverian nobles and princes, according to Brennan, received their education under this devoted and distinguished Irishman. Tamburini, who administered the University of Pavia, in which Dr. Lanigan was one of the professors, was accustomed to designate him as the "pillar and brightest ornament of the establishment." Father Francis Slingsby, of the Society of Jesus, who was so much loved and admired by Cardinal Barbareni, was the eldest son of Sir Francis Slingsby, Knight, and was one of the most distinguished mathematicians of his time.

Maurice Wise, a Waterford boy, was professor at the Roman College. David Woulfe, a native of Limerick, was rector of the Modena College, Papal Nuncio, prisoner, a writer, and was classed by Stanihurst, who wrote a history of his country, among "the learned men and authors of Ireland. He was a most distinguished divine, and a man of great reputation for austere sanctity. Christopher Holywood, from Artane, County Dublin, was an ardent patriot and a great scholar. One of his books was condemned from the throne. He was an able professor of Philosophy and Theology at Padua, and at several other famous schools. Bryan O'Carney, of "Cashel of the Kings," took away the highest honors of Douay. He was professor of Greek and Rhetoric, a writer, a fervid preacher, and gave most successful missions in Ireland. Patrick Lenan, from Drogheda, the scene of Cromwell's carnage, was an accomplished theologian. He was a gradnate of Oxford, an M. A. of Douay, and a B. D. of Louvain. He was for six years a pupil of Stapleton, the great English controversalist, and had Leonard Lessius as professor. James Everard, born in Fethard, was professor of Theology in Portugal. John Lombard, of Waterford, was professor of Theology at Ipres and Antwerp. Robert Queitrot, called in Portugal *Cotinho*, was an able professor at Coimbra in its brightest days. William McCrach, known in Portugal as *Da Cruz*, was professor of Theology and Philosophy, and rector at Lisbon. William Malone, who is stated by Nathaniel Southwell to have been born in Dublin,* but who is claimed by others as a native of England, was rector both in Rome and Seville. Father Hogan, the distinguished Irish Jesuit, proves to my satisfaction that Malone was an Irishman. Brother Henry Foley, editor of the *English Records*, for whom I have the greatest personal regard as a religious and a writer, I think is mistaken on this point. But I will not now stop to dispute the question. Granting that Malone

---

* Sir James Ware and Harris say Malone was born in Dublin.

was English, I have more undoubted Irishmen to speak of in connection with my subject than I can make place for in one article, or that my readers would wish to hear of for the present. Paul Sherlock was rector of Salamanca and Compostella, and was appointed Censor of Books by the Inquisition of Spain.

George Dillon, son of the Earl of Roscommon, and "uncle of the poet Earl," taught philosophy and mathematics in Belgium. Peter Redan, from "Royal Meath," was rector of Salamanca, was acknowledged to be an excellent Greek and Hebrew scholar, and was professor of Scripture and of Controversies at Salamanca. Simon Jordan was rector of Polotzk, in Poland. Ignatius Tellin was a great *litterateur*, and was for some time professor of philosophy at the University of Ingolstadt. Peter Talbot calls him "a miracle of learning." James Relly is praised by Dr. Peter Talbot. He defended theses *ex universa theologia* in the Roman College in the year 1667. Michael White was rector of the Madeira College for years. Thomas Brennan, of Dublin, professed theology in the *Grand College de Poitiers*. John St. Leger, from the banks of the Suir, taught Humanities to Jesuit students in Spain during five years. Thomas Weldon, of Drogheda, was professor of Philosophy and Rhetoric in France. James Power was professor of Philosophy at the Jesuit College of Paris. Bryan O'Kelly publicly defended theses in philosophy at the University of Evora. Joseph Ignatius O'Halloran, brother of the famous Dr. Sylvester O'Halloran, was professor of Scholastic Theology at La Rochelle. James

O'Connell was master of Humanities in the Roman College, and was for years chaplain and secretary of Rinuccini, who treated him with singular courtesy. Richard Lynch, of Galway, taught Theology for twenty-five years at Valladolid and at the University of Salamanca. "He was," says a recent writer, "one of the first three Jesuits honored with the degree of D. D., by the University of Salamanca. He was the admiration of this school, and was so subtle, brilliant and eloquent in the chair of Theology, that he was constantly called on by the acclamation of his hearers to prolong his lectures."

Henry Fitzsimon, no mean judge, in the Preface to his remarkable book on the Mass, thus refers to Bishop David Rothe and Thomas Deis: "Of two, among others, for future imitation and present admiration, I will make mention, although I hazard to incur thereby their grievous indignation. Both are Graduates, yea, Doctors of Divinity in the two most famous universities of Christendom. Both are, for piety, virtue, edification, sufficiency, if not incomparable in all the nation, are yet in the highest rank of the foremost. Both are pillars and planters, ornaments and upholders of our country's religion and credit, and are held among natives and foreigners in great authority, love and reputation."

These are some of the proud Irish names that rush upon us to-night and "star the field of memory." They are the names that help to shed a radiance and a glory around the brow of our own "loved Island of Sorrow." We love them, we cherish them, and will not easily let them drop into the coldness and darkness of oblivion.

A HYMN TO FAITH.

O! holy Faith; O! Sacred Light,
  Forever beam on me;
O like a star, shine on my night,
  And light me o'er life's sea.

The deep I sail is fierce and dark,
  A wide, unbounded way,
I cannot steer my wandering bark
  Without thy saving ray.

The shore is far away, I know,
  And rocks and shoals are nigh,
Among a thousand wrecks I go,
  O! star, my starless sky.

I sail, and sail, but know not where—
  Before me, death and night;
O! holy Faith, now hear my prayer,
  And show thy blessed light.

Shine on the waves that 'round me roar,
  Shine on the far-off strand,
Be thou my light-house by the shore,
  My sunshine on the land.

LINES TO IRISH STUDENTS.

I.

O! tell me, students—ye of Irish blood—
  Are ye never sad in gay France or Spain?
Do ye never sit in a lonely mood
  In the classic halls of renowned Louvain?

II.

Do you never wish for a dear old friend
  To unload your hearts of their hopes and fears?
Do ye never wish for a speedy end
  To the long, hard chain of your exiled years?

III.

Do ye never think of the Shannon's tide,
  Or the lovely banks of the Boyne or Suir?
Do ye never feel in your hearts a pride
  At the thought of Erin, so fair and pure?

IV.

Do ye never dream of Old Ireland's hills?
  When the stars light up soft Italian skies?
Do ye never weep over Erin's ills
  When ye hear that in sorrow deep she lies?

V.

When dear Christmas comes, or the Easter bells
  Speak aloud from each lofty tower and dome,
Do ye never sigh, in your foreign cells,
  For the love and joy of your Irish Home?

THE HOMES OF OLD TIPPERARY.

I will not pray for wealth or power,
    For fleeting fame or glory;
I will not pray that I may live
    In Ireland's sacred story:
But I will ask my Patron Saint,
    And my sweet Mother, Mary,
To guard, and bless, and ever love
    The Homes of Old Tipperary.

I'll ask a blessing on the Suir,—
    The river of my childhood;
I'll ask a blessing on loved scenes—
    On mountain, field, and wild-wood;
To-night I'll ask my Patron Saint,
    And my sweet Mother, Mary,
To gladden with their brightest smiles
    The Homes of old Tipperary.

I've wandered much in foreign lands,
    But still my heart is swelling
With all its love for early friends,
    And for my boyhood's dwelling;
So now I'll pray my Patron Saint,
    And my sweet Mother, Mary,
To guard, and bless, and love for me,
    The Homes of Old Tipperary.

IRISH CHAPLAINS WITH THE IRISH BRIGADES.

> In Nothern Spain and Brittany, our brethren also dwell—
> O! brave are the traditions of their fathers that they tell.
> The eagle and the crescent in the dawn of history pales,
> Before their fire, that seldom flags, and never wholly fails.
>   One in name, and in fame
>   Are the sea-divided Gaels.

SINCE Strongbow's haughty standard was reflected in the waters of the Suir up to the time of the Violated Treaty, Irish soldiers swelled the ranks of every European Army. Some were to be found fighting under the banners of Russia, some under those of Spain and Austria, while a large number of them marched under the *Fleur-de-lis* of France. But it was immediately after the Siege of Limerick that whole regiments of Irish soldiers were to be met in France and Spain and the Netherlands.

This state of things, of necessity, opened a new field to the zeal of Irish priests. The Irish troops desired to have their own *Soggarth Aroon* by their side in the camp and on the battle-field. Hence wherever we find our Irish soldiers there, too, we find our Irish Chaplains. No battle was fought, no battle won, by the sons of Ireland,

> "From Dunkirk to Belgrade."

at which one of Erin's priests was not present with the Crucifix in his hand. No soldier fell wounded on the gory ground above whom an Irish priest did not bend, to whom an Irish priest did not impart an Absolution.

As we do not intend to make this a lengthy article we shall merely refer to a few of the Irish Continental Chaplains who easily come to our minds. Father Henry Fitzsimmon and Father Hugh MacCaghwell had much to do with the Irish soldiers stationed in the Low Countries.

Of the last-named priest we may say here that he wrote some works in the Gaelic tongue, for the use of the regiment to which he was Chaplain. The name of Father James Archer, of Kilkenny, is one of the dearest in Ireland. The patriotic deeds of this Jesuit have been often made the theme of ballad and of song. The part he took in Ireland during the war of Tyrone is known to all. After having been chosen the first Rector of Salamanca, he became Chaplain to the Irish troops in the service of Spain. With the fleet sent to Ireland he also set sail. Father Francis Bray, of Clonmel, a man of great courage and piety, was Navy Chaplain in the service of Spain. He was killed by a cannon ball in a naval action between the Spaniards and Dutch in 1624. Father Peter McCarthy, who made his Novitiate at Mechlin with Blessed John Berchmans, was Chaplain-in-Chief, or Head Camp Missioner, in the Netherlands. Father James Fullam, a Dominican, who on two occasions was thrown into prison by the English, was made Chaplain to the regiment of the Duke of Berwick. He filled his post faithfully, and was slain in a battle in the Milanese, between Prince Eugene, of Savoy, and the Duke of Vendôme. Father Simon O'Fallon, of Galway, was appointed by the King of Portugal, not only to attend to the spiritual welfare of the soldiers, but likewise to inspect the fortifications. Father Bryan McDavitt, a most talented priest, was Chaplain to Owen Roe. The Confederates used for national purposes a printing-press, which this Father had bought in France for the Irish Jesuits. Father William Boyton, a native of Cashel, was military Chaplain for some time in Holland. In an article on *Dominicus de Rosario*, we mention him as being slain while administering the last Sacraments to a dying soldier on the taking of the Rock of Cashel. The most reliable historians say that he was either cut down or shot, while hearing the Confession of a wounded soldier. Father Augustine Fitzgerald "was for many years Professor of Moral Theology at the Azores, and was dear to all for his amiability and virtue; on his return home he was Chaplain in the Fleet which was sent against the French, and in which were many Irishmen; after sundry escapes he was exiled from Ireland, and in the College of Faro looked after the spiritual interests of his countrymen." Father Lawrence Moore was in the Golden Fort with the Spanish soldiers when it was treacherously surrendered to the English Commander, Lord Grey. Father Moore, after being hanged, had his body cut into fragments. We read in the examination of James Roche, an Irishman of the Lord Roche's country, "that in the Irish regiment there are many priests that have pay out of the army, amongst which McEgan, Flahir O'Mulconry and father Cusack are the chiefest; the first whereof, in reputation, is not inferior to the other, but the other two are more stirring, and therefore employed in directions and plots betwixt the Spanish Court and the Low Countries. The lord Henry hath another priest, named doctor Chamberlayne, who still attends him, and is used in the secrecy of all their works." Father Thomas Carve, a native of the county of Tipperary, spent much of his life at St. Stephen's Cathedral, Vienna. During his earlier years he was Chaplain to a regiment and traveled through many parts of Germany "during the War carried on there by Gustavus Adolphus, and continued after his death." The Colonel of the regiment to which he was attached was Walter Devereux. Carve was a writer of some repute, and among his works he left an account of his experience as an army Chaplain. Father Lawrence O'Ferrall, a Dominican, who studied at Prague, in Bohemia, died piously, while serving as Chaplain to Berwick's regiment in Spain. O'Ferral is justly placed among the Confessors of Ireland, having twice suffered imprisonment for the sake of his religion. His life, if full of perils, had something of romance in it. On one occasion he was sent into Portugal as a German. His companion on this trip was the Archduke Charles, afterwards Emperor of the Romans. It is well known in this country that the first regularly settled priest in New York city, the Rev. Charles Whelan, an Irish

Franciscan, " served as Chaplain on board of one of the French ships belonging to Admiral De Grasse's fleet, engaged in assisting the cause of the colonies. Father Whelan was much esteemed by Lafayette, and was recommended by that soldier to the favor of the State.

THE SWORD ALONE.

(A Song of 1641.)

The Sword alone can right your wrongs,
All brave men now must own it;
The Sword to Freedom's cause belongs,
All history past has shown it.
   Then grasp the Sword,
   And say no word,
Bright steel must plead for Ireland.

In vain you weep, in vain you pray,
Your masters smile, and heed not;
You sigh in vain for freedom's ray
While Erin's foemen bleed not.
   Then grasp the Sword,
   And say no word,
Sharp steel must speak for Ireland.

Fling out your banners to the sky,
Place swords around them gleaming;
Your tyrant foes can scare deny
What's asked by sabres beaming.
   Friends, grasp the sword,
   And say no word,
Bare steel must plead for Ireland.

With arms in hand now claim your right,
Your arms alone can serve you;
Your Justice yet will vanquish Might,—
But your arms first must nerve you.
   Unsheathe the Sword,
   And say no word,
With steel now strike for Ireland.

IRISH CHAPLAINS IN EUROPEAN COURTS.

IRISH monks and priests, from the very dawn of Christianity on their Island, were found to be no strangers in the Courts of Europe. St. Virgilius was high in the esteem of King Pepin, who much admired his mildness and erudition. Claude Clement, and John Scott, the famous "Wisdom-Sellers," who, according to the monk of St. Gall, were "men incomparably skilled in human learning and in the Holy Scriptures," were greatly beloved by Charlemagne. Many Irish monks were to be met in the Court and Council of Charles, the Bald. We read that, long before, St. Columbanus enjoyed the hospitality of Clotharius, King of the Soissons, and that St. Kylian was honored by Gozbert, the ruling Prince of Franconia.

As we glance through the history of the Penal Times we are surprised to find how many of the poor exiled priests, who had been hounded from their country, became the friends and advisers of kings and queens. Doctor Plunket, a graduate of the College of the Lombards, Paris, and afterwards Bishop of Meath, was Almoner to the beautiful, but ill-fated Marie Antoinette—the unhappy queen whose misfortunes inspired Burke and Carlyle to write two of the most eloquent passages to be found in all their works. Father Florence Conry, famed as a theologian, writer, and patriot, received many royal favors from different princes, and was held in the highest esteem by King Philip III., of Spain. Father Daniel O'Daly, *alias* Dominick a Rosario, a native of Kerry, was so greatly admired for his learning, piety, and prudence by the King of Portugal that that sovereign sent him, in the year 1655, as his special Ambassador to the brilliant Court of Louis XIV., on affairs of great importance. Father O'Daly was also in great favor with the Spanish Kings, and was for a time Chaplain to Portugal's Queen. The celebrated Peter Talbot, Archbishop of Dublin, possessed great influence with the Spanish Ministers in Flanders, and particularly with the Count de Fonsaldagna, who was the actual Governor of the country, though the Archduke Leopold enjoyed the title. While Charles II. was exiled at Cologne, according to some respectable authorities, Father Talbot frequently visited his Majesty. After some conversations on religion, the Irish priest had the consolation, it is stated, of converting England's King to the true Faith. Talbot was sent on an embassy to the Court of Spain, by his royal convert. On the marriage of the King of England to the Infanta of Portugal, Father Talbot was appointed one of the Queen's Almoners, officiated in her family, and became one of her household. Though Catholic priests "were hunted down like wolves," during the Penal Days, both in England and Ireland, foreign Catholic Ambassadors frequently brought their Chaplains with them into the very heart of London. Father Gerard Robinson, an Irish Priest, and a student of Salamanca, was high in favor among the royal personages at Madrid. After his ordination he was attached to the Spanish embassy in London. The patriotic Irish Jesuit, Father Archer, was Confessor to the Archduke of Austria. Father Bonaventure Baron, a native of Clonmel, and a distinguished classical scholar, was the historiographer of Cosmo III., Grand Duke of Tuscany. Father Nicholas Donnellan was also greatly loved and highly appreciated by the Grand Duke. Bartholomew Archer, of Kilkenny, was Almoner to the Duchess of Orleans. Dr. Thaddeus O'Rorke, Bishop of Killalla, held the post of Private Chaplain to Prince Eugene, of Savoy, and this illustrious commander, who held him in the highest esteem, presented him with a gold cross, and a ring set in diamonds, and obtained a letter from the Emperor Leopold, recommending the newly-consecrated Bishop to his ally, the Queen of England. Father Ralph Corby was highly regarded at the Court of France. While this holy man was confined in a horrible cell in Newgate prison, awaiting a terrible and disgraceful death, he was honored by a visit from the French Ambassador. Father Ignatius Brown, of Waterford, was a Jesuit of great literary ability, taught *Belles Lettres* in Castile, was made Rector of the Irish Seminary at Poictiers, and held other important offices in different educational establishments. So highly was he rated for his virtue and learning that he was chosen as Confessor to the Queen of Spain.

Is it not strange, we will ask here, that Irishmen, who are so often said by the English to be unfit to rule their own little country, should so frequently be prayed to guide the kings and queens of Europe? Is it not strange that the priests who were outlawed in their native land, who were hated and despised, and driven out of their country at the point of the sword, should rise, like Joseph, to such favor in the eyes of foreign rulers? Is it not strange that for centuries Irishmen have had a large share in ruling the world as priests, writers, orators, warriors, and statesmen? It is not so strange, after all, when we know that Englishmen are grossly mistaken in their estimate of Irish character, when we remember the brain, and blood, and Faith of Ireland's sons.

THE CROSS.

I

Tell me, strong Faith, I asked,
Which is the fairest tree?
Faith smiled, and said to me :
"The fairest Tree to Faith—The Cross."

II

Tell me, bright hope, I cried,
What lights the skies for thee?
Hope shone, and answered me :
"Hope's ever-burning star—The Cross."

III

Tell me, chaste Love, I breathed,
What is thy mystery?
Love sighed, and whispered me :
"Love's deepest mystery—The Cross."

IV

Tell me, pale grief, I said,
What can bring joy to thee?
Grief wept, and said to me :
"My only fount of bliss—The Cross."

V

O, budding Earth, I sang,
What makes all nature free?
Earth singing said to me :
"My son, thou knowest well—The Cross."

VI

Sweet Peace, I touched my lyre,
What must my palm-branch be?
Peace thought, and answered me :
"The Palm of all God's sons—The Cross."

WHEN NIGHT COMES ON.

I.

The hour is still, the scene is fair,
   But night comes on ;
A glory mild fills sky and air,
   But night comes on ;
With flowers the blooming trees are crowned,
With softest green the meads are bound,
The woods shed music all around,
   But night comes on.

II.

Sad is my heart, and moist my eye,
   For Night comes on;
I watch the landscape, and I sigh,
   For Night comes on;
Much that I love will pass away.
When pass the beauties of this day—
In darkness soon my steps will stray,
   For Night comes on.

III.

Sweet Jesus, take me by the hand,
   When Night comes on ;
Oh, lead me to my Promised Land,
   When Night comes on
Let Thy Fair Face illume my eyes,
Let Thy Bright Throne before me rise,
Ah, let me enter Paradise
   When Night comes on.

IRISH HAGIOLOGY.

"Through storm, and fire, and gloom, I see it stand,
    Firm, broad and tall,
The Celtic Cross that marks our Fatherland."
            —*T. D. M'Gee.*

"THE chief glory of Ireland is Christian," says Father Victor De Buck, the distinguished Belgian writer. No higher encomium than this can be given to any land. The glory of ancient Greece arose chiefly from her perfection in literature, in sculpture, and in architecture; the pride of old Rome lay in her code of laws, in the might of her armies, the majesty of her emperors, and the wideness of her dominion; but Ireland's glory springs from a purer, loftier, diviner source—*her Christianity.* Ireland's glory lies in the holiness of her sons and the chastity of her daughters. It lies in her likeness to the Divine Model; in the firmness of her hope; in the warmth of her charity; in the brightness of her Faith. It lies in the innocence of her people; in their love of prayer and mortification, and in their fidelity to their God. The glory of Ireland falls upon her bent and reverent head from the Cross of Calvary. It falls upon her from the golden lamps of her sanctuaries, and from the white tapers burning on her altars. It shines above and around her convents and monasteries, her chapels and her cells, her cradles and her tombs.

> O ! Erin chaste, O ! Holy Isle
> The Cross is still thy glorious sign ;
> O! bear it bravely for awhile,
> It crowns thee with a light divine.

> What though thy tears must nightly fall
> On rocky beds and thorny ways,
> What though thy chiefs must pine in thrall,
> And sorrow sadden all thy lays.

> Thou art the chosen Isle of God,
> The home of holy Faith and love,
> With sainted dust in every sod,
> And saints in every star above.

It was the full conviction that Ireland's glory sprang from her Christianity that inspired the hagiologists of the penal times—Ward, Fleming, Colgan, O'Clery, Wadding and White—to search in foreign libraries and ruined monasteries for the records of her saints. It was this conviction that encouraged them to travel along the Rhine, the Tagus, the Dyle, the Rhone, and the Tiber in search of the footprints of Irish apostles. It was this conviction that made them examine crumbling walls and fallen pillars, mouldering chapels and oratories, and broken tomb-stones, for the names of Irish Bishops, priests, and virgins. They beheld Ireland's banner lying in the dust, her harp-strings mute, and the sceptre and crown of her ancient kings in the hands of strangers, and they resolved—oh, glorious resolve!—to rescue for her the glory of her saints and martyrs, the glory of her Christianity. England having robbed her of her power and rights as a nation, Scotland tried to deprive her of the fame and honor of her holiest and most glorious sons and daughters, those faithful servants of the Lord who are venerated on the altars of the Church. This fired the energy of Ireland's student-sons, and made them hasten from library to library in search of documents to refute and destroy Scotland's claims. They had learned in childhood that Ireland was the "Island of saints;" they had been inspired by the thought to lead pure and holy lives; they had gloried in the knowledge that their native land was the mother of saintly men and women, and now were they to be cruelly undeceived? Was Ireland's claim to Rumold, and Dympna, and Fridolin based on no solid foundation?

Was it a mere dream of their fathers? Dusty volumes and obscure manuscripts were heaped up at St. Anthony's Convent of Louvain, and Hugh Ward, a Franciscan priest, the son of the Lord of Letter and Bally-Ward, undertook to publish the "Acts of the Saints of Ireland," in which he conclusively proved that *Ireland*, and not *Scotland*, was anciently known as *Scotia*, and consequently, that those called in old books *Scots*, were Irishmen and not Scotchmen. Michael O'Clery made reverential pilgrimages to all the old ruins in Ireland; he visited the deserted monasteries of Ireland's monks; he lingered around silent churches and holy wells; he dug into the dark mines of Gaelic lore; he gathered up old songs and old traditions that still flourished among the people, and after having sent much of the fruit of his excursions and labors to his brethren in Louvain, he, together with Ferfessius O'Conry, Pelerin O'Clery and Pelerin O'Dubgenman, composed the "Annals of Donegal." Patrick Fleming, a scion of the noble family of Slane, visited France, Italy and Germany, and rifled their libraries of all the knowledge relating to Ireland. His zeal was unflagging. Now we find him in the cell in which St. Malachy died at Clairvaux; now we find him in the monastery of Ratisbonne; and again, we find him at Harfleur, or at St. Peter's Convent at Regensburg. Besides the valuable information, books, and manuscripts, which he sent to Father Ward, he wrote the lives, from original sources, of several Irish saints. From his fertile pen we have the "Life of St. Comgall," founder of the great monastery of Bangor; the "Life of St. Columbanus;" the "Life of St. Molua," patron of Killaloe, and founder of Clonfert-Molua, in the Queen's County. "The Works of St. Columban," by Fleming, had the honor to be reprinted in the "Bibliotheca maxima Patrum," and in the "Patrologie de Migne." His "Life of St. Mochvenog" was inserted in the great work of the Bollandists. The indefatigable John Colgan arose with the might of a giant to defend Ireland's claim to her saints. To his care in transcribing from original documents, and his zeal in visiting libraries, several distinguished Jesuit professors of Louvain bear honorable testimony. In his time Belgium was rich in grand libraries. At Tournay and Brussels were found many rare and precious volumes. But it was in the library of Louvain, then one of the most beautiful libraries in Europe, he passed most of those leisure hours which he could spare from his professorial chair at St. Anthony's Convent. To him we are indebted for the lives of St. Patrick, St. Columba, and St. Brigid.

All the Irish talent on the Continent was engaged in building up and glorifying the lives of the ancient monks of Erin. Some of the most distinguished scholars in Europe spent their leisure hours, or spare moments, in casting new light upon the Christian heroes of Irish history, in snatching from oblivion the fading records of the sainted children of the Apostle Patrick. Father Stephen White wrote of Ireland's saints in glowing language on the banks of the Moselle. Thomas Messingham put forth in Paris his "Garland of Irish Saints." Henry Fitzsimmon, with a power and clearness which were all his own, vindicated Ireland's right to the apostles of nearly every country in Europe. David Rothe, Bishop of Kilkenny, in the shadow of the church of St. Canice, collected the proud details of many a holy life which were fast sinking into oblivion. The memory of Ireland's saints aroused all the enthusiasm, awoke and stimulated all the talent and energy of every Celtic scholar in the halls of Europe and in the glens of Erie.

Oh, beautiful and holy, as fair as the dawn, was the Ireland of the Celtic hagiologists of the seventeenth century. Their studies led them into the cells, and caves, and woods, in which the mortified and zealous

Irish monks spent their peaceful and sublime lives. They brought before them the virgin daughters of Erin, wrapt in divine contemplation, or singing sweet canticles of love and praise before the chaste altar of the Immaculate Lamb.

Our noble hagiologists watched with streaming eyes the holy missionaries marching out from Ireland in glorious succession to bring light, and peace, and joy, and life to the peoples who sat in the darkness of error and in the shadow of death. They saw St. Arden preaching to the Northumbrians in England; they saw St. Colman among the Northern Saxons; they beheld St. Arbogart seated and ruling in the Episcopal Chair of Strasbourg. Sts. Maildulphus, Cuthbert, Killian, Virgilius, Finden and Columba rose up before their entranced vision, and they blessed and glorified the land that bore such flowers. They deeply felt the truth of the words of St. Adelnus to Elfride, "that Ireland is no less stored with learned men than are the heavens with glittering stars." With Egiwold, they agreed "that Ireland, though fruitful in soil, is much more celebrated for saints." With Henry of Huntingdon they knew "that the Almighty enriched Ireland with several blessings, and appointed a multitude of saints for its defence." They delighted in old, holy Ireland. Ireland of the Cell, and the Church, and the Monastery, and the Convent, and the Well, and the Celtic Cross, claimed the deep devotion of their hearts. No wonder that the names of our hagiologists are loved and cherished by every true child of Ireland. Would that we could inherit some of their love for our forefathers in the Faith! I can think of few blessings greater than the grace of devotion to the dear servants of God. To love the saints who prayed, and watched, and fasted, and bled, and died to transmit the Faith pure and bright to us ought to be our great aim. Sons of Ireland, do you always remember that the chief and lasting glory of your country is Christian? Do you always remember that the brightest halos that shine upon your country are those that surround the heads of your saints? Alas! I fear not. To many the angelic vision of Ireland's beauty during the days when St. Columb preached in Scotland; when Columban taught in France; when St. Clement spoke in Germany; when St. Buan bore the light into Iceland; when St. Killian prayed in Franconia, and St. Suiwan in the Orcades, when St. Gallus stood amid the snows of Switzerland, and St. Brendan shone upon the Fortunate Isles, is covered with mists and clouds.

THE PATRIOT'S ADDRESS.

(Supposed to be written when first the "Red Hand of Ulster" was unfurled.)

Do you wait for the swords of seraphs to flash in your holy cause?
Do you wait for a heaven-sent Moses to free you from alien laws?
Do you look to the skies for manna to feast you in famine years?
Do you hope for the hands of angels to dry up your fount of tears?

Do you think that the graves will open and yield up hosts 'gainst your foes?
Do you dream that Red Seas will cover the tyrants that cause your woes?
Look not for these favors, my people; look not for miracles grand;
Arise like the waves of the Ocean, and strike for your own dear Land.

Trust now to your valor and virtue; trust now to your flashing steel,
Charge down on the black-hearted foeman,— in this is your only weal.
Pray, yes pray to the God of Battles to nerve you for deadly strife;
If you fall on a field blood-reddened,—to God offer up your life.

In vain you have begged from the tyrant to live
    in your own Green Isle.
You may beg till the Day of Judgment,—the
    Saxon has naught but guile,
Think, oh think of the sword of Judith, think
    of the brave Machabee,
Think of your wrongs, your homes, your altars,
    and strike that you may be free.

Join hands with each foe of England, join hands
    with brave France or Spain,
Dye red the green folds of your Banner in blood
    of your Saxon slain,
If you bleed in the fight for Ireland, not rebels
    but martyrs you,
If you fall for your homesteads warring your death
    will be brave and true.

Remember the blood of your martyrs! Remember
    the tears of your maids!
Remember the Strongbows and Cromwells!
    Remember the fires in your glades!
Remember the exiles who perished—the priests
    and the bards, and chiefs,—
It is yours to avenge their exile—it is yours to
    avenge their griefs!

IRISH COLLEGES FOUNDED ABROAD.

And call to remembrance the works of the fathers, which they have done in their generations; and you shall receive great glory, and an everlasting name. 1 Mac. Chap. II., v. LI.

NEARLY all the famous Irish schools that had escaped the ravages of the Danes were destroyed by the Protestant "Reformers." The blackest laws ever framed by any government were enacted against Catholic education in Ireland by the ministers of Henry, Elizabeth, and James. It is needless to mention here the numerous statutes against "lectors or schoolmasters," not Protestant. Almost every one has read them. It is sufficient to say, that it was the penal enactments against Catholic schools and teachers that forced our students to retire to the old Continent, there to found new asylums for learning. Schools that should flourish in Irish valleys, and by Irish rivers, had to rise and flourish in the different parts of Catholic Europe. And they did soon rise and flourish in France, Spain, Portugal, and Italy. Ireland's love for learning cannot be extinguished. Irishmen at all times love and seek the Light. Schools were founded at Lisle, Antwerp, Tournay, Douay and St. Omer. Seminaries were established in Bourdeaux, Toulouse, and Nantes. Irish scholars opened new seats of learning at Louvain, Lisbon, Madrid, Rome, Paris, Seville, Valencia, Valladolid, Alcala, and Salamanca. The Irish secular priests had their seminaries abroad, as well as the different religious Orders. In all these colleges were found men of wide experience, of deep and solid learning; men renowned for the sanctity of their lives and the purity of their doctrine. Fervent youths who were anxious to take the places of martyred pastors flocked to the schools abroad in defiance of all the laws and threats of the dominant party. The foreign schools soon defeated the object of the Penal Laws against Catholic education. Though the ranks of the brave priesthood at home were cruelly thinned by persecution, death, and unheard of suffering, still new recruits were anxiously waiting in the halls of distant lands to rush into the thick of the combat. Through these recruits the Church of St. Patrick was saved, through them, under God, the Faith of Ireland was victorious. All through the Penal Days many an Irish student turned his back on sunny Italy, on gay France, on generous Spain—many an Irish student left pleasant homes in foreign schools and courts to keep alive among his people the glorious fire of religion and patriotism. At one time nearly every priest, bishop, and archbishop of Ireland could be numbered among "the Irish Scholars of the Continent." On returning to their native shores, many of those who had spent years abroad in pursuit of knowledge devoted themselves in a special manner to the instruction of their less fortunate people at home. It was a strange and edifying sight to see during the Penal Days some of the most distinguished of Europe's professors seated in the ruins of some old abbey or under the white branches of the blooming hawthorne bush or hedge teaching the elements of religion and science to the children of the persecuted Irish peasantry, or to the scions of rob'ɔed, impoverished, noble houses. We find in the glorious catalogue of "hedge schoolmasters" the names of even archbishops. History tells us that Nicholas Skerret, Archbishop of Tuam, as well as other distinguished ecclesiastical dignitaries, taught school at Galway in the worst of times. Father Charles Lea, a distinguished Jesuit, who shone as a student in the halls of Rome, Oxford, Paris, and Cologne, was happy to be able to teach a school in Youghall about the end of the Sixteenth Century. In many an Irish hut in the wildest and most solitary parts of the country, all through the Penal Days, could be found schoolmasters who had won many a medal in the most famous schools and universities of Europe.

> His altar was an uncarved rock,
>   The Priest of Penal Days;
> His choir the waves upon the lough,
>   The Priest of Penal Days;
> His incense rose from flowerets wild—
> His temple—Nature undefiled—
> His acolyte— a peasant child—
>   The Priest of Penal Days.

> His garden was the lonely moor,
> > The Priest of Penal Days;
> His bread came from the poorest poor,
> > The Priest of Penal Days;
> He scorned the earth and all it gave,
> His mansion was a gloomy cave,
> His goal—a glorious martyr's grave.
> > Grand Priest of Penal Days.

It would go beyond the scope of this book were we to give a full account of the several Irish Colleges founded abroad during the Penal Days. We shall, therefore, treat only of a few of them, of whose history we have made a special study. Before treating at large of any particular establishment, we venture to give our readers a few interesting details concerning some of the colleges of which we will not treat in detail. "In various parts of the continent," writes Father Walsh, "colleges for the reception of Irish students were in a short time established. Under the protection of Philip II., King of Spain, and other benefactors, who munificently endowed them, they soon multiplied, and while the Irish Church could thus calculate on a regular succession in the ministry, the malice of England was confounded and her name became a by-word of contempt and scorn throughout Europe. In 1595, the Irish Seminary at Lisbon was founded by Cardinal Ximenes, who had ever taken a lively interest in its welfare, and who was, according to his own directions, honorably interred in its church. Another establishment was founded about the same time at Evora, by

Cardinal Henriques. In 1596, the Irish College at Douay, was founded. Christopher Cusack, a learned priest of the Diocese of Meath, had through his influence contributed much in advancing this literary retreat. He also through his exertions founded the Colleges at Lisle, Antwerp, Tournay, and St. Omer. Seminaries were established in Bordeaux, Toulouse and Nantes, for Irish students, under the patronage of Anne, Queen of Austria. The Irish College, on the Hill of St. Geneviève, in Paris, was a gift from the French Government, and to which the Baron de St. Just had been a great benefactor. In 1582, the College of Salamanca was founded for Irish students by the states of Castile and Leon, Philip III. being its principal patron; and about the same time two extensive Seminaries were erected, one of them a royal establishment, at Seville, for the education of Irish missionaries, to which Sarapater, a learned canon of that city, was a principal benefactor. In the last year of this century, the Baron George Silveria, founded the Irish College at Alcala de Henares; he afterwards richly endowed it, and it became, in the seventeenth century, a source of incalculable benefit to the Irish Church." Thomas White, a native of Clonmel, belonged to the Society of Jesus, and "was a great pillar of the Irish Church and of extraordinary piety and zeal." He died at Santiago, in 1622. He founded the Irish Jesuit College of Salamanca, and became its Rector. We do not know whether the Jesuit, Cornelius Carrig, founded a house of studies in Portugal, where he long resided, or not.

He is at all events praised by Henry Fitzsimon, as a benefactor of Irish education. John Houling, a native of Wexford, was an able writer, a good linguist, a man of zeal, and is said to have died a martyr of charity. He is highly praised in the controversial writings of Copinger and Fitzsimon. To Houling we are indebted for the founding of an Irish Jesuit College at Lisbon. The celebrated Jesuit, Father Parsons, also founded a College for Irish students, in Spain. All honor to his name. Father James Archer, the patriotic Jesuit, if he did not found a College, was a great promoter of the education of Irish students abroad. Archer was "a most celebrated man, whose name was very dear to Irishmen, with whom he possessed an unbounded influence. He was a famous missioner in Ireland during the war of Tyrone." In 1628, Luke Wadding prevailed on Cardinal Ludovisius to found a College at Rome, for the benefit of those youths who wished to study for the ranks of the Irish secular priesthood. "The Cardinal hired a house," says Harris, "for the use of this foundation, opposite the College of St. Isidore, and placed the youths under the care and inspection of the Friars of that house. He allotted six hundred crowns a year for their support, and laid out one hundred and fifty crowns in providing it with furniture. Wadding had the charge committed to him of drawing up a book of statutes for their government, to be approved of by the Cardinal, which was done. The College was opened on the 1st of January, 1628, and the students were immediately introduced." Owen Callanan was chosen first Rector, but died after six months in office. He was succeeded by Martin Walsh, a native of Waterford. Walsh was a young man at Madrid, when Charles, Prince of Wales, afterwards King Charles I., arrived at the Court of the Infanta of Spain. He made himself known by a poetical work which he published at the time. He afterwards went to Naples and read philosophy in the Convent of Mount Calvary in that city. He was thence called to Rome, and became Divinity Lecturer in the College of St. Isidore. He was also Guardian of this College for some time. John Ponce was the third Rector of the Ludovisian College. This Franciscan was a native of Cork, and spent part of his life at Paris and Louvain. He was an able and voluminous writer. He composed several works on philosophical and theological subjects.

The students of the Ludovisian College attended all the exercises and lectures at St. Isidore's. A watchful eye was kept over their conduct. They were never allowed to go out except in the company of some of the Franciscans. Even in death the Cardinal did not forget the College of his heart. He left for its benefit a farm situated about twelve miles from Rome, and a yearly rent of a thousand crowns. He obliged his heir to pay this forever, and to purchase the house in which the Collegians resided for their use.

"Wadding," says Harris, "founded another College or Convent, as an Irish Franciscan Novitiate, at Capranica, in the Patrimony of St. Peter, about twenty-eight miles from Rome. For this he obtained the

Pope's License by Bull, dated the 8th of May, 1656, and six days after he solemnly took possession of it for that use. The intention of this foundation was, that it should serve as a seminary for the instruction of Irish novices as a supply for the College of St. Isidore. The Pope made some grants in favor of this house. Wadding provided vestments for the altar, books for the students and other furniture necessary for the first inhabitants, which he took care to increase as long as he lived." The first guardian of this novice-home was Maurice Matthews, a "Lecturer of Divinity."

ERIN, DEAR!

I.

Bright gold sleeps in thy mountains,
                Erin, Dear!
In silver leap thy fountains,
                Erin, Dear!
Thy skies with light are glowing,
Thy winds in music blowing,
Thy buds in beauty growing,
                Erin, Dear!

II.

Thy streams are sweetly singing,
                Erin, Dear!
Thy chapel bells are ringing,
                Erin, Dear!
Thy vales of song and story,—
Thy castles strong, though hoary,
To me still beam with glory,
                Erin, Dear!

III.

Pure as Avoca's waters,
                Erin, Dear!
Are they brave sons and daughters,
                Erin, Dear!
Thy great heart throbs the Ocean,
With its sublime emotion—
Chaste Temple of Devotion,
                Erin, Dear!

ST. ISIDORE'S COLLEGE, ROME.

A GREAT IRISH FRANCISCAN CONVENT.

THE Roman Pontiffs have always fondly cherished the Irish nation. But it was during the Penal Days that they showed their deepest love for her. It was then, when she most needed friends, that they gathered to the Eternal City the exiled Irish chiefs and scholars; it was then that they sent Nuncios, missionaries, material help, and Papal Benedictions and Indulgences to her struggling sons. The Spanish banner, blessed by Papal hands, still lies hidden on the hills of Kerry, at Smerwick, by the ancient Fort of Gold. How many "an Irish exiled lord" found a home in the capital of the Christian world, and lived in peace and plenty through the munificent bounty of the Popes! Can Ireland ever forget the brilliant reception accorded the fugitive Earls of Tyrone and Tyrconnell, on their arrival under the shadow of St. Peter's? Can she ever forget the honors and gifts bestowed by the Vicars of Christ on her Conrys, her Waddings, and her Lombards?

Rome and Ireland are bound in love by the holiest and strongest ties that can exist on earth, and nothing in the future can sever the golden links of their affection. The high interests of Rome, "the City of the

Soul," and of Ireland, "the Island of Saints," are one and inseparable. Even in our own day the devotion of Ireland's youths to the Holy See could be read in the light of the swords of the Irish Papal Brigade. The appointment of Dr. Walsh to the See of Dublin, and of Dr. Kirby to the archbishopric of Ephesus, is but one of many proofs of the devoted love of the present glorious Pontiff, Leo XIII., for the Irish race and nation.

St. Isidore's Franciscan College, Rome, will ever remain dear to the hearts of all patriotic Irishmen. From the beginning it was a source of countless blessings to Ireland. Its guardians, professors and students were religious who united great piety with deep learning, who devoted their talent to the service of the universal Church, and yet never waned in their love of the hapless land of their fathers.

"Here," says Thomas Darcy McGee, "had gathered Irish professors whose names are distinguished in the Church literature of their age. Here, in after times, were bred many of that race of clergymen who lived in martyrdom under penal legislation, refusing to fly the land for royal proclamations, refusing to recant at the gallows."

St. Isidore's was founded by Luke Wadding, on June 13th, 1625. "It was intended," says Sir James Ware, "for the education of Irish students of the Franciscan Order in the study of the liberal arts, divinity, and controversy." It was also destined as a seminary, out of which the missions in England, Scotland and Ireland might be supplied. Wadding bought for this purpose a plot of ground on which an hospital or place of reception for the Franciscans of the Spanish nation had been erected. He paid off large sums with which that house was incumbered, framed orders proper for the government of a college, and procured the Bull of Pope Urban to give them strength. He entered into possession of the premises on June 24th, the same year. He was the first guardian of it himself, and appointed Anthony Hickey the first principal lecturer of Divinity, and Patrick Fleming lecturer of Philosophy. Wadding called indifferently into it the native friars of all the four provinces of Ireland, who were dispersed in Spain, Flanders and Germany. So in a short time the college increased to the number of thirty, who acquired such an opinion for religion and learning that they began to be very acceptable to the Romans, and their fame spread in other countries. The founder purchased of all the reserved rent and incumbrances to which the ground was subject under the first agreement, and bought in other contiguous plots of ground to enlarge the site. He improved the former buildings, erected many new ones, surrounded the whole with a firm wall, elegantly adorned both the inside and outside of the church and buildings, and enlarged the former by annexing to it six chapels. He furnished the college with a noble and well-chosen library, not for ostentation, but use; the library consisted of about 5,000 printed books, for the most part folios, and about 800 manuscripts, all of which he settled and disposed into classes in an alphabetical method.

The money to supply these expenses was obtained, for the most part, from the munificence and charity of the Romans out of the affection and love which they bore Wadding, who lived to see this, his newly-erected college, grow in great splendor. The office of Guardian was elective, and he enjoyed it five times. He took exact care to keep the college out of debt, and the last time he was Guardian he made a present to the body of a great number of his "Annals," and others of his writings, that, even after his death, the Superiors found from thence considerable aid to answer their expenses. So great was his virtue and industry, that though he was a poor friar, and a stranger from the remotest island of Europe, yet from the time he arrived at Rome, in the thirtieth year of his age, he acquired such friends and patrons in a short time that, from their voluntary beneficence, more than from his importunity, from June 13th, 1625, when he took possession of the Hospital of St. Isidore, to August 2d, 1630, he found means to expend 22,000 Roman crowns on the area, buildings, books and furniture of the sacristy only, when the portico of the church, the choir, the wall inclosing their whole possessions, were not built, nor the larger garden levelled, nor the lesser garden purchased, nor one stone laid in the second cloisters, nor the sacristy enlarged or adorned. For these and other things he provided the expenses afterwards.

Father Luke Wadding, the founder and first Guardian of St. Isidore's, rises up in Penal Times like a pillar of light. Among the great sons of Ireland he is one of the greatest. Among the great men of all Christendom he holds a high rank. His fame was a new glory to his Order, and was long the common property of all the learned men of Europe. The favorite of several nations, distinct in laws and language, he was highly honored on various occasions by dukes, kings, Archbishops, Cardinals and Popes. A man of consummate prudence in difficult embassies, a great preacher in several of the European tongues, a distinguished professor, he was a writer who may well be compared to the most indefatigable and learned among the Bollandists. "From the time of the Spanish Embassy," says Ware, "he grew into such authority, and the world had conceived such an opinion of his wisdom, dexterity, industry, and his good fortune in transacting business, that every person was fond of courting his advice and aid in the most difficult matters."

A true religious, he bore in his heart a deep veneration for the Mother of God, and most learnedly defended her Immaculate Conception; a devoted Son of St. Francis, he threw a flood of glory upon the saints and distinguished members of the Franciscan Order; a faithful soldier of the Church, he published the "Lives of the Popes" and many glorious things relating to the Holy See of Rome. As was natural to him as a Franciscan and an Irishman, he took a deep interest in the works of Scotus. He collected the fragmentary writings of this great man, examined them carefully, rejected spurious papers attributed to the Subtile Doctor, and added many marginal notes of great importance.

He ably defended Scotus against the charges made against him, and had his works properly brought out with a dedication to Philip IV., King of Spain.

Like all truly great minds, Wadding bore a deep and lasting love for his native land. To her sacred cause he generously devoted his learning and his influence. He wrote with a burning pen when he treated of her great sons, or when he defended her rights and depicted her bleeding form. It is deeply to be regretted that he did not live to compose his intended "General History of Ireland." No man of his time was better qualified than he for this grand task. The active part he took in the great rebellion of 1641 endeared him to all patriotic Irishmen, and sheds immortal glory on his name. "By his industry," writes Ware, "he solicited and procured supplies of money, arms and expert Irish officers from France and Flanders to be sent to Ireland, before the rebels had any thoughts of either demanding or receiving them; and he sent over a person to bring him an exact and certain account of affairs there. *These were the first foreign aids received by the Irish from abroad,* which he obtained by soliciting the wealthy and such as were well disposed to sustain what they thought the cause of religion. The Supreme Council, then established at Kilkenny, returned him thanks *'for his seasonable zeal to the Catholic religion and his country.'* In 1642 they gave him a commission to act as their agent to the Pope, Cardinals, and other princes of Italy, sealed with the new seal of the newly-erected Commonwealth. They sent him also dispatches to be delivered to those who, at his instance, had contributed to their first aid, namely, to Pope Urban VIII., to the Cardinals Onuphrius, Francis and Anthony Barberini. In the dispatches they laid open their condition, implored their patronage and the Pope's benediction and aid. They also extolled the wisdom, religion and zeal of Wadding.

"Animated with this commission, he employed his whole power with the Pope and Cardinals, and was instant with them in season and out of season to succor his distressed country. Among other graces, he obtained the favor of the Pope to send Peter Francis Scarampi, priest of the Oratory of St. Philip Neri, at Rome, to Ireland, with the Pope's Benediction, and large supplies of money and ammunition to animate and comfort the rebels, and to give seasonable notice to the Pope's ministers in other countries in what manner they might best aid the Catholic cause. By his own industry he promoted a charitable collection among some of the Cardinals and prelates for the aid of his brethren, by which, upon several occasions, he seasonably relieved them. He obtained a particular congregation of Cardinals to be appointed to deliberate from time to time on ways and means to aid and direct the Irish rebellion. Wadding himself was always admitted to assist at the meetings of the Cardinals. Some time after he obtained from the new Pope, Innocent X., that an Apostolic Nuncio should be sent to Ireland, and John Baptist Renuccini, Archbishop and Prince of Firmo, was appointed for that office. Besides the aid which he carried from the Pope, Wadding delivered into his hands 26,000 crowns out of the collection which he made for the pious cause, and a year after sent another considerable sum by Dennis Massario, auditor to the Nuncio, for the like purpose. The Supreme Council sent a deputy to Pope Urban VIII., and to Francis and Anthony Baberini, his nephews, with letters subscribed by three Archbishops, five secular peers, the secretary of the Council, three of the Commons, and one Bishop, humbly entreating His Holiness, that he would condescend to call to the College of Cardinals Father Luke Wadding, a native of Ireland, illustrious by birth and merit, whose other praises and virtues are not unknown to the Apostolic See.'" Wadding, being a man of humility, and for other reasons, did all he could to escape the intended dignity. In this he was successful.

Wadding was so successful in defending the Immaculate Conception at the Holy City, "that his labors acquired him the acknowledgments of the Spanish King's* ambassadors at Rome, of Cardinal Sandoval, Archbishop of Toledo, in his own name, as well as in the names of the Council of Madrid and of the Chapter of the Metropolitan Church at Seville. And, above all, King Philip IV. himself gave him thanks in a letter written with his own hand; which he also commanded the Duke of Terra-Nova to do in His Majesty's name."

"Wadding," says Thomas Darcy McGee, "had left Ireland at fifteen, was bred in the Peninsula, his fortune was cast in Rome, yet his heart and hopes turned

---

* King Philip III.

more frequently to Ireland than to any other land. We can well believe him when he declares that he valued any subsidy gained for her over any honor that could be conferred upon himself."

Paul King, for some time guardian of St. Isidore's, is said by Harris "to be a very zealous man for the Nuncio's party and that of O'Neill, and a bitter enemy to his sovereign and the loyalist." A work of his was published at Brussels, "and dispersed over all the Popish countries of Europe, with design to instigate these powers against the English and Protestant interest in Ireland." He was also a philosophical writer. James Miles, a native of Drogheda, also made a name for himself in the same college and at Naples. He wrote a Catechism in English, for the instruction of those of the English nation who should be converted in Italy. He was also the author of a few books on music. These, we are told, were held in high esteem "among the adepts in music." Bonaventure Baron, whose true name was Fitzgerald, a native of Clonmel, was also professor in the college founded by Wadding. He was considered "the first Latinist of Rome, by the unanimous concurrence of the best judges" He ably defended the system of Scotus, and was a prolific writer. He composed works on Philosophy, Theology, History, Controversy, and even put forth a volume of poems. The name of Francis Porter, from Meath, reflects no small share of glory on St. Isidore's. He was professor of Divinity and Jubilate Lecturer in that college. He was also for some time president of it, and was undoubtedly an able controversial writer. In one of his books he resolves all difficulties between Catholics and Protestants to the one question of "the Perpetual Infallibility of the Visible Church of Christ." He loyally devoted his pen to the service of the ancient Church of Ireland, and proudly spoke of the love and reverence which his countrymen always bore the Holy See of Rome. His invectives against Martin Luther, as the author of countless evils to Christianity, were by no means mild or agreeable to the arch-heretic's friends.

Francis Birmingham, from Galway, taught Philosophy with distinction at Milan. Thence he went to Rome, and was Jubilate Lecturer of Divinity at St. Isidore's, and Definitor-General of his Order. Francis Harold, like Bonaventure Baron, was the nephew of Wadding. He first distinguished himself as a Divinity lecturer at the Irish College of Prague, in Bohemia. The latter part of his life he spent at Rome, devoting his time and talent to the completion of his great uncle's works and other writings of his own. Anthony Hickey, from the County Clare, was another of St. Isidore's distinguished scholars. He was a renowned Greek student, and "very learned in Scholastic Divinity," which he taught at Cologne and Louvain. He was for a time Superior of St. Anthony's Convent, and was elected Definitor of the Franciscan Order, in 1630. "His dear friend, Luke Wadding, carried him to Rome in 1619, being thereto solicited by Benignus à-Genua, General of the Franciscans, in order to be an assistant to Wadding, in collecting and disposing materials for his 'Annals and Writers' of that Order. He died on June 26th, 1641, much lamented by all his acquaintances, especially by Wadding, who gives him the highest character for his many excellent virtues and qualities."

HER ROSARY OF WELLS.

Ireland is enriched and beautified by a vast number of wells. The following verses poetically account for their origin.

The Angel spread her gleaming wings
   Upon the golden light ;
A sweet "adieu" to heaven she sang,
   Then sailed from visions bright.

Like winged star she crossed the sky,
   She fanned the fields of blue ;
She passed the moon with heedless eye—
   Down, down to earth she flew.

She saw the nations of the earth
   In error's baneful shade ;
She saw the fairest isle below
   In sinful pomp arrayed.

"Is this the destined home of saints?
   The chosen isle of God?"
The Angel dropped a holy tear
   That purified the sod.

She wept upon the mountain peak,
   She wept in secret dells ;
She placed on pagan Erin then
   Her Rosary of wells.

GOOD-NIGHT.

My bark of life now gains the shore,
    Gently she glides along;
Behind—she hears the breakers' roar,
    Before—sweet angels' song;
Thick darkness falls upon the sea,
    Upon the land soft light.
To all who sailed the deep with me,
    To friend and foe—Good-Night.

I bless the lips that shone with smiles,
    When stars forgot to glow;
I bless the hundred sunny isles
    That broke my sea of woe;
The shore is struck, a golden land,
    The sea fades on my sight,
My faithful bark is on the strand—
    To friend and foe—Good-Night.

THE IRISH DOMINICAN CONVENT, ON MONT-CESAR, LOUVAIN.

In all Belgium there is scarcely a more romantic, a more interesting, or a more sacred spot than the summit of Mont-Cesar, Louvain. Its "Castrum Cæsaris," is as solid, as gloomy, as mysterious, as the Tower of London. According to popular tradition, the Chateau Cesar was built by Julius Cæsar, during his sojourn among "the bravest of the Gauls." Historians, however, tell us that it was built by the Emperor Arnulf, about the year 885, to protect Louvain from the incursions of the Normans. Whether tradition or history be right, in this instance, we are unable to decide. Clouds and mists have long since gathered over the early history of the Chateau Cesar.

In the beginning of the sixteenth century a little boy was brought from Ghent, where he was born, to the Chateau Cesar, whose name was destined to fill Europe. This was Charles, Archduke of Austria, the son of Philip and Joanna, of Castile, known in history as Charles the Fifth. On Mont-Cesar Charles had his dreams of future power and glory. There he spent his boyish days in innocent amusement and in planning grand plans which he was to execute when the crown should be placed upon his youthfnl head. With him dwelt his two beautiful sisters — Mary, afterwards Queen of Hungary, and Eleanor, the Consort of Francis the First, King of France.

Little the youth dreamed, when he longed for royal power, when he told his pious sisters of his great ambition, that a day would come when he would grow weary of his sceptre, and find nothing but thorns in his jeweled crown. Little did he dream that a time would come when he would kneel before the Convent of Yuste and say:

> "'Tis night, and storms continually roar;
> Ye monks of Spain, unbar for me the door.
>
> Here in unbroken quiet let me fare,
> Save when the loud bell startles me to prayer.
>
> Make ready for me what your house has meet,
> A friar's habit and a winding-sheet."

Yet, so it was, in fact. Charles the Great resigned his purple robes for the humble habit of a monk.

If the Chateau Cesar was a suitable home for an ambitious and warlike prince, it was no less a home for a poet and historian like Puteanus, the worthy disciple of the illustrious Justin Lipsis. The silence, gloom and mystery of the Chateau at times helped the mind in serious thought, at times excited the imagination and courted that high inspiration without which no one can sing a deathless song.

Puteanus well deserves the name of a great Christian

philosopher. During more than forty years he devoted his time, his varied and brilliant talents, his energy and zeal, to the training in virtue and the advancement in science of the students who confided to his care. At an early age he filled a chair of eloqueuce in Milan; but his fame having spread to Spain, he was chosen by Philip III. as his historiographer. The Archduke Albert, wishing to have him in the Low Countries, invited him to Louvain, and had him appointed successor to Lipsis. He also gave him charge of the Chateau Cesar. Here Puteanus wrote several of his great works, and wore the collar of gold—not which he won from the proud invader—but which he received from the fair hands of the beautiful and virtuous Archduchess Isabella III. The style of Puteanus was not that of the ancients, but that of his master, Lipsis.

Puteanus was endowed with great qualities of head and heart, and won fairly all the honors conferred upon him. He died at Louvain in 1646, in his seventy-second year.

In 1607, the great Hugh O'Neill and his fellow-exiles, having passed through many dangers and hardships, and after having been feasted by the most illustrious personages in France and Belgium, arrived in Louvain. We can easily imagine the joy and enthusiasm of the Irish University students, and the patriotic Irish Franciscans, at seeing the noble princes of Ulster and Tyrconnel in their midst. But we cannot easily depict their sorrow when they called to mind that these illustrious men were exiled from their crowns and country. Did not tears fill the eyes of many a brave Irish student at Louvain when he thought of the pains of exile to be suffered by the sons of Hugh O'Neill and by Nuola, the accomplished and beautiful sister of Hugh O'Donnel? We know too much about the generosity, sympathy and tenderness of the Irish heart to doubt it for an instant.

Tyrconnel and his friends had suitable accommodation provided for them in the city of Louvain, but by the express wish of the Archduke Albert, O'Neill took up his abode in the old Chateau Cesar. There he received letters of congratulation and sympathy from illustrious Irish prelates and scholars at Rome, Paris and Douay. Crowds of Irish students and professors hurried to the Chateau to shake hands with the great Hugh, and to look upon the glorious banner of Ulster— the stainless "Red Hand."

O'Neill and O'Donel were obliged by circumstances to remain several months at Louvain. Though exiles, in truth, though rebels and firebrands in the eyes of England, who had robbed them and driven them to revolt, they were honored at Louvain by its generous and spirited inhabitants in a manner worthy of noble princes and Christian heroes. "When Christmas came," says the gifted author of "The Fate and Fortunes of Tyrone and Tyrconnel," "the burgomeister and the chief citizens waited on O'Neill, and according to custom paid him and O'Donel all the usual compliments, making them presents, and sending minstrels to perform in their residences."

How the heart of O'Neill must have been gladdened

as he sat in the spacious hall of the old palace of Charles V. and listened to Irish martial airs played in his honor by the countrymen of "Godfrey the Great, the shining western star!"

There is a gate, or rather the last relic of one, on the ramparts, within sight of Chateau Cesar, which has a special interest of its own for the Irish historian. It was there that Preston and some of his countrymen proved true to the martial renown of Irish soldiers.

About 1330, "those lions of the war," the Hospitallers of St. John of Jerusalem, exchanged their property, "Le Kesselstein," for a house on Mont-Cesar. The convent, which the Duke gave them, consisted of a house and a chapel, built in 1140. Here those noble champions of the Cross devoted themselves to the sick and neglected poor. Was Schiller thinking of the Knights of Mont-Cesar when he so beautifully wrote:

"Oh, nobly shone the fearful Cross upon your mail afar,
When Rhodes and Acre hailed your might, O! lions of the war,
When leading many a pilgrim horde through wastes of Syrian gloom,
Or standing with the Cherub's sword before the Holy Tomb.
Yet on your forms the apron seemed a nobler armor far,
When by the sick man's bed ye stood, O! lions of the war,
When ye, the high-born bowed your pride to tend the lowly weakness—
The duty, though it brought no fame, fulfill'd by Christian meekness."

The chapel served the congregation as an oratory. "La Commanderie"—this was the name the Hospitallers gave their house—was placed under the invocation of St. Nicholas. The chapel was entirely reconstructed in 1457. It was then dedicated to St. John the Baptist. This chapel was of considerable dimensions. Its principal façade was surmounted by a square tower of a remarkable height. Near the altar of the chapel was a wooden statue representing St. John weeping at the foot of the Cross. This statue was held in great veneration by the people of Louvain. They styled it St. John the Weeper—"St. Jan Gryzer." The women whose infants could not be prevented from weeping continually, were accustomed to make a pilgrimage to it. The Feast of St. Gregory was a gala day for the young and old of Louvain and the surrounding villages. Crowds of musicians and peddlars could be seen on that day all around Mont-Cesar. The young, who had hoarded up their money for St. Gregory's Feast, freely spent it in buying toys, fruits and cakes. The aged citizens of Louvain could be seen seated on the green sward in front of the chapel, telling wonderful tales about the Knights of St. John, or giving fabulous accounts of the venerable Castrum Cæsaris.

The English Jesuits, being driven by fire and sword from their own country, rented a house on Mont-Cesar adjoining "La Commanderie," in 1607. This house was opened as a Novitiate for young Jesuits by Father Parsons, the same year, with six priests, two scholastics and five lay brothers. Here Father Andrew White, the "Apostle of America," began his noviceship on the 1st of February, 1607.

Only two years after its foundation this novitiate gave its first martyr to heaven in the person of Father Thomas Garnett, nephew to the Provincial, who was executed at Tyburn, in June, 1608. Father Thomas was a true son of St. Ignatius. On reaching the gallows he kissed it in a transport of joy, declaring that it was the happiest day of his life.

In 1614, in consequence of the remonstrance of the English Government, the novitiate was transferred to Liège. The English novitiate at Louvain was established through the munificence of the pious Dona Louisa de Carvajal. Father Thomas Talbot was its first Rector. Father Henry More, the distinguished historian of the English Province, and the great grand-son of the martyred Chancellor, Sir Thomas More, entered the novitiate on the 19th of November, 1607. He was remarkable as a linguist. Father Gerard said of him: "Father Henry More hath French well, Dutch prettily, and Italian sufficiently, besides Spanish very well, and Latin as I would wish him."

Father More became Provincial of the English Province, and was cast into prison for his services to religion. He was twice declared rector of St. Omer's College. He died at Watten, of apoplexy, December, 1661, aged seventy-five.

Father More faithfully described the novitiate as seated on "high ground, commanding the whole city; below was a walled garden, and on the slopes of the hill pleasant walks among the vines, which were arranged in terraces, and the whole, though within the city walls, as quiet and calm as befitted a house of prayer."

In 1626 the Convent of the Hospitallers and the adjoining Jesuit novitiate were rented to the Irish Dominicans. These remained there only until 1656. After that period a secular took care of the convent belonging to the Hospitallers. This convent was sold in 1799 for 80,000 livres, and was immediately afterwards destroyed.

The Dominican Convent stood to the north of the Castrum Cæsaris, between the rocky stairs and the road which leads to the canal. We can still see some of the cloistered outbuildings of that establishment.

Where the Dominican Church was built now stand three or four private houses. One of these houses, a few years ago, was in the possession of an old French captain. This gentleman assured me that a piece of fine-cut stone, which he pointed out to me near the top of his residence, was the only relic preserved from the Church of St. John.

I visited with a Irish-American student of philosophy—a young gentleman who took great interest in the archæology of the Irish convents on the Continent—an old stable near the above mentioned private buildings, and which was connected with one of them by means of a covered gallery. This was the English Jesuit novitiate. After examining the premises closely by means of match lights—we had to use lights, for the place was dark and gloomy—we had the good fortune to find pasted against an old door, whose cobwebs were almost as old as the door, a plain picture, representing St.

Andre, St. Eligio and St. Bartolo. St. Andre was embracing his cross; St. Eligio held a hammer and a crown in his right hand, while in his left he held a book and a crozier; St. Bartolo had his right hand lifted, and seemed to be pointing towards heaven.

Underneath the picture were some Flemish verses, a prayer to "Heyligen Eloy," and a brief sketch of that saint's life.

It was Richard Birmingham, of the Convent of Athenry, who procured for the Irish Dominicans their house on Mont-Cesar. Its first Rector was Oliver Burke, a native of Galway. Father O'Daly, *Dominicus a Rosario*, was lecturer of divinity in it.

I believe it was before taking the house on Mont-Cesar that the Dominicans lived in a house on Rue St. Jacques. That they had a house on that street I learned from some old maps furnished me by Fr. De Backer, the Belgian writer. After leaving Mont-Cesar they opened a house on a street which is called to this day "Rue des Dominicains Irlandais." Scarcely the last relics of this house, or of the church of St. Thomas Aquinas, can now be seen. The present writer while searching for them was directed by a Fleming to the house of the Little Sisters of the Poor, on the adjoining street. The Louvain Dominican houses produced several men of great learning. Christopher French, of Galway, completed his studies at Louvain, and took out his degree as Doctor of Divinity. He became Master of Students, and wrote several theological works. He afterwards became one of the professors at Rome. He was highly esteemed for his virtue and learning by Cardinal Palavincini, who invited him to Osimo, in Ancona, as professor. Edmund Burke, also of Galway, reflects honor on the convent of his Order at Louvain. He began his studies in his native place, and afterwards continued them at Pampheluna, Salamanca, and Madrid. He took all his degrees at Louvain with great applause. In this city he became the principal Regent of the Dominican College. "He was," says an old author, "well skilled in sholastic Divinity, and doctrine of St. Thomas Aquinas, as the Theses he published, and the Treatises he wrote on these subjects show." Burke was a prolific writer, and devoted his pen to elucidating the most difficult points in the Angelic Doctor. The Right Rev. Dominick De Burgo, of the Dominican Order spent some time with his religious brethren in Louvain. "In the war of rebellion against King James II. he was compelled to take refuge in the city of Galway, out of his diocese, which was Elphin. King James and his queen esteemed him much. When he was driven into exile, King Louis of France offered him an abbey, but he preferred to go to Louvain, and share the poverty of his Order in the college of the Holy Cross there."

ERIN'S PRAYER.

I.

O ! Master of the ocean vast,
    Let ocean drink my sorrow;
Speak but the word, and night shall pass,
    And bright shall shine my morrow.

II.

Some vainly fear that were I free,
    Were I a rich, great nation,
I'd basely turn away from Thee,
    And lose my Christian station.

III.

Some fear to break my galling chains,
    They fear from Thee I'd sever;
Thou art my Lord—in freedom's light
    I'll do Thy will forever.

IV.

I clung to Thee in woe and want,
    Thy cross shines through my story;
Why should I leave Thee in the blaze
    Of freedom, or of glory?

V.

Kind Master, show poor, erring man,
    That freedom comes from heaven,
That with the gift of liberty
    Thy grace is always given.

THE IRISH DOMINICAN CONVENT, LISBON.

THE Spanish Rulers of Portugal favored the Irish students in that country as well as in their own, and in the Netherlands. They did not consider the *mere* Irish as firebrands, rebels, and traitors. King Philip IV. being anxious to found an Irish Dominican College in Lisbon, Father Dominick O'Daly, *Dominick a Rosario*, was called to that city. The new establishment was called *Corpo Santo*, and was situated in *Rua Nova de Almada*. O'Daly was chosen first Rector of this house. He afterwards founded a convent for Irish Dominican nuns, called *Bon Success*, at Lisbon.

"When Portugal," says Harris, "had thrown off the yoke of the Spaniards, and advanced John, Duke of Braganza, to the throne, O'Daly was appointed Confessor to the new Queen, and was in such high esteem with the King, that he employed him in many weighty affairs during his reign. In 1655, the King sent him as Ambassador to Louis XIV., King of France, to treat of a league of affinity between the two Crowns. Having arrived at Paris, he would not depart from the Rules of his Order, but took up his residence in the Convent of St. Honoratus. Yet he complied so far as to go to audience with the usual state of an Ambassador. When the King died on the 6th of November, 1656, he celebrated the ascension of his son and heir, Alphonsus, to the throne of Portugal with great solemnity at Paris, gave public largesses to the people, and had splendid fireworks on the Seine." He was recalled the same year. He died in 1662, at Paris. He was a man of singular piety, great zeal, a skilful writer, and an ardent lover of his country, the story of whose wrongs he laid before Europe in one of his books. The celebrated Cardinal Baronius gives him a high character for his integrity, modesty, and contempt of worldly honors. "He came a youth from Ireland," writes Baronius, "to Spain, where being received into the Dominican Order, he pursued his studies in the Province of Castile, and there drew in such seeds of piety and wisdom, as became the admiration of Louvain, Madrid, France, and almost of all Europe. In the name of the Catholic King, Philip III., he transacted affairs of great weight and moment with Charles I., King of England. Being clothed with the title of Archbishop of Goa he refused the promotion, and was afterwards sent Envoy of Portugal to the Most Christian King ; where he became the love and veneration of the whole Court, and carried with him this character, *that nobody ever was more happy in uniting piety with prudence, a religious modesty and humility with the gravity and wisdom of an Ambassador.* Why then should I mention the three bishoprics refused by him?" The bishoprics he refused are supposed by Ware, to be Goa, Coimbra, and Braga. Many honors were conferred on O'Daly in Portugal. He was Censor of the Inquisition, Visitor-General and Vicar-General of the kingdom. In the galaxy of Irish students of Penal Times, *Dominick a Rosario*, is a star of the first magnitude. In him shone the brightest virtues and the highest qualities of a man and of a religious. He was undazzled by honors, and maintained his vigor and zeal even when crowned with success. In the midst of the splendors of foreign Courts he still cherished in his heart a deep tenderness for the blessed "Homes of Ireland." While in the company of kings and queens his mind was wandering back to the princes of his native land, his mind was filled with the glory of the brave Geraldines. In festive halls his eyes filled with tears as he pondered on the wrongs and sufferings of his Irish Catholic countrymen. With a pen of fire he depicted the butcheries of the reign of Elizabeth.

Father James Arthur died in the Dominican Convent, Lisbon, about the year 1670. He joined the sons of St. Dominick in the Abbey of St. Stephen, at Salamanca. He was a distinguished author and teacher. He lectured with great applause in several convents in his Order in Spain, was Doctor and Professor of Divinity for many years at Salamanca. He was afterwards solicited to go to Portugal to teach the first chair of Divinity in the University of Coimbra. He fully answered the high idea conceived of him as to learning and merit and held his chair with great applause until the Portuguese separated from the Spaniards. He wrote a Commentary on the Summa of St. Thomas. When overtaken by death he had in preparation a work on the Angelic Doctor to consist of ten volumes.

THE IRISH PEASANT'S SONG.

I bless Thee, God, who gave me love
   For this, my humble home;
I find sweet joys within this cot
   Ne'er felt by those who roam.

I hear at noon our chapel-bell,
   At eve, my childrens' prayer;
I have a friendly face to see
   Around me everywhere.

I know each voice that greets me here,
   I know the hands I take;
I read the eyes that look on me,
   I know how free to make.

My little field is blessed clay,
   The dust of monk and nun;
The morning air is loaded still
   With hymns of saints long gone.

I've often heard that those who go
   In foreign lands to roam,
With eyes all wet, and hearts full sore,
   Sigh for their Irish home.

Then tell me not of happy lands
   Far o'er the raging sea;
My Irish roof, my Irish cot
   Make Paradise for me.

REFUGE OF THE WRETCHED.

(One of the titles given our Lady, in the old Gaelic Litany, is *Refuge of the Wretched.*)

Refuge of the Wretched, my soul is dark with woe,
Refuge of the Wretched, no light around me glow,
Refuge of the Wretched, my heart with pain will break,
Refuge of the Wretched, no joy from life I take;
Help me, help me, Mother, O! let me hear thy voice,
Thy tone alone, Mother, can make my soul rejoice.

Mother, were I happy, did my hours in sweetness roll,
Were there sunshine in my heart, and music in my soul,
Were I never pierced by sorrow, never touched by pain,
Were I like a seraph, all free from every shade of stain,—
Refuge of the Wretched, I could not hope from Thee
More true love, more sure love, than in my Misery.

THE CONVENT OF SAINT ANTHONY OF PADUA, LOUVAIN.

No Irish convent, founded during the Penal Days, is more renowned, or more venerated than the Franciscan School of St. Anthony of Padua, Louvain. This venerable home of learning and piety is crowned with a glory such as enshrines the hallowed ruins of the famous Schools of Lismore, Clonard, and Bangor. With feelings akin to awe the patriotic Irish tourist, or student, stands beneath its holy roof. Many of its students and professors were distinguished as theologians, renowned as Celtic scholars, and are honored as martyrs for their country and religion. The glorious memory of our early Irish churches, schools and monasteries, founded on Europe's continent, is, alas, unfortunately passing away. Who now thinks of the Irish monastery raised by St. Fridolin on the banks of the Moselle? Who now dreams of the great Irish monastery, founded by St. Gall, by the waters of the Stinace ? Who now is mindful of the hermitage of Cataldus that once stood near the hamlet of San Cataldo? The Irish monasteries at Alt-Munster, at Ratisbon, at Wurtzburg, Nuremberg, and Vienna, are almost all forgotten;—but the fame of St. Anthony's Convent grows brighter day by day.

While searching in the Jesuit library of Louvain for

some documents relating to this great college, I met, in a work by Father De Backer, the distinguished Belgian writer, the following note: "Voyez une dissertation trés remarquable du P. Victor De Buck intitulée, 'L'Archéologie Irlandaise au Convent de Saint Antoine de Padoue à Louvain;' dans les Etudes Religieuses, etc., Paris, 1869. p. 408–437 et 586–603." This note proved most useful to me; I went immediately to see Father De Backer, who resided in our college, and who always received me most kindly, and asked him if he had the article, spoken of in the note, at his command. To my great pleasure he arose from behind his large pile of old books and pamphlets and procured for me, from a select library adjoining his room, *Les Etudes Religieuses*. In this magazine was contained the grand article of Father De Buck: "L'Archéologie Irlandaise au Couvent de Saint Antoine de Padoue à Louvain."

Though we intend to give all the interesting facts and reflections of Father De Buck relative to St. Anthony's Convent, we will take the liberty of interspersing them with facts gleaned from other trustworthy sources. The archæologists of whom we are about to speak, says Father De Buck, who is referring to Ward, Colgan, Cleary and Mooney, were priests and religious, professors or missionaries; the study of the religious antiquities of their country was a mere accessory occupation for them. Their central point was the Convent of St. Anthony of Padua, at Louvain, which served the Irish Franciscans as a Novitiate and Seminary, and which they sometimes called a *College*. The erection of this convent was due to Florence Conry, Archbishop of Tuam. This prelate, who had been a member of the Order of St. Francis, saw with grief the manner in which the young Irishmen of his Institute were formed. They were scattered throughout the different convents of Spain, France, Italy and Belgium. Though their brethren on the continent received them with great charity, and gave them the ablest masters in sacred and profane sciences, still it was a serious disadvantage to them not to be united, and formed together, for the one grand Mission for which they sighed. The Irish Province, from the year 1601, had acquired at Louvain, near the church of Saint Jacques, a residence occupied by young students. Conry obtained in 1606, or 1609, from King Philip III., the means of building a regular convent. That was a proud and joyous day for the Irish Franciscans, in 1616, when the corner-stone of St. Anthony's convent was laid. They did not know then how famous their new home would one day become, what a source of benefit it would be to Ireland, what a glory it would be to the Order. Though good religious, they were weary of wandering from city to city, from country to country, in search of an asylum, a resting-place. They could not help, at times, of growing tired of strange tongues and strange faces. They knew how sweet and pleasant it is for brothers to dwell together. They longed to be in a home of their own where they could cultivate with advantage the studies they loved ; where they could hear, at least in time of recreation, the music of their native tongue. To increase the exultation of the poor exiles, the Prince and Princess, Albert and Isabella, came from Brussels, attended by many distinguished Irish soldiers and scholars, to lay the foundation. We may be sure, too, that many distinguished Professors from the University, and many famous warriors from different parts of the Netherlands, out of compliment to their brother-officers of Irish blood, and out of regard for the exiled sons of St. Francis, were present on the occasion. When St. Fridolin rebuilt the monastery of St. Hilary, at Poictiers, he was assisted by King Clovis. This was a great honor; but we are inclined to think that the Irish Franciscans felt as happy in having the Governors of the Low Countries present on the commencement of their convent as the saint was to have the great King of France present at the rebuilding of his monastery. Albert, the seventh son of Maximilian II., emperor of Austria, and Isabella, daughter of Philip II., of Spain, were far more illustrious on account of their virtues than by reason of the currents of royal blood flowing through their veins. Albert, by his kindness and generosity, won the hearts of his subjects, while his virtuous consort edified them by her great piety and zeal for religion. According to all writers, the palace at Brussels, during their government, resembled more a monastery than a court. Purity of manners and perfect order were found there. When reading of the regal home of the Governors of the Netherlands we are reminded of the days of St. Louis. Like the holy King of France, these two royal consorts were fond of study, and were great patrons and friends of the devoted sons of literature. They delighted in the company and conversation of religious and priests. It is with no small share of pride—we hope to be forgiven for it—that we recall the fact that two Irish priests were chosen by Albert and Isabella as their chaplains. Father Archer, the patriotic son of St. Ignatius, was one of them, while the famous literateur, Father Richard Stanihurst, was the other.

The Governors of the Netherlands were very friendly towards the persecuted Irish Catholics. When Hugh O'Neill and Rory O'Donel visited Brussels, the most distinguished personages of that city gathered around them. The illustrious General Spinola, the hero of Ostend, and the captor of Aix-la-Chapelle, Wesel, and Breda, tendered them a banquet, "of which," says O'Keenan, "a king might be proud; and there was plate, gold and silver, of which no crowned head in Christendom could have been ashamed." Father Meehan tells us that there were present at this feast, "among other celebrities of the time, the Duke d'Aumale, the Marquis of Ossuna, the truly eminent Cardinal Bentivoglio, then Nuncio of Paul V. in the Netherlands, Colonel Henry O'Neil, the Spanish Ambassador from the Court of Madrid, and many others not less known to fame. O'Neill occupied Spinola's own chair at the centre of the table, the Pope's Nuncio on his right; Tyrconnell, the sons of O'Neill and Maguire being placed in due order on the same side; while the opposite one was filled by the Duke d'Aumale, the Spanish ambassador, the Duke d'Ossuna, Viceroy of

Sicily, the host himself, and many other noble and distinguished personages."

But the best friends of the exiled princes were Albert and Isabella, who not only showed them every mark of esteem and friendship, but appointed O'Neill a home on Mont-Cesar while he stayed at Louvain. The generous Princess took Bernard O'Neill as one of her favorite pages, and the Archduke promoted Henry O'Neill to the command of an Irish regiment then in their service. As the reader knows, both of these were the sons of the great Hugh. They honored also with high positions in their armies, Rory O'Dougherty and Daniel O'Cahan, afterwards lieutenant-general to Owen Roe O'Neill.

We hope the reader will pardon this digression, as we trust it will not prove wholly uninteresting to him.

St. Anthony's convent soon became a school to which Ireland owes a deep debt of gratitude. "With the annals of Hugh Ward, in 1632," says a writer in the "Irish Ecclesiastical Record," "began the golden era of historical studies in St. Anthony's. For fifty years the religious of that convent pursued these studies with unrivalled activity, although more than once their material resources were quite exhausted; and they merited for their convent the eulogy bestowed by no partial writer in our own days: 'No Franciscan college has maintained, with more zeal than this, the character of the order as expressed in their motto: *Doctrina et Sanctitate.*'"

The community was generally large, having on an average, about forty brothers. At the time of its suppression, however, in 1797, its members numbered only fifteen. According to Paréval, the historian of Louvain, their diet and apparel gave evidence of their poverty. Paréval wrote in 1667. A century later the "Guide fidéle de Louvain" says: "we have often seen, and still can see among these religious, a number of distinguished men of the first nobility who make themselves capable, by study and virtue, to go and defend the Catholic Religion in England and Ireland.... there are even many of them who have undergone trials, imprisonment and cruel tortures for their faith." Among the Bishops and Archbishops sent out from St. Anthony's were Hugh MacCaghwell, appointed Archbishop of Armagh on the 2d of April, 1626 ; Thomas Fleming, appointed Archbishop of Dublin, 23d of October, 1623; Florence Conry, appointed Archbishop of Tuam, in 1608; Boetius MacEagan, appointed Bishop of Elphin in 1625; and Hugh (Bonaventure) Magennis, appointed Bishop of Down and Connor on the 9th of April, 1630.

Dr. Hugh MacCaghwell was a learned prelate, and the author of several works. "His Mirror of the Sacrament of Penance," which was printed at Antwerp in 1618, while he was professor of divinity at St. Anthony's College, is the only one destined for popular reading. His other publications were intended for scholastic readers, by whom his name is still remembered and highly esteemed. He made his novitiate in Salamanca, where he had among his fellow novices, eleven, who were afterwards Bishops in different parts of the globe. "Dr. Hugh MacCaghwell, called in Latin, Cavellus," writes a modern Irish author, "succeeded to the Primacy immediately after the death of Dr. Lombard. MacCaghwell was born in the County Down, in the year 1572, studied in the Franciscan Convent of Salamanca, and took out his degree of Bachelor licentiate, and Doctor of Divinity, with great *eclat*. Believing himself called to the religious state, he gave himself to the Observantine Friars Minors of St. Francis, and co-operated by his influence and exertions with Dr. Florence Conry, in establishing at Louvain the College of St. Anthony of Padua, for Irish Franciscans. It is probable that he also contributed his meed of assistance to the establishment founded at Rome by Luke Wadding, although it would seem that Wadding derived much more efficacious aid from his relative Dr. Lombard, who then enjoyed much favour and influence at the Roman Court. Dr. MacCaghwell taught theology for about nine years; first at the college of St. Anthony, of Padua, immediately after the foundation, and afterwards, from about 1623, at the convent of Ara Cœli at Rome; and was, moreover, for some time Definitor General of the Observantines or reformed Franciscans. In his theological lectures he adopted the method and opinions of his brother-Franciscan and countryman, John Duns Scotus (the Irishman), whose airy abstractions, refined subtleties, and infinitesimal distinctions he delighted to expound, and whose opinions he defended with much metaphysical ingenuity against one of the most voluminous writers of that age, Abraham Bzovius, a Polish Dominican. He possessed very superior talents, and was highly distinguished as an acute metaphysician and a perfect master of scholastic divinity; the matter and manner of which as then taught he greatly admired. But what was still more worthy of praise, 'he was,' says a modern Protestant writer, 'a man of singular humility, piety, zeal, and personal courage.' Recommended by these qualifications, he was appointed to the see of Armagh, by Pope Urban VIII., March 17th, 1626. This noble-minded prelate, with a disinterestedness and intrepidity, worthy of a successor of the apostles, did not 'make his life more precious than himself;' but offering it in sacrifice on the altar, at which he was consecrated, determined to brave all dangers and risk every torture for the flock of Christ committed to his care. He eagerly hastened to repair to his diocese, completed his preparations for the journey, paid his parting visit to his friends in Rome, and bid them a last farewell. But just when he had overcome every obstacle to his return, and his will had rejected every fear and fully completed the merit of the sacrifice, he was suddenly called to receive the reward. He died after a few days' sickness, on the 22d of September, 1626. His remains were interred in the cemetery of the convent of St. Isidore, where, a few years after, a monument was erected to his memory."

Abraham Bzovius, against whom MacCaghwell defended the opinions of the Subtle Doctor, taught philosophy at Milan and theology at Bologne. He was the continuator of the *Annals of Cardinal Baronius*. He occupied for some time an apartment in the Vatican, but died in his seventieth year, 1637, in the Dominican convent of Minerva.

We owe lasting gratitude to MacCaghwell for the encouragement he gave to the hagiologists of his Order. Without his aid, as Superior, many of their works would be incomplete indeed.

Our Franciscan was a great favorite with Hugh, of Tyrone, who appointed him tutor to his sons, and sent him to Salamanca with Henry, who went there for the purpose of receiving an education suitable to one of his rank.

Dr. MacCaghwell's edifying death is thus described by Fr. Meehan : "At his bed side, in the poor cell of St. Isidore, were two brothers, Edmund and Anthony Dungan, both Franciscans, and his most intimate friends. Turning to the former he calmly observed : 'I have always been weak of body, and am now about to leave this world; to you, then, I bequeath my cross and ring, and to your brother I leave this poor habit, all that I have to give.' Then fixing his last look on a picture of St. Anne, which was sent him from Sicily, and grasping the crucifix, he resigned his soul to God, and his renown to the schools. No one could have been more affected by his premature death than Pope Urban, who, on hearing it, remarked, 'We have lost not a man but an angel.'"

When the news of MacCaghwell's demise reached Louvain, great was the distress of his Franciscan brothers. But it was not among the sons of St. Francis alone there was grief. Many distinguished professors mourned his loss and his obsequies were performed by the classic city on the Dyle as well as by the gorgeous city on the Tiber. His pangyric was delivered before a learned audience by no less an orator than Nicholas Vermulaens. The style of this distinguished man was harmonious and easy, and when lit by the fire of passion, rolled on like a majestic river in the gold of fullday sunshine. We may easily imagine the effect he produced on the vast assembly of scholars and religious gathered before him, when he sketched the career of MacCaghwell from the time he dwelt in the princely halls of Tyrone to the moment he expired at St. Isidore's with the crucifix in his hands. "The life of great geniuses is," he said to his audience, "like that of flowers, brief and transitory; and the purple is oftener the apparel of death than of life."

Thomas Fleming, Archbishop of Dublin, deserves well of Ireland. In the face of the Penal Laws against Catholic education in Ireland he opened schools not only for the youth of his diocese, but likewise aspirants to the priesthood. He did everything in his power to mitigate the sufferings of his flock. Though belonging to the noble house of Slane, he became the father of the poor, and "the servant of all." "Passionately fond of the ancient literature of Ireland," writes Father Meehan, "he generously entertained Michael O'Clery in the convent of Dublin, and it was under that poor roof that the chief of the Four Masters found bed and board while transcribing a goodly portion of the material which was subsequently incorporated in the 'Annals of

Donegal.' To his brethren in Louvain he extended the same patronage, and it is to his fostering care we are indebted for Colgan's '*Triadis Thaumaturgus,*' a fact gratefully acknowledged by the author, who states that the Archbishop transmitted to him many a rare book and valuable record, without which he could not have completed his noble work. These, surely, are evidences of an intellectual nobility, which, in that transition period, strove to maintain the honor of Ireland, by preserving and perpetuating its ancient literature."

Fleming was but a mere boy when he went to Louvain for the purpose of studying for the priesthood. He made great progress in his studies, and while still young became a professor at St. Anthony's. It is no mean fame to him to have been the preceptor of John Colgan and his near kinsman, Patrick Fleming. But to come back to the history of St. Anthony's. During almost a century it was forbidden to the Irish Franciscans to beg in Louvain, and the annual alms promised by the Spanish Court did not arrive regularly; but this was atoned for by extraordinary gifts. The years 1686 and 1687 were particularly severe; however, God did not abandon his servants. Thanks to the charity of the faithful, and the donations of the Government, this sacred refuge for Irish science, and Irish piety, was preserved until the second invasion of Belgium by the French Republicans.

Dr. Conry's "first care," says the Ecclesiastical record, "was to petition the Spanish monarch for the erection and endowment of a convent of the order in the city and University of Louvain. This request was readily granted; and Philip III., by letters dated the 21st of September, 1606, signified his pleasure to the Archduke Albert, Governor of the Low Countries, as also to the Marquis Spinola, commander of the forces there, that the petition of Father Conry should be granted without delay, and that one thousand Spanish ducats per annum should be allotted for the support of the new college. Some difficulties, however, arose in Louvain about the erection of this national Franciscan convent; and early in the following year we find Father Conry addressing a petition to the reigning Pontiff, Paul V., soliciting 'apostolicke authoritie for building the intended colledge,' and asking at the same time, a confirmation of the royal pension accorded by Philip III. A brief of his Holiness, granting all the requests of the Franciscan Provincial, was published on the 3rd of April, 1607, and the letters of the Archduke Albert and of Isabella, commanding that this brief should be put into immediate execution, are dated on the 17th of August, 1607. The erection of the building was at once proceeded with, and just two years from the date of the papal Brief, that is, the 3d of April, 1609, an official, deputed by the Archbishop of Mechlin, visited the new college, and in canonical form declared it duly 'erected and instituted for the Franciscans of the Irish nation.'"

Paul V., whose Brief proved so beneficial to the Irish Franciscans at Louvain, was a great friend of religious bodies in general. He seemed fully persuaded that there could not be too many asylums for piety in the midst of the corruption and slime of this world. But this should not in the least lessen our gratitude towards him for the kind favor he showed the founders of St. Anthony's college. When the great benefactors of that college are mentioned, the name of Paul V., Pope and Bishop of Rome, must not be passed over in silence.

"If the new Irish foundation at Louvain was fortunate in having such a founder, it was, perhaps, still more fortunate in having Father Donatus Mooney for it first guardian. He was a man earnestly devoted to the study of the antiquities in Ireland, and to him we are especially indebted for that Irish historical school which soon became characteristic of St. Anthony's, and enabled it, in after times, to render such service, and shed such light on the early monuments of our history."

While as yet a Franciscan novice, Father Mooney suffered imprisonment for the faith. He was living with the Provincial of the Order, Father John Gray, in the monastery of Multifernan, and the aged Bishop of Kilmore, Dr. Richard Brady, had chosen the same sanctuary as a safe retreat. They were, however, all seized in 1601, and dragged to prison, where our young novice lingered for some months. While yet in prison he completed his novitiate, and was admitted to the holy vows of his Order by his fellow-captive, the Father Provincial. Soon after, he was liberated, but on the condition that he should seek a home in exile on the continent.

The chronicle of the Order adds that "he was a man of great ability and learning. After teaching philosophy and theology in France, he was appointed the first guardian of the Convent of St. Anthony in Louvain, and subsequently he held a similar office in Drogheda. He was a distinguished preacher, and strenuously labored for the conversion of the heretics, and the salvation of the faithful. Being elected Provincial of the Order, in the chapter held in Waterford in 1615, he for three years faithfully discharged the duties of that arduous post." Father Mooney seems to have had a special talent for the reconstruction of the walls of the sanctuary in Ireland.

In 1610 he was sent as superior to Drogheda, to restore the house of the Order, which, from the middle of the 13th century, had flourished till the year 1546, when it was reduced to ruins by Moses Hill, one of the unprincipled agents of the lawless Monarch, Henry VIII. From an account of this Franciscan mission in Drogheda, which was forwarded to Rome in 1623, we learn some interesting details regarding the Irish Church of that period of its desolation.... It was also through the exertions of Father Mooney, the Franciscan Order was re-established in Dublin, in 1615. Father Mooney, as we have seen, was chosen Provincial of the Order in Ireland, in 1615. The following year he proceeded to St. Anthony's at Louvain, to watch over the growth of that institution; and during the leisure months that he enjoyed there, composed the history of his Order in Ireland—a work of vast research and full of invaluable details, not only regarding the early foundations of the various Franciscan convents, but still more illustrative of the desolation and ruin that fell upon the Irish Church during the sad era of the Reformation, under Henry VIII., Elizabeth, and James I. It has been embodied and popularized in the interesting "History of the Rise and Fall of the Irish Franciscan Monasteries," by Rev. P. C. Meehan—a work full of interest to all students of Irish literature.

There is another Franciscan Father who merits to be mentioned among the first promoters of Celtic studies at St. Anthony's. This was Giolla-Brigid, or Bonaventure Hussey, a native of Ulster, who, in the chronicles of the Order, is described as a man held in great esteem for his singular skill in the language and history of Ireland."

In a manuscript list of the first religious who received the habit in the convent of St. Anthony, we find the name, "*Bonaventura Hosaeus, antea Brigidus*, diocesis Cloghorensis, admissus die 1 Novembris 1607." O'Reilly, in his "Irish Writers," states that in 1608, Father Hussey published his prose Irish Catechism in Louvain, the first book printed on the continent in Irish, and that it was re-printed at Antwerp in 1611. We suspect, however, that the date of its publication in Louvain should be 1618, in which year an edition of it, under the title of "The Christian Doctrine," is mentioned by Anderson. At all events, it was only in 1611 that the Irish typographical press was established at St. Anthony's, as we learn from the following passage of the history of the Order, written in 1630 : "The Irish convent of Louvain, for the salvation of souls in the kingdom of Ireland, established in the year 1611, a printing-press, with the proper type for the Irish letters, which, on account of the prevailing heretical rule, was heretofore impracticable to the Catholics of that kingdom, and printed some books in the Irish language, to the great advantage of the faithful." Father Hussey also composed a metrical catechism, in two hundred and forty verses, which, a century later, was published by Donlevy, as an appendix to his own famous catechism, in the Irish language. O'Reilly mentions several other unpublished poems composed by the same writer, some of which are preserved in the Royal Irish Academy.

The extract from the history of the Order just cited mentions *some books* printed in the Irish language at St. Anthony's. It is not easy now to determine what these books were; one of them, no doubt, was the Irish catechism of Dr. Conry; another was the "Mirror of Penance," published in 1618, by Hugh MacCaghwell, O.S.F., who was subsequently appointed to the primatial See of Armagh—as we have already seen. In a manuscript catalogue of the books of the Irish convent of Louvain, made about the year 1675, we find mention of another work, with the title, "Acta Sanctarum Virginum Hiberniæ," which some time before had been lent to the convent of Donegal. Perhaps this, too, may have been one of the books referred to in the above extract. At all events the Irish type of St. Anthony's continued for many years to render good service to

Irish literature. The illustrious annalist, Michael O'Clery, availed himself of it when publishing his "Glossary," in 1643. Father Anthony Gernon, another Irish Franciscan, made use of it in 1645, for his "Paradise of the Soul," a Jesuit, Father Richard MacGillacuddy (better known by his Anglicized name of Archdekin), printed with it a "Treatise on Miracles," in 1677; and Colgan and his brother hagiologists made frequent use of it in the Irish extracts inserted in their various Latin works. The type was still preserved at St. Anthony's in 1675, but there was then but little encouragement for Irish publications. In the manuscript list of the books belonging to the convent, of which we have already spoken, the following passage is added, as precious as it is concise, giving the only reference to this Irish type which we have been able to discover in contemporary records:

"In a plain chest is preserved the type of the printing-press; the key is over the chest. In the pulpit there is one silver chalice belonging to the convent of Donegal, a small case of the relics of various saints, and the silver seal belonging to O'Donnell. In the first of the upper rooms, in a small chest is the Irish type, with its own forms; also several copies of Colgan's works, Ward's *St. Rumold*, the *Fochloir* (i. e. O'Clery's Glossary), and some skins for the covers of books."

We are told by writers on the subject, that St. Anthony's convent was not always a peaceful asylum for the Irish exiles. Its tranquillity was more than once disturbed by the wars that so long raged in the Netherlands; the Emperor Joseph II., 1782, made some intolerable laws regarding it, while two years later an inundation of the Dyle swept away its cattle, wood and property of every kind. The Convent, which was rebuilt in 1753, was suppressed in 1797. The dark, and for Ireland the sad day on which this act of injustice and folly took place was the 8th of January. The Superior, at the time of the suppression, was James Cowan, of Newry, Ireland. It was publicly sold at Brussels, on the 22d of April following. The Guardian bought it by means of some money which was sent to his religious. But in 1822 he made it over in favor of Father J. Van Andenrode, doctor of theology, for the benefit of the English missions. Father Van Andenrode gave it into the hands of the brothers of Charity. There is no difficulty for the visitor to Louvain, if he wishes to visit this convent. It stands on "La place St.-Antoine" or "St.-Antonius-Plaets," near the Convent of the Daughters of Mary, or as it is called by the people—"Paridaens." The excellent Brothers of Charity are very kind to strangers ; without the least hesitation they show them the inscriptions on the slabs in the wall and on the floor, the old refectory, the chapel, etc.

It may interest the reader to know that "Paridaens," which was once the Dutch College, had the notorious Jansenius for its President. The " Tower of Jansenius," where he wrote his *Augustinus*, is not far from "Paridaens."

"But a few months since," says the Dublin *Freeman's Journal*, on the 1st of Jan., 1879, " the Rev. James Ryan,

D. D., of the archdiocese of Cashel, appealed to the Irish public through our columns for funds necessary to restore some interesting monuments of distinguished Irishmen and Irishwomen resting beneath the cloisters of the old Irish Franciscan Convent of St. Anthony, Louvain. The sum asked for was only £20, which was promptly subscribed, and the subscriptions were acknowledged at the time in our paper. The patriotic priest of Cashel lost no time in getting the work accomplished, by engaging the services of the Rev. Dr. Ruyssens, Professor of Archæology in Louvain, and in procuring correct copies of the effaced inscriptions, which have been faithfully restored on the tombs. These have been taken up from under foot in the common cloister passage, and placed as mural adornments, safe from further effacement. The Rev. Mr. Ryan had the great pleasure of finding the whole projected work completed last October, and to the perfect satisfaction of all the Irish University residents and archæologists of Louvain. The work, however, although based on the most moderate estimate, cost somewhat more than had been at first supposed, some marble inlaying and repairing the cloister being required ; yet we are happy to announce that the sums collected by the Rev. Fr. Cary, O. S. F., and the Rev. Father O'Hanlen, C. C., sufficed for the work, leaving a small balance in the Rev. Mr. Ryan's hands. This gentleman is at present in Rome, but he purposes returning to Louvain, when he would be exceedingly anxious to procure means to achieve a still greater work for Ireland. The celebrated preservers of our country's history in the sixteenth century, Father Hugh Ward, Father John Colgan, etc., are buried in St. Anthony's Convent, yet no monument marks their respective graves. The Brothers of Charity have promised a place in their chapel for a mural tablet to commemorate them ; and if Irishmen are willing to furnish the small amount required, the Rev. Mr. Ryan, who returns to Belgium next summer, would most cheerfully complete a work, creditable alike to himself, to the illustrious dead, and to Irishmen all the world over. In any case, he means to erect a tablet, with an inscription commemorating the late restoration. We hope, however, he shall be encouraged to accomplish all he desires, and in a manner to delight his countrymen at home and abroad."

LINES ON THE DEATH OF MAURICE EUSTACE, S. J.

(Maurice Eustace, a youth of great promise, entered the society of Jesus at Bruges, in Flanders, and having returned to Ireland was seized by the cruel soldiers of Elizabeth, and put to death for the Faith, on the 9th of June, 1588.)

I.

In abbeys gray, and ivied towers,
   The sweet toned bells are slowly ringing—
      Martyr-Novice, sleep in peace ;
In chapels dim, and cloistered bowers,
   The holy nuns are sadly singing—
      Blessed Novice, rest in peace.
Thou, Ignatius' loyal son,
Palm and crown hast nobly won—
      Saintly Novice, rest in peace.

II.

Blessed the land that bore thee,
Blessed the flowers now o'er thee,
Blessed the friends that knew thee;
Red the hands that slew thee ;
Slew thee in thy lovely youth,
Slew thee for thy God and Truth—
      Noble Novice rest in peace.

III.

True disciple of the Cross,
Erin weeps thee as her loss,
Exiles near the Herbrides,
Exiles on dark India's seas,
Brown-cowled monks at Papal Rome,
Prelates 'neath St. Romold's dome,
Pale- faced students at Louvain,
Hoary chiefs in France and Spain;
All now join the sad refrain—
    Youthful martyr, rest in peace.

IV.

Hear that voice from street and steeple,—
    Erin's loved one, rest in peace.
Hear their voice—the Irish people—
    Noble Eustace, sleep in peace ;
O'er thy fate we must not sigh,
Martyrs bleed but never die,
Martyrs fall by axe or blade,
But *no grave* for them is made —
    Erin's Martyr, rest in peace,
Thou hast fallen for thy sireland,
For the Faith of virgin Ireland,
    Thou hast fallen, torn, gory,
But undying is thy story,
But unclouded is thy glory—
    Hero-Novice sleep in peace.

OUR CROSSES AND SHAMROCKS.

RUDE nations may boast of their might and their treasures,
    They may count in their pride their ships and their men,
But virtue and faith are a country's true measures—
    The shamrock and cross are a power in each glen.

The swords of our sires often won us pure glory,
    But from crosses we borrow the best of our light.
Take away from Queen Erin her grand Christian story
    And you snatch from her crown the jewel most bright.

Our lyres may be broken, our keen weapons rusted,
    And trampled the banners our forefathers bore,
But we'll hold the loved faith to our country entrusted—
    Our crosses and shamrocks we'll keep evermore.

St. Patrick's grand "Credo" by law was forbidden,
    His altars were razed through the land of the Gael,
But Masses were chanted in caves deep and hidden,
    And faith lit the heart of our sweet Innisfail.

The blood of our saints often dyed Erin's crosses,
    And shamrocks grew green 'neath the rain of their tears,
But no suffering nor tortures we name as deep losses;
    Our faith is the triumph of dark penal years.

Loved faith of old Ireland, how fair is thy glowing
    Thy light is the purest that mortals can see;
The high throne of God is the source of thy flowing,
    No land is in bondage that thou hast set free.

Full vain is the tyrant, full vain his endeavor,
    Who would drive away faith from Erin's brave shore ;
Nor fire, nor the sword, nor white famine can sever
    Our hearts from the crosses and shamrocks of yore.

Ye may hew down the oaks in our deep valleys springing,
    Ye may level our cots by each dark wood and sward ;
Ye may exile each bard that we love for his singing,
    But our crosses and shamrocks for ever we'll guard.

We scorn all your racks and your "scavanger's daughters,"
    We smile at your axes, your blocks, and your chain ;
Ye may chase us with blood-hounds through brakes and o'er waters,
    But true to our faith we shall ever remain.

The waves of wild ocean may sweep over our island,
    And only the hill-tops of Erin be seen ;
Even then, even then these emeralds of dry land
    Will glow 'neath our crosses and shamrocks of green.

When we sleep the long sleep by some bright Irish river,
    Or lie in cold clay on some far stranger shore,
Be the cross our true friend to stand near us ever,
    May shamrocks grow green on our hearts evermore.

THE IRISH COLLEGE AT PARIS.

THE Capital of France was always a favorite retreat for Irish students. They did not seek it on account of the gaiety and brilliancy of its society, but on account of its friendliness towards their country, and the renown of its University. Men who are preparing themselves for a fierce and unequal combat, men who look forward to the prison and the scaffold, men who are the sons of murdered sires, and who look for the palm and crown of martyrdom, are not easily carried away by a fondness for the vanities and frivolities of this life. It is only those who have no exalted purpose in view, it is only those who do not deem life a warfare, it is only those who never reflect on eternal truths, that follow with eagerness the shadowy pleasures of this world. Historians like Thomas Messingham, the pious author of a "Garland of Irish Saints," or John Mageoghan, who wrote a History of Ireland and its sufferings, a great divine and controversialist like Cornelius Nary, men like Archbishop Queely and Geoffry Keating, were not the kind of men that go to form the vain society of a showy and thoughtless metropolis.

In 1578, John Lee, an Irish priest, and some students who had escaped with him from the persecution of Elizabeth, founded the community afterwards known as the Seminary of Irish Clerics. They were first established in the College of Montaigu and afterwards in the College of Navarre. The President de Lescalopier purchased a house for them in the Faubourg St. Germain, where they remained until 1667. In that year Malachy Kelly and Patrick McGinn, both Irish priests, obtained possession from the Government of the old College of the Lombards, founded by four Italians for students from Italy in 1330. The buildings, which had almost fallen to ruin, were repaired, a seminary of Irish priests established, and to it was united the Seminary of Irish Clerics of the Faubourg St. Germain. The two communities remained in the same building for one hundred years, but in 1776, the members of the establishment increasing to one hundred and sixty, of whom one hundred were priests, the Superior, Father Kelly, purchased for the accommodation of the Irish Clerics a new site, and erected the college at present occupied by the Irish students—Rue des Irlandais. Both colleges were suppressed at the Revolution. The Seminary of Irish Clerics was restored under the Consulate, and obtained possession by the decrees of 1801, 1802, 1803, and 1805, of the suppressed English and Scotch Colleges and of the College of the Lombards.

The English Seminary, Rue des Postes, was founded during the persecution of Cromwell, and recognized as a secular community by letters patent of Louis XIV. In 1685 the college was placed under the direction of the Irish Seminary. It was suppressed in 1792, and its buildings are at present occupied by private families and by the Seminary of St. Esprit.

The College of the Lombards had the honor of a visit from the illustrious Edmund Burke in 1775. In his famous letter to a Peer of Ireland, February 21st, 1782, he thus alludes to that college : "It seemed to me a very good place of education, under excellent orders and regulations, and under the government of a very prudent and learned man, the late Dr. Kelly. This college was possessed of an annual income of more than a thousand pounds a year, the greatest part of which had arisen from legacies and benefactions of persons educated at that college and who had obtained promotions in France, from the emoluments of which promotions they made this grateful return ; one in particular, I remember, to the amount of ten thousand livres annually, as it is recorded on the doner's monument in the chapel."

Tradition says that the chapel mentioned in Burke's letter was one of the last, if not the very last place where Mass continued to be said after the abolition of Catholic worship by the infidels in 1793. We are informed by the able editor of Renehan's "Collections on Irish Church History" that when he visited it in 1840 it was used as a storehouse.

The Abbé McGeoghgan, writing about the Irish students on the Continent, thus speaks of the foundation of their College at Paris: " France generously afforded an asylum to these voluntary exiles, and gave them a house on the hill of St. Genevieve. They were kindly received by the people of Paris, who in this imitated their illustrious fellow-citizen, Baron de St. Just, and President of their Parliament. This virtuous nobleman and true Christian was deeply affected by the state of religion in Ireland, and much interested for the fate of the Irish priests who were banished from their country on account of their religion. These were looked upon as martys for Christ and laborers destined to cultivate his doctrine. They were brought by this illustrious Frenchman from an obscure dwelling, and settled in a more commodious place, while he was providing a regular seminary and funds necessary for its support. Retirement was a favorite virtue of this pious and good man. Every day that could be spared from public business he passed with the Irish exiles. Devotion to God and his saints, the conversion of heretics, the propagation of the faith and the salvation of souls, were always favorite subjects of conversation between him and the novices. He was frequently with them in the refectory, where his humility was such that, forgetful of his rank as first magistrate of France, and as a proof of his respect for the exiled clergymen, he always chose the last place at table. According as they had completed their studies, and were prepared to return to their country, their illustrious patron had them examined by Père Binet, a learned Jesuit of the time; he then himself presented them to Cardinal Retz, Bishop of Paris, to receive their mission from him, after which they were furnished with clothes and everything necessary for the voyage at his expense."

It may interest our readers to know that Cardinal

Retz, who was accustomed to give the Irish priests their mission, had received a part of his education from St. Vincent de Paul.

Father Binet, S. J., the examiner of the Irish students, was born at Dijohn. He wrote the "Lives of the Saints" and an Essay on "The Wonders of Nature." This last work was highly esteemed by the learned.

What a writer in the *Irish Ecclesiastical Record* for November, 1870, says of the present Irish College at Paris, can be truthfully said of the old College of the Penal Days: "It is manifest that no foreign institution could be less French on French soil than is the Irish College, nor could it be more Irish. Even though words should be silent on the subject, the College itself proclaims the fact. Let any one approach it by the street 'Rue des Irlandais,' in which it is situated, and, entering the building, let him inspect the national emblems of Ireland, the Irish cross, the Irish harp, the Irish round towers, the Irish wolf-dog, the titles of the Irish dioceses, the statues and pictures of titular saints of Ireland, the Irish mottoes, etc., etc., and then let him mingle with the professors and students, who are exclusively Irish—if the visitor be an Irishman, he forgets for the moment that he is in France, and feels as he were at home in old Ireland; or, if he be a Frenchman, he feels as if he had gone out of his native land and as if treading upon foreign soil. So little is the Irish College a

French establishment—so completely is it, and has it always been an Irish Institution."

Not to mention the rash Scotus Erigena, many Irish students distinguished themselves at Paris. Thomas Palmer, usually styled Thomas Hibernicus, a native of Kildare, and who flourished about the year 1229, was a Fellow of the Sorbonne, and was famous as an author and as a professor of that University. The celebrated John Duns Scotus was a Doctor of the Sorbonne; and it was while delivering his pulic lectures at Paris that he defended the dogma of the Immaculate Conception. Thomas Messingham, for some time Rector of the Irish College at Paris, was a native of Leinster. He was a writer of great authority on Irish subjects. More distinguished still than Messingham was a youth who often played in Bridge street, Dublin. This was Michael Moore, who did much for the advancement of Irish literature. Before leaving his native city Moore had received a good classical education. When he grew towards manhood he repaired to France and commenced his ecclesiastical course in the Irish College at Nantes. After having spent some years in this College he removed to Paris, and there completed his theological studies. Moore was an accurate and profound Greek scholar. On this account he was appointed Professor of Rhetoric in the Grassan College, which office he filled with marked ability. On account of ill-health he was obliged to return to Ireland, and was there ordained priest by the learned Luke Wadding, Bishop of Ferns. He soon became Prebendary of

Tymothan and Vicar-General of Dublin. Having returned to Paris he was caressed by the learned, and won the patronage and friendship of Cardinal Noailles. This great Cardinal is represented by French writers as one who loved what was good, and did it. He was amiable in his manner, agreeable in society, full of candor, and brilliant in conversation. By his influence our Irish student was nominated Professor of Philosophy Greek, and Hebrew, and became soon after President of the College of Navarre and Rector of the University of Paris. When King James II. was in Ireland, Tyrconnell recommended Moore to him. He preached often before the monarch, and for a time was high in his favor. Pope Innocent XII. was so well pleased with his government of the College at Montefiascone that he made a donation of two thousand crowns a year to that seminary. Clement XI. so much esteemed Moore that he declared in the presence of several Cardinals, that he would place his nephew under his tuition. Moore's heart was always in Ireland. His interest in her welfare never diminished. He took a special care of Irish students who wished to study for the Irish mission. With the assistance of Doctor John Farelly, he purchased a house near the Irish College for them. Some years before his death he had the misfortune to lose his eyesight, and was obliged to employ a person for the purpose of reading to him. This wretch, however, proved to be heartless and dishonest, and pillaged some hunreds of the Doctor's books. The volumes that remained were bequeathed to the Irish College, for the benefit of his countrymen. Doctor Moore died in the College of Navarre, on the 22d of August, 1726, and was interred in the chapel of the Irish College. Doctor Moore was distinguished, not only as a professor, but likewise as an author. He left several learned works behind him.

While Dr. Moore was at the summit of fame in Paris, another Irish student shone in the halls of that city's university. This student was Cornelius Nary, from the county of Kildare. Young Nary received an early classical education at Naas. He was ordained in his twenty-fourth year, by Dr. James Phelan, Bishop of Ossory, and proceeded to Paris. He became an alumnus of the Irish College. After some time he was appointed provisor of the same establishment, the duties of which office he continued to discharge for seven years. "His transcendent talents, enhanced by unremitted application, soon opened the way for further literary honors; in 1694 he acquired superior distinction as a canonist, and took out a degree of Doctor of Laws in the University of Paris. With a view of contributing assistance to the exigencies of the Irish mission, he resolved to return to his native country, but when he reached London he was prevailed upon by his friends to remain for some time in that city, and became domestic chaplain to the Earl of Antrim. Notwithstanding the discouraging state of Ireland at this period, the love which he cherished for the religion of his native land, and his anxiety to co-operate with his fellow-countrymen, would not permit him to prolong his stay in London; he soon after proceeded to Dublin, and was appointed parish priest of

St. Michan's in that city. The reputation of Doctor Nary was soon universally established; he ranked as the leading and most successful controvertist of the day; by his writings as well as by his discourses he contributed to the triumph of truth and to the conversion of numbers. During the registration of 1704, Doctor Nary clung with the affection of a father to his flock; he was one of the 1,080 priests who submitted to the process of that penal ordeal, his sureties on that occasion being Nicholas Lincoln in Capel street, and John Butler, of Ormond-quay. This learned and truly valuable pastor continued unmolested in the government of his parish until his death, which occurred on the 3d of March, 1738." Doctor Nary was a prolific and able writer. He wrote books of devotion on several subjects, as well as historical and controversial works.

Another distinguished Irish student who won laurels at Paris was Malachy O'Queely. "There is little to be said of O'Queely's literary tastes or labors," says Father Meehan, "but we may state that they were appreciated by John Colgan, who was indebted to him for the 'Description of the three Islands of Arran and their churches.'" Geoffry Keating, the Irish historian, was also a Paris student. He was a man of marked abilities. He wrote on various subjects. His "Defence of the Mass," and the "Three Shafts of Death," were written in Gælic. He was the author of some short poems, one of which was an eulogy on the death of Lord Decies. "Dr. Keating," says an unknown author, "was a fine preacher, and in such high repute, that people flocked from all parts to hear him."

Besides the Irish students of Paris already spoken of we may mention the honored names of the two great historians, Sylvester O'Halloran and John Megeoghegan, the illustrious physician, Neil O'Glacan, and Dr. William Coppinger, the ascetic writer.

The present century saw several distinguished natives of Ireland in the Irish College at Paris. Among them we may name Dr. O'Higgins, subsequently Bishop of Ardagh, who was one of its professors; Archdeacon Hamilton of Dublin; Dean Gaffney, of Maynooth; Dr. Kirby,* made by our present glorious Pontiff Bishop of Lita, and the famous and patriotic Edward Maginn, Bishop of Derry.

Dr. Maginn seems to have known well the history of his *Alma Mater*. In his letter to Lord Stanley he asks: "Who, my lord, was amongst the first to welcome the royal refugee to the shores of France? An Irish friar, my own name-sake, afterwards chaplain to the queen-mother, Henrietta. The hard earnings of a long life, which he kept by him for the pious purpose of educating for the holy ministry his proscribed race at home, on bended knees, with the generous devotion of an Irish heart, he poured into the lap of poor exiled royalty. So much, my lord, for an Irish, denouncing, confessing, secret-keeping Christian friar. The same was afterwards the founder of the Irish College of the Lombards, which

---

* Now Archbishop of Ephesus.

supplied Ireland for centuries with priests and martyrs, who kept the faith, and mark you, my lord, royalty alive, in spite of the united efforts of the powers of darkness and of your own non-confessing Christians to extinguish both."

The following passage from the eloquent pen of Thomas D'Arcy McGee is highly pertinent to our present subject. "Of the faculty of the Irish College at Paris," he writes, "were the Abbé Kearney, who, with the better known Abbé Edgeworth, had escorted Louis XVI. to the scaffold, and whose reminiscences of the first revolution, when he chose to indulge them, are pronounced by a recent writer to have been ample and interesting.

"The Irish College at Paris possesses many claims to the affectionate remembrance and respect of all Irishmen. Originally founded with the sanction of the exiled Stuarts, under the auspices of the Bourbons, it was necessarily a very loyal and legitimist institution. It possessed, from the accident of its location, a patriotic as well as a royalist influence. Every Irish soldier in the service of France some time or other came to see its inmates; every Irish tourist, especially if a Catholic and a patriot, was desirous of being introduced to its faculty. In its library were deposited some valuable relics of our Celtic literature, carried abroad in the Jacobite exodus, and destined to be resorted to after many days, by such zealous students as the Abbé McGeoghegan, and the Chevalier O'Gorman. In 1792 it shared the fate of all the ecclesiastical institutions of France—was confiscated and closed; with the consent of the Consuls it was re-opened as a secular academy, having the Abbé McDermott for principal, and Eugene Beauharnais and Jerome Bounaparte among its scholars. The studies were wholly unlike those designed for its original inmates by the original founders. The practice of religion had not yet been tolerated! Voltaire and Rosseau were more read than sacred history. On the restoration of the Bourbons this school was fully restored, and has ever since remained sacred to theological studies. Its importance in that respect, to the insulted Church it recruited and sustained in the worst of times, can hardly be exaggerated."

MEMORIES OF THE CONTINENT.

God bless those pictured college-walls,
    We loved upon the Continent;
God bless those glorious college-halls,
    We loved upon the Continent;
God bless our friends of France and Spain,
God bless old Rome, God bless Louvain,
God bless each gifted heart and brain,
    We found upon the Continent.

How peaceful passed our college-days,
    Upon the grand, old Continent;
How sweetly rose our vesper lays,
    Upon the noble Continent;
How dear to us each blushing vine,
From Tiber to the kingly Rhine,—
How dear to us each sacred shrine
    Upon the good, old Continent.

THE PASTORAL COLLEGE, LOUVAIN.

As the precise spot on which the Irish Pastoral College stood should be dear to each Celtic heart, I took particular care, while in Louvain, to find it out. At the present moment there is a hospital for orphans, "L'Hospice des Orphelins," in the street called "Rue des Orphelins." The ancient Jesuit College stood on the ground now occupied by this Hospital. On its left, and adjoining it, was the Pastoral College. The large archway, or entrance, with "Collegium Hibernorum" over it, has long since disappeared.

In 1773 a masonic lodge was formed at Louvain. This lodge was transferred to the Irish Pastoral College in 1806. The Freemasons held their first banquet at Louvain in the dear chapel of the Pastoral College. It was in 1835 that the venerated "Collegium Hibernorum" was changed into private houses.

But we must give the early history of the College. During the seventeenth century the Irish Catholics had no means of educating their sons at home. Barbaric laws forbade them the rights of education. The Catholic schoolmaster was considered a most dangerous enemy to the state. "Amidst the political and religious troubles," says a writer in the *Dublin Review*, "which succeeded the expulsion and outlawry of the parochial clergy, and monastic orders, we can catch, but at intervals, and from scattered spots, the fitful glimmerings of the torch of Catholic science, now escaping through chinks of caverned rocks and other hiding places, where aged priests and friars, unable or unwilling to flee, lingered about to teach the poor persecuted children of the land; and at another time gleaming dimly, like expiring beacon-lights on the sea-coast, when learning, banished from all its accustomed haunts, was forced to take its mournful departure from the shores on which, in days of old, it had welcomed the strangers who had come in quest of knowledge, from every clime, to the schools of Lismore, Armagh, Cloonard, Ross, Clonfert, and Bangor. Now the Irishman is to be the exile and wanderer, in quest of learning denied him at home, and every Christian land, save that which was nearest, returns the rights of hospitality; and every university, college, school and convent abroad, emulously contending for the honor of enrolling the poor, homeless Irish student amongst its doctors, scholars, or brethren, throws open wide its gates, and compels him, with generous violence, to enter, and throw aside his pilgrim's staff, and rest his weary feet, and abide in peace, as in more ancient times strangers were wont to find a home in the schools and cloisters of his fatherland. Spain, France, Italy, Portugal, Belgium—may it never be forgotten how each of your people succored Irish genius in the hour of its need and sheltered it when harborless, and slaked its thirst for knowledge at the fountains of living waters, and broke to it the bread of every science."

About the year 1622 Eugene Matthews, Archbishop of Dublin, being obliged to fly from his country, or die the death of a traitor, knowing what his countrymen were suffering on account of their devotion and Faith, represented the case to Urban VIII., and pressed upon the sacred college the necessity of providing a seminary, with a view of preparing missionaries for the Church in Ireland. The Cardinals at once entered into his views, and accordingly it was settled that a college should be founded in Louvain; and by the Pope's bull of the 14th of December, 1624, the preliminaries were all arranged, Urban himself having endowed it with a considerable grant, a house was purchased, and the College was opened; the course of study was rhetoric, philosophy and theology. The college was at first supported by the generosity of the congregation of the Propaganda. Archbishop Matthews himself established a bourse for the benefit of students from his diocese. The good accomplished by the learned and zealous priests sent to Ireland from this college was great and lasting. The persecuted Irish people found in them fathers, consolers, fortifiers and spiritual directors. Who can picture the joy of the poor peasants and plundered nobles, when they saw amongst them devoted fathers who had gone to distant countries to prepare themselves in order to be able to labor for the hunted, reviled, down-trodden children of St. Patrick.

It is not difficult for one who has spent any length of

time in a University-town to see the utility and high importance of such a college as the Irish Pastoral College. The dangers to which youths were exposed, who, being free to choose their own abodes, in the midst of luxury and worldliness, were not few nor trifling. It is not easy to gather into one city thousands of young men, students of law and medicine, as well as students of divinity and aspirants after University honors, without having, at least, a few of them without good morals or good manners. Hence the danger of bad company and of bad example to the young and innocent.

The students of monastic orders who attended at the courses given in the great universities were removed from a thousand dangers to which other students were exposed. Though far away from their own province or country, still they found themselves at home under rule and discipline in one of their conventual houses. The Irish Dominican who attended at the University of Paris went to his daily class from a French Dominican convent; the Irish Franciscan in Louvain or Rome, dwelt amidst his Flemish or Italian brethren. "Not so in those early days of the universities was the condition of the secular clerk, whether lay or ecclesiastical. Then there were no colleges except those possessed by the regular clergy in their convents, which suggested the expediency and the plan of erecting similar collegiate homes for secular students. Inns and hospices and hostels abounded in all the streets and alleys, where youths of gentle blood and varlets of low degree congregated for brawls and carousals, and the peace of the community was disturbed by frequent day outbreaks and midnight feuds, between turbulent academicians and officious bailiffs and sturdy burghers; and serious issues therefrom arose between the authorities of the universities and the magistrates of the cities for violated privileges on the one hand, and municipal order broken and public officers maltreated on the other."

Again there was another reason for the existence of the Pastoral College. The students there were to prepare themselves for a hard and arduous mission—the Irish mission. They were to prepare themselves for all kinds of trials and sufferings.

"The duties of the Irish priest," says the Dublin *Review* for May, 1862, "who had forced the lines were different, as we before had occasion to remark, from those of the English missioner, but they were identical in this respect, that they were performed in secret, and that in many instances all the heroism of their performances is lost to history. The course of the Irish priest or Bishop from Louvain or Paris to Ireland, and thence to the Birmingham Tower or the Tower of London, although not marked in log or journal, may be tracked without any effort of imagination, and yet with sufficient certainty. Having escaped the English cruisers and the still more alert and dangerous spies who swarmed in the foreign and Irish ports, he reached his diocese under favor of a secret understanding and difficult correspondence with friends too numerous for perfect safety or discretion, through a country beset with enemies, vigilant, blood-thirsty and keen-scented. Being at length at home, his labors, his dangers and his unrest seemed only to begin. A new lodging every night, a new disguise every day, a new congregation every Sunday; high treason to be committed in every cabin by absolving the sinner or anointing the sick; a correspondence to be kept up with Rome, with Spain, with the Irish colleges everywhere upon the Continent; relations to be preserved with influential Catholics at home differing in judgment, in feeling and in interests; provision to be made for succession in the ministry; a learned controversy, perhaps, to be maintained with clever disputants at a distance from books of reference and other appliances of study, and all this without other resources at his command than the alms of a poverty-stricken people, and with hourly chances of capture and its inevitable consequences : such were the duties well understood, coolly undertaken and resolutely performed by the Bishop who could set foot in Ireland. In the great majority of cases, the historical detail of much that we know to have taken place are, for the present, wanting; and we can learn nothing more of many great and laborious Bishops or priests than that they reached Ireland, lived there for a time, and died. But there can be no doubt, from what we know of others concerning whom something is preserved to us, and from the condition of the times, that the life of every Irish priest and Bishop worthy of the name must have been something very nearly resembling what has been described."

Among the early Rectors of the Irish Pastoral College may be mentioned Edmond O'Reilly, Archbishop of Armagh. This patriotic and pious prelate was born in the year 1606, and after having made some studies in Ireland, was sent to Louvain by Dr. Fleming, where he studied Sacred Scriptures and Moral Divinity under the Jesuits, and Canon Law under the Franciscans. It is very probable that O'Reilly had the good fortune to attend the lectures on the Sacred Scriptures given by the celebrated Jesuit commentator, Cornelius à Lapide, who taught at Louvain about his time. Corneille Cornelissen Van Den Steen (à Lapide) was born in 1566, and having become a Jesuit, devoted himself to the study of languages, to literature, and especially to the understanding of the Sacred Scriptures. After having explained the Scriptures with great success at Louvain and Rome, he died at the last-named city, full of renown for his learning and virtues, aged seventy-one years. Whether O'Reilly had so distinguished a professor, or not, among the Jesuits, we are certain that he had a renowned professor among the Franciscans—"the Honorable and Rev. Thomas Fleming (the eldest son and heir of Lord Slane), who, renouncing the pleasures of earth, had exchanged the titles and estates of this world for the cloister here and the 'hundred-fold hereafter,' and was now Professor of Divinity in Franciscan College of St. Anthony of Padua, at Louvain."

O'Reilly, by his piety and other good qualities, won the esteem of his professor, Father Fleming. When about to return to Ireland, this latter priest wrote to his uncle, the Archbishop of Dublin, commending him most highly. The life that O'Reilly led in Ireland was hard and perilous, but always great and glorious. He suffered many tribulations and persecutions, and was banished several times from his native land. He was the steadfast friend of the famous Owen Roe O'Neill, and of the Papal Nuncio, Rinuccini. It was while Dr. O'Reilly was in exile, at the Irish College of Lisle, in Flanders, that he received notice that the Pope, in approbation of his virtues and constancy, had appointed him to the Primatial See of Armagh.

"Dr. O'Reilly," says Renehan, "was not 'a reed shaken by the wind,' he was not a man clothed in 'soft garments,' nor versed in that *finesse* and pliancy which prevail in the 'palaces of kings;' he knew not how to temporize, but he knew how to contend and 'suffer for justice' sake.'"

The last days of O'Reilly were spent in exile, and, like many another Irish Bishop, he sank to rest far from the land that gave him birth.

"On the 27th of September, 1666, he was sent off to London, under the custody of the City Mayor, Stanly, and thence was sent, without trial or accusation, to Dover, whence he took shipping for Calais."

Do not the white cliffs of Dover grow more interesting to us when we recall the host of "O'Reillys" who, as they sailed into eternal exile, saw for the last time that stainless portion of the land once ruled by Alfred and Edward? While mindful of O'Reilly's fate, we can appreciate, with a peculiar appreciation, Matthew Arnold's poem on Dover Beach:

> "The sea is calm to-night,
> The tide is full, the moon lies fair
> Upon the straits; on the French coast the light
> Gleams and is gone; the cliffs of England stand,
> Glimmering and vast, out on the tranquil bay.
>
> * * * * * * *
>
> Listen, you hear the grating roar
> Of pebbles which the waves draw back, and fling
> At their return up the high strand,
> Begin, and cease, and then again begin,
> With tremulous cadence slow, and bring
> The eternal note of sadness in."

And the "Calais Sands," do they not grow dear to us, and seem like precious relics in our eyes, when we remember the pilgrim bands from Ireland that walked up and down the French shores in the days gone by?

> "A thousand knights have rein'd their steeds
> To watch this line of sand-hills run
> Along the never-silent strait
> To Calais, glittering in the sun."

Ah! more than a thousand Irish lords and ladies fair—ah! more than a thousand Irish chiefs and soldiers, priests and students, turned their gaze with rapture, mingled, indeed, with sorrow, towards the friendly forts of "Calais glittering in the sun."

O'Reilly being "banished forever from his diocese

and his country, studied how he might best provide for the interests of religion and the spiritual instruction of his people. His first care was to revisit the Irish Colleges in Belgium. He passed, therefore, from Calais to Louvain, and thence to the other seminaries; and in the beginning of 1667 reached Brussels, where he ordained several priests for the Irish mission. It was in the Jesuit chapel of Brussels that he himself, with the utmost secrecy was consecrated Bishop. From Brussels he came to Paris, in the summer of 1667, and making that city his principal place of residence, he occasionally journeyed, at a very advanced age, to the different Irish seminaries through the country. In these he exhorted and instructed the young candidates for the ministry, and held several ordinations, the last of which I find any mention took place at Paris, in January, 1669. It was probably the excessive fatigue of one of these visits of pastoral zeal that abridged the term of his pilgrimage here, and hastened the reward of his manifold virtues. The expatriated confessor was seized with his last sickness at Saumur, in France, on the Loire, and there, with great sentiments of piety, he resigned his heroic soul into the hands of its Creator, about the spring of the year 1669."

We wonder if O'Reilly found a resting-place in the chapel of the ancient royal college of Saumur? Another distinguished rector of the Pastoral College was Thomas Stapleton, he who had the sad privilege of delivering the funeral oration of Nicholas French, Bishop of Ferns. This great scholar was on several occasions elected to the highest academical honors that could be conferred upon any university student, namely, "Recteur Magnifique." He was born in the little town of Fethard, in Tipperary, and was consequently a fellow-townsman of the famous John Baptist Hacket, a Dominican, the author of several books, and an esteemed professor of theology at Milan, Naples and Rome. Dr. Stapleton was the grandson of Thomas, Lord of Thurlesbeg, Knokane, Nenagh and Karrighine. His mother was one of the Meaghers of Barnane. Dr. Stapleton enjoyed the esteem and friendship of some of the greatest men of their time. Having departed this life, August 14, 1694, at the Pastoral College, he was laid to rest in the Chapel of St. Charles Borromeo, in St. Peter's Collegiate Church, Louvain. Dr. Stapleton is numbered among the great benefactors of the Pastoral College.

Nicholas French, Bishop of Ferns, a native of Wexford, was one of the chief benefactors and glories of the Pastoral College. The life and writings of this great and patriotic Prelate are the national property of Ireland. It is not necessary for me to give a detailed account of his varied and brilliant career from the time he left the shores of Ireland until he expired at Ghent. McGee grows more eloquent than usual the moment he begins to touch upon the character of this giant among Irish students. "Wolsey, Ximenes, Richelieu," he exclaims, "there was a church man born to be a fourth among you, a man of iron will and lofty genius, who planned and well nigh achieved things as great as any you have attempted or effected. He, too, was a boy-bachelor, could have rivalled in learning the Polyglott of the Spanish cardinal, and in the magnitude of his political views was scarce inferior to the great cardinal statesman of France. He was banished into a strange land, and the tide of oblivion, which has swept away so many minor names and histories of the Catholic Confederacy, at reaching its flood almost hid his form from our eyes. But he held his ground firmly on the confines of Fame, like that rude Colossus on the Antrim shore, told of by tourists, which is supposed to be a giant of old, petrified in the act of stepping on Irish soil. The waves and the winds of heaven have beaten upon it; little men have climbed to its summit, to pluck the lank, green grass, which falls like discolored hair over its granite brows; they have broken and carried away fragments of its base, still it keeps its post, rising just above the tide-mark, broad and brave-looking as a tower of strength.

"The life of French is so filled with incident, with scenes so constantly shifting, that it is no easy matter to form an accurate judgment upon it. He had been an Ambassador to four different courts. He had ruled with episcopal power in four different countries. As a public man and an ecclesiastic there can be no doubt of his powers, his address, the extent of his accomplishments, nor of the greatness of his labors. He was the leader of all work to the Catholic Confederacy. He was one of the best known Christian bishops of his age.

As an author, it was no unformidable degree of success which could call Clarendon against him to the lists. At a time when Europe was occupied with the greatest affairs, when the most remarkable men that a single generation ever saw were all actively operating upon its theatres of peace or war, he forced by the strength and sincerity of his writings, this Island and its fortunes on the general attention."

Harris tells us "that all along during the Rebellion French was a violent enemy to the king's authority."

THERE IS HOPE FOR ERIN.

There is hope for Erin,
While in ten thousand cells,
Where devotion ever dwells,
The meek-faced nuns are telling,
While their hearts with love are swelling,
Ten thousand rosaries for Erin.

There is hope for Erin,
While monk and saintly priest
Offer up the Sacred Feast,
With tears and nightly sighing,
For an Isle in sorrow lying,
An isle whose music-name is Erin.

There is hope for Erin :
Her sons, to virtue true,
By their holy actions sue
From God the choicest blessing,
From the Sacred Heart caressing
For the Sacred Heart's own isle, Erin.

There is hope for Erin:
While angel-censers wave,
While her saints for mercy crave,
While Virgin-Mother's pleading
Can move the Victim bleeding
On thy altar's sacred stone, Erin.

PONT-A-MOUSSON, LORRAINE.

Pont-a-Mousson, in Lorraine, in olden times, was not without beauty. Its venerable religious houses, and especially its magnificent Premonstratensian Church and library, would be ornaments to any city in Europe. The Moselle, which is spanned by a fine old bridge, divides the town into two parts.

In the year 1573, Cardinal De Lorraine established at Pont-a-Mousson a University* modelled after the best schools of the period. The first Chancellor of this University was an Irish Jesuit, Father Richard Fleming. Father Fleming was a native of Westmeath, of a noble family. He was a distinguished writer, and a man of great virtue, and of "a religious bearing." "Of him," says Stanihurst, "I hear a great report, to be an absolute Divine and Professor thereof." Father Fleming was so highly esteemed for his learning that he was appointed to succeed the celebrated Maldonatus, in the Chair of Theology at Paris. He died at Pont-a-Mousson, on the 25th of August, 1590. His death, says Father Carayon, threw a gloom over the whole College.

Another Irish Jesuit, whose name is connected with Pont-a-Mousson, where he made part of his studies, is

---

* This University was transferred to Nancy on the 3d of August, 1768.

Florence More, of Armagh. This Father was particularly beloved by Primate Creagh, and was highly thought of as a Spiritual Director. He was born in 1552, and died at Neuhaus College, in Germany, 1616.

While John Barclay, a prose-writer and poet of some renown, was a pupil of the Jesuit College at Pont-a-Mousson, Christopher Hollywood from Artane, in the County Dublin, studied with him. Great success attended young Hollywood in his studies. He was admired not only by his Jesuit masters, but also by the distinguished professors of the university. Having completed his course of study at Pont-a-Mousson, he removed to Padua, where for years, he delivered lectures on dogmatical theology. This great Jesuit became a Confessor for the Faith, having been cast into a prison while passing through England on his way to his Irish mission. Hollywood was powerful with the voice and pen. His preaching and writings were so disagreeable to the fanatical James I. that that monarch denounced him by name. The works of Father Hollywood were published at Antwerp in 1604. After presiding with great ability for twelve years over the Society in Ireland, he died in 1626.

Another illustrious Irish student was at Pont-a-Mousson about Barclay's time. This was Father Stephen White, whom Victor De Buck styles a "very remarkable man." Father White was born at Clonmel, on the pleasant banks of the Suir, Spenser's favorite river. His birth took place about the year 1570. After finishing a brilliant course of studies White was appointed professor of philosophy at the Irish college of Salamanca. So great was his success in teaching and lecturing that he was soon called to Ingoldstadt, in Bavaria. A famous university had been founded at Ingoldstadt in 1471. Father White was appointed professor of dogmatic theology in this renowned school. After teaching for years with unbounded applause at Ingoldstadt, the great Clonmel student became a professor of the University of Dillingen. The Dillingen University was established in 1549, by the illustrious Cardinal Othon Truchses. After leaving Dillingen, White next appears as a professor at Pont-a-Mousson, at the College of the Jesuits. In the years 1627 and 1628 we find Father White in a residence of his Order in Metz, the birth-place of Sebastian Le Clerc and the distinguished Jesuit, Father John Francis Baltus. White returned to Ireland in 1640, and proceeded to Dublin, where he expired in 1662.

White was distinguished not only as a professor of philosophy and theology, but also as an archæologist. He was in continual communication with Father John Colgan, of Louvain. We may be certain that the famous Franciscan hagiologist received many a useful piece of information from the learned Irish Jesuit, who, in his studies and travels, must have found treasures of Irish history.

The Irish Fathers at the Jesuit College of Pont-a-Mousson were often visited by a brilliant young university student. The youth was noble in appearance, and frank and generous in character. This was nothing to be wondered at, for his name was Emer McMahon, a worthy scion of the princely house of Farney. McMahon after studying with distinction at Pont-a-Musson, and having been ordained priest, was honored with the doctorate in civil and canon law. After some years as missionary in Ireland Emer was created Bishop of Clogher, which See he afterwards exchanged for the perilous See of Dublin. After many trials and labors in Ireland, Bishop McMahon removed to Rome, where he died of a fever, on the 24th of August, 1622, about two years before the demise of the great Peter Lombard.

About the year 1754 a young man from Kells, in the county of royal Meath, entered a French novitiate of the Society of Jesus. Having proved himself not only a brilliant student but also a deep and solid scholar, Thomas Betagh was chosen by his superiors to teach at the public schools attached to the Jesuit College at Pont-a-Mousson. Here he distinguished himself as a professor. His mind was clear and acute and his language rich, yet precise and simple. There was nothing cloudy about his explanations; even the dullest of his pupils could immediately catch his meaning. About the year 1762 Doctor Betagh returned to his native country and devoted himself to the glorious cause of education. For years he taught hundreds of the Dublin youth in School-house lane and Skinner-row. Father Betagh was not like the Reformers who believed in faith without good works. He well knew that charity covers a multitude of sins, and so he was accustomed anually to clothe out of his scanty resources at least forty of his most destitute pupils. As a moralist Betagh ruled an audience at will; as a champion of Catholic doctrine he might well be ranked with the most illustrious men of his Order. "After a most successful mission of upwards of forty years Doctor Betagh died on the 16th of February, 1811. On the announcement of his death, the metropolis was turned into one general scene of mourning, and at this day his name and his virtues remain embalmed in the recollections of a grateful people."

His preaching much, but more his practice wrought—
A living sermon on the truth he taught.

THE ISLE OF THE LIVING.

(It was believed that no one could die while on the island in Loch Cre.)

I.

I sailed around the blue Loch Cre,
And watched the Isle that ever blooms;
The sun was mild, and soft each ray
Fell o'er the Isle that knew no tombs.

II.

The hymns of monks stirred all the air,
The soul of flowers rose to the sky,
I heard the plaintive voice of prayer;—
"*Grant, Master, grant, that we may die.*

III.

"This Isle is rich in fruits and flowers,
One Summer here forever reigns,
Peace smiles upon our quick-winged hours,
Our joys are great, and rare our pains.

IV.

"But still of earth we tired have grown,
We long to be with Thee, our King,
We long to see Thy shining Throne,
And in Thy court Thy praises sing.

V.

"O ! saddest Isle, where none can die,
Whence none can reach man's destined goal
Our Home is far beyond yon sky,—
'Tis Heaven alone can fill our soul."

III.

I dared not touch the fatal shore,
It is too sad to live for aye,
My heart would bleed, if evermore
Death had no power to come my way.

SOME IRISH AUTHORS OF THE PENAL DAYS.

WHILE the swords of Irish chieftians flashed in the glens of Ireland, the pens of Irish priests in the cells and halls of Europe seemed to blaze like so many torches, and throw lurid lights upon the iniquity and tyranny of England. What England always dreaded was the light. She is fond of sinning, but she wishes her crimes to be hidden under the wings of night. She is desirous of a good name, and like the Pharisee, she proclaims in the highways her deeds of mercy and charity. In secret she loves to grind and pillage and plunder. It has ever been the aim of England to misrepresent the state of Ireland, to deny the existence of suffering in that country, and to blacken and slander its inhabitants. For this reason she has always encouraged lying and ignorant writers on Irish subjects. How happy she would feel if she could only make Ireland a "howling wilderness," if she could raze its altars and desecrate its holy graves without a fear that the rest of the world would hear of her dark deeds. I am not writing in passion. I merely state what I know, from a cool and patient examination of her seven-centuried treatment of my country, to be a clear and positive fact. How she longed during the Penal times to turn the heart of Europe away from Ireland and the Irish. How she prayed—but prayer without faith and charity is of no avail—that France and Spain would not hear the sorrowful cry of their Catholic brethren, who were being slaughtered by her miscreant soldiers in the ruins of their shrines and in the caverns of their mountains. But fortunately the Irish students on the Continent had pens, and could use them as skilfully as their brothers did their swords at Beal-an-atha-Buidhe and Benburb. Scattered through all parts of Europe they were masters of every living language. One published his book at Paris, another sent forth his volume at Rome or Vienna; others wrote in Spanish or Portuguese; others, again, wrote in German or Bohemian. All Europe learned the true state of Ireland's cruel slavery and martyrdom, and looked with horror and indignation on England. The mask of hypocrisy was rudely torn from the face of the mock philanthropist, and she was exposed to the scorn and contempt of the nations. What Ireland owes to her priestly authors of Penal times cannot be over estimated.

Speaking of these writers, Thomas Darcy McGee says: —"It may not be improper to add a word or two as to the influence of their Irish works upon the European mind. It is certain that these occasioned in all the Catholic states strong anti-English sentiments. It is equally certain that they whetted the swords and fed the passions for distinction that animated the hearts of the Irish soldiers of France and Spain and Austria. They kept alive in no slight degree the spirit that formed and sustained those noted brigades, who are visible whenever danger appears on or glory brightens the page of European history during the past two centuries. The men whom George II. had cause to curse his ministers for banishing, and for whom the Bourbons had reason to be grateful; the men who bore away tattered, but untaken, the Austrian banner from Austerlitz; the men who revolutionized South America, were in a great degree sustained in their integrity, and stimulated onward to fame, by perusing the pages of their brother exiles of the pen. And to them also is due much of that respectability which is attached, and so long has been attached, to the Irish name among the well-informed of those nations. It is the boast of many a Continental man that his father was from Ireland, and so well is this truth known that our oppressors masquerade beneath it into favor on their travels. The bravery of our banished captains alone could not have established this *prestige* round the character of our country; but the writings of our exiled authors aiding, it was achieved."

A catalogue alone of the names of Irish authors of the Penal days would fill a large volume. Of necessity, therefore, I will be forced to confine myself to some few writers who achieved more than an ordinary amount of fame in their time. It may be said in passing, that nearly every Irish scholar of note in Penal times was more or less distinguished as a writer. It may also be added, that though many of our Irish authors wrote in the language of the country in which they resided at the time, most of them addressed the learned world at large, and therefore used the Latin language as a medium of conveying the knowledge they wished to impart.

Thomas de Leon, whose proper name was Dillon, was a brilliant Jesuit whose memory was long honored in the learned halls of Spain. He taught philosophy, and was both dogmatic and moral professor for many years at Seville and Granada. He became eminent as a linguist. He received a high encomium from Athanasius Kircher for his profound knowledge of Hebrew, Greek, and the Arabic tongue. Like Lynch and other Irish students, he is placed by Nicholas Antonio among the famous Spanish writers. Peter Talbot, no mean authority, calls him "the oracle of Spain, not only for his profoundness in divinity, but for his vast extent of knowledge in other sciences, and his great skill in the languages." He composed his works principally in Spanish.

John Lynch was a secular priest and a native of Galway. His great work is "Cambrensis Eversus," a refutation of Gerald Barry. Harris says that Lynch, "with a judicious and sharp pen, exposeth the numberless mistakes, falsehoods, and calumnies of that writer; showing, in confuting him, that he was well qualified to undertake the subject by a great compass of knowledge in the history of his country, and in other polite learning. His work is not properly a history of Ireland, yet it contains many choice collections out of Irish antiquities."

Augustin Gibbon de Burgo, D.D., an Austin hermit, was a native of Mayo, and provincial of his Order. He resided principally in the University of Erford, in Germany. He was a well-known author. Besides several works on theology, he published a large volume of sermons.

Nicholas Comerford, of Waterford, was a famous Jesuit in his time. He wrote in English "a pithy and learned treatise, very exquisitely penned," and addressed to the inhabitants of his native city. Anthony Wood says that he "wrote and published divers other things." Constantine O'Mahony, known by the *alias* Cornelius á St. Patricio, in Portugal, was a priest burning with an ardent patriotism. He wrote a book to prove the right of Irish Catholics to the Irish nation. "The object of this book was to excite the Irish to persist in their rebellion." He proves conclusively that the kings of England never had any claim to Ireland, and that their title was mere usurpation and tyranny. He adduces a Bull of Pope Gregory XIII, granted to Owen Roe O'Neill in 1642, in which the chiefs and soldiers of the preceding year are blessed, and a Plenary Indulgence granted to all in the future who will assist in freeing the Irish Catholics from the tyranny of England. He boldly asserts the right of Irishmen to crown a king of Irish blood; nay, he even binds them in conscience to do so, and tells them openly that they must cast off the hated yoke of heretics and foreigners. It is said that the Nuncio favored this advanced doctrine.

Paul Sherlock, as a youth of great promise, entered the Jesuit novitiate in Spain. "He passed through his course of philosophy and divinity with great reputation, became a very learned man, and was raised to the government of the Irish seminaries of Compostella and Salamanca." In this last-named college he taught dogmatic theology. He lived altogether in Spain, and Nicholas Antonio ranks him among the writers of that country. He published three volumes on the Canticles. He also wrote some works on difficult theological subjects, in which he showed his deep and varied knowledge and his linguistic skill.

Anthony Bruodine was a recollect from Clare, and Jubilate lecturer of divinity in the Irish convent of the Holy Conception of the Blessed Virgin, at Prague, in Bohemia. He wrote much on theological subjects, yet did not forget to devote some of his time to illustrating the history of Ireland. Anthony Gearnon, of St. Anthony's Convent, Louvain, wrote an Irish ascetic book which bore the title of the "Paradise of the Soul." Father Martin Green, a distinguished Jesuit, was the author of "The Life and Doctrines of the Society of Jesus against the Calumnies of the Evil-Minded." He had also commenced a "History of the Church of England," but death came before he could proceed far in this undertaking.

Father William Bath, a learned Jesuit, wrote at the age of twenty-five many articles of deep and lasting interest to the members of his Order. He is said to have been very fond of music. While still a young student at Oxford he wrote "An Introduction to the Art of Musick, wherein are set down exact and easy Rules with Arguments and their Solutions, for such as seek to know the Reason of the Truth." In 1611 he published at Salamanca his "Gate of Tongues," by which he opened to students an easy entrance to all languages. This work was published by the Jesuits of Salamanca, and was highly prized as a class-book throughout all Spain. He also published the "Methodical Institution of the Principal Mysteries of the Christian Faith," with a method annexed for the exercise of general confession. This work was sent forth to the world of literature in English and Latin. The author also, under the assumed name of Peter Manriques, translated it into Spanish.

James Piers, D.D., was royal Professor of Philosophy in the Aquitanic College. He was a pious and learned man and wrote an ascetic work, "To the Greater Glory of God, and the Blessed Virgin Mary." Peter White, of Waterford—commonly called the *lucky schoolmaster*, as he had for students Richard Stanihurst, Peter Lombard, and other great literary lights—was the author of several prose works. He was also a poet of some repute.

John Dowdall, an Austin hermit, who was appointed one of the preachers to King James II., was an author. He wrote "The Infallibility of the Catholic Church" and the "Life of St. Augustine." Richard Lynch, a native of Galway, taught philosophy, explained the Holy Writings, and lectured on dogmatic subjects, both at Valladolid and Salamanca. He died in 1676, being at the time rector of the college of Salamanca. He published a volume of sermons in Spanish, and had his works on philosophy and theology printed at Lyons and

Salamanca. Father John Travers, D. D., published a book in "Defence of the Pope's Supremacy." For this work he had his hands cut off. He was afterwards executed at Tyburn, for what the English tyrants were pleased to call high treason. Cornelius Dovan, who was also executed for high treason, was the author of a book which was fitly written by him on the Irish Martyrs. Father Jerome Malone, a friar of St. Jerome, wrote several ascetic works, the principle of which were on the sufferings of our Blessed Saviour.

Sebastian Shortal, a native of Kilkenny, became a Cistercian in "the monastery of Nucale, in Gallicia, Spain, where he was held in great reputation." A distinguished Cistercian writer assures us that he was "a man of sharp wit, a good disputant, and one of the best poets their society ever had; and that his writings had obtained a high character." Shortal was the author of some prose works. Father John Clare, a Jesuit, was highly esteemed by his superiors. He was the author of "The Converted Jew," which he dedicated to the two universities of Oxford and Cambridge. Father Purcell wrote "The Right Way to God." Florence Grey published an Irish grammar at Louvain. Richard Rochford, a native of Leinster, and a Franciscan at Louvain, published in English "The Life of the Glorious Bishop, St. Patrick, Apostle and Primate of Ireland." He also wrote the Lives of the Holy Virgin, St. Bridget, and St. Columb, patrons of Ireland. His works were sent from the press at St. Omer's.

Thaddeus Dowling was a great canonist. He gave

much of his time to the study of his native land. Besides the "Annals of Ireland," he also had printed an Irish grammar. Richard Creagh, Bishop of Limerick, wrote several able works. He was the author of an "Ecclesiastical History," wrote a controversial work, and published the Lives of the Irish Saints and also an Irish catechism. John O'Farrell, a native of Munster, and a Franciscan in the Irish college of Louvain, was a great preacher, and acquired a reputation as a poet. He composed some elegant elegiac verses on the glories of the Geraldines. He also wrote some good verses on the Stigmata of St. Francis of Assisium. James Shiel, a Franciscan also, and a native of Down, and titular bishop of Down and Connor, wrote an answer to Dr. Jennings' "Challenge." Shiel's work was a great success, and went through several editions even in London. Barnaby Kearney, a Jesuit priest of Douay and Antwerp, was esteemed as a powerful preacher. He published some volumes of his sermons at Paris, Lyons, and Rome. Edmund Dwyer, titular bishop of Limerick, wrote some poetry. One of his poems had for subject the "Fire of Kildare's holy fane." Father Henry Ryan, a Dominican, who lived at Rome during the pontificate of Pope Urban VIII., wrote some creditable poetry. "One of his poems," says an old author," is reckoned a very elegant piece." Robert Chamberlain, a native of Ulster, a "secular doctor of divinity at Salamanca," was an able theologian. He composed some excellent tracts on his favorite study.

Francis Matthews, a Franciscan from Cork, who held

responsible offices in his Order, is praised by Luke Wadding for his abilities in divinity and canon law. He was the author of several theological works. He was a very zealous man, and was put to death in his native city. The Jesuit, Peter Wadding, was a versatile writer. He defended his Order with great success against the malicious attacks of its enemies. He composed some volumes of moral and dogmatic theology, and also published several poems. Francis O'Mellaghlin, of Athlone, so famous in Irish story, was a Franciscan, and jubilate lecturer of divinity in the Irish college of Prague, and afterwards public professor of that faculty in the cathedral seminary at Imola, in the Roman states. So highly was he esteemed for his learning that he was ordered by the archbishop of Imo'a to write a work on philosophy. This he did in an able manner. Dr. Timothy O'Brien, of the county Cork, wrote some controversial works. He ably answered the vile attacks of Rowland Davis, dean of Cork. One of his books was styled "Goliath Beheaded with his Own Sword." O'Brien also published some sermons, Richard Archdekin, of Kilkenny, was a distinguished member of the Jesuit Order. He professed divinity and philosophy at Louvain and Antwerp. He soon acquired a great reputation as a theologian. Besides other works, he wrote "Theologia Tripartita Universa." This work was favorably known in all parts of Europe. As early as 1700 the eleventh edition of it was published at Venice.

John Harting, of Waterford, a member of the Cistercian Order in Spain, wrote much and well about the distinguished men who had adorned his society. Father William Malone, a Jesuit, "was esteemed a dangerous person," and so was arrested and cast into prison. But having made his escape, he fled to Spain and became rector of the Irish college of Seville. He wrote a masterly controversial work, called the "Jesuits' Challenge." This book was deemed worthy of answers from several learned Protestants, among whom were Usher, "the great pillar of the established church," as Dr. Johnson calls him, Dr. Joshua Hoyle, Divinity Professor in Trinity College, Dublin, Roger Tuttock, an English Protestant minister, and Dr. Synge. Peter Redan, also a learned Jesuit, and a native of Meath, was educated at Salamanca, where he became famous for his Erudition. He was considered a profound Greek and Hebrew scholar. He died at the age of forty-four. He was the author of an able work against the Manichæans.

David Rothe, D. D., of the University of Douay, bishop of Ossory, and vice primate of Ireland, was a most patriotic prelate, "a man of great natural parts, and very well accomplished in learning." Usher speaks of him highly as a scholar, and calls him a "curious inquirer into the antiquities of his country." The great Protestant archbishop also confesses that he owes much to Rothe in matters of learning and information. Messingham says, "that he was well versed in all sorts of learning, was an elegant orator, a subtile philosopher, a profound divine, an eminent historian, and a sharp reprover of vice." Bishop Rothe was certainly an able and voluminous writer. His "Hibernia Resurgens" was directed against Dempster, the ambitious Scotchman, who made claim to the saints of Erin as natives of his own country. The vigor of his pen and his Irish hagiological knowledge are clearly shown in this little work. "David Rothe," says Father Meehan, "whose works were destined to elevate and perpetuate the name of his progenitors and kindred, and whose chequered life—extending over so considerable a portion of the first half of the seventeenth century—would be sufficient to interest us without his celebrity as a writer." McGee says of this prelate: "Among the churchmen of the age who gave themselves up to research and authorship, scarcely any if we except Nicholas French, has a clearer claim to remembrance. His book, more than any other, prepared the minds of Ireland for the confederacy, and the Irish abroad for co-operation in its projects."

THE MONKS OF ERIN.

The Irish monks, the Irish monks, their names are treasured still
In many a foreign valley, on many a foreign hill,
Their preaching, prayers, and fastings are still the peasants' themes
Around the coast of Cornwall, and along old Flanders' streams;
Their lives austere and holy, and the wonders of their hands
Still nourish faith and sanctity through fair Italia's lands,
The cross they bore in triumph still bright as ever shines
Above the domes of Austria, among the Tuscan vines.

Sedulius, the poet, and Columbkille, the dove,
At Rome and Hy are honored, and remembered still with love;
At Lucca, St. Frigidian, in a church ablaze with lights,
Is honored with pure worship, 'mid the pomp of Roman rites,
Even still the British miners exult on Piran's feast,
And though they hate the Church of Rome, they venerate her priest.
The bells of sweet Tarentum, as they wake the matin air,
Still tell in tones of gladness that Cataldus' faith is there.

Quaint Mechlin's noblest temple to an Irish monk is raised,
In every home in Mechlin St. Rumold's name is praised;
Virgilius, the gifted, in his glorious Salzburg tomb,
Is honored by the silent prayer and by the cannon's boom;
Old hymns are sung to Fridolin in the islands of the Rhine,
And the relics of Besançon's saint sleep in a silver shrine;
The voice that roused Crusaders by the Tagus, Rhone and Po,
Seems ringing still o'er Malachy at the convent of Clairvaux.

The Irish monks, the Irish monks, their spirit still survives
In the stainless Church of Ireland, and in her priesthood's lives,
Their spirit still doth linger round Holy Cross and Kells—
Oh, Ireland's monks can know no death while gush our holy wells.
High Cashel's fane is standing, and though in the spoiler's hand
Like the captive ark of Judah, 'tis a blessing to our land,
For proudly it reminds us of the palmy days of yore,
When kings were monks and monks were kings, upon our Irish
    shore.

IRISH GENIUS ABROAD.

(Before taking farewell of the Penal Times, I wish to devote a few pages to some illustrious Irishmen, not ecclesiastics, who reflected glory on their land and race in diffcrent foreign countries.)

THE Irishman is the *eagle* of the human race. He is proud, daring, and born to soar. Give him a fair opportunity, do not fetter him, and he will take his place among the stars, he will not rest until he is bathed in the light and glory of the sun. The blood of Irishmen seems to partake of the immortality of their souls. It may be spilled in torrents by successive English tyrants; it may be poured out like water on every battle-field of Europe, and America; it may be drunk up by famine-fevers, and still it does not seem to diminish, it preserves all its glorious vitality. What other race but the Irish could have passed through the fiery furnace of Penal Times, and live? What other people, could have squandered so much blood in wars not always their own, and still exist: "From calculations and researches that have been made at the War-office" says an older writer, "it has been ascertained, that from the arrival of the Irish troops in France, in 1691, to 1745, the year of the battle of Fontenoy, more than four hundred and fifty thousand Irishmen died in the service of France." When we consider all the sufferings, the persecutions, the exiling, and the ten thousand nameless wrongs that the sons of Ireland have endured for long centuries it looks like a miracle that there now exists one genuine Irishman in all the wide world. And yet Erin's children are multiplied as "the stars in the heavens." Surely we may say,—"the finger of God is here." Their defeat in one field only made their victory in the adjoining one more glorious. Driven from their own little Island, the rest of the earth became their inheritance. They soon shared in the glory of all civilized nations. In the competition for honors—literary—civic—martial—they often bore away the laurels. Clancy writes: "O'Sullivan, Lawless, Gardiner, O'Donnell and O'Reilly became grandees of Spain; and men yet living can recall the time when O'Donnell was Dictator at Madrid. Lacy and Browne were Marshals of Russia, and won the most brilliant victories of their era. Admiral O'Dwyer commanded the Russian fleet in 1787. Marshal Maurice Kavanagh was Chamberlain of Poland; Colonel Harold filled a similar position in Bavaria. Patrick Lawless was Ambassador from Portugal to France; O'Reilly represented Spain at the Court of Louis XVI." The following extract from a newspaper published in Vienna, in March 1766, gives us an account of some of the distinguished guests who were present at a banquet given by Count O'Mahony: "On the 17th of this month his Excellency, Count O'Mahony, Ambassador from Spain to the Court of Vienna, gave a grand entertainment in honor of St. Patrick, to which were invited all persons of distinction that were Irish descent—being of an illustrious Irish family. Among others were present—Count Lacy, President of the Council of War; General McDonnell, General Brown, General McGuire, General Plunkett, General O'Kelly and General McElligott; four chiefs of the grand cross, two governors, several knights military, six staff officers, four privy councillors of Austria, with the principal officers of state—who, to show their respect for the Irish nation, wore crosses in honor of the day, as did the whole court of Vienna."

As, is well-known, O'Reilly, Kavanagh and Prince Nugent are historic names in Austria, in which country their bearers were Aulic Councillors. Sarsfield, who is so greatly admired by Macaulay, and O'Brien, became marshals of France; Hamilton, Lally and McCarthy, Generals; Sheldon, Galmoy, O'Carroll, O'Gara, Fitzgerald, O'Mahony, O'Neil, Power, McMahon, Burke, Murphy, Maguire, Dillon, Roche, McDonnell, Lee, McElligott, and a host of others commanded regiments, many of them founding families whose representatives play an important part even still in France.

According to Sir Bernard Burke, the organization and tactics of modern armies in Europe were perfected by a Franco-Irish colonel, named Daniel O'Connell. Marquis McMahon (grand-sire of the late Marshal-President), was one of the first agents to investigate the condition of the American colonists, and suggest plans for their liberation. "It is strange," said Napoleon, on his second entry into Vienna, (1809), that now as in 1803, on entering the Austrian Capitol, I find myself in intercourse with Count O'Reilly." It is said that Napoleon "had good reason to know the Count, for it was he, with his band of exiled '98 men, that saved the broken army of Austria after Austerlitz. In that army at that time there were over forty Irish names, ranging from the grade of colonel to field-marshal; and when Maria Theresia of Hungary instituted fifty Crosses of the Legion of Honor, forty-six of them were worn on the breasts of Irishmen."

The following citation, though long, is so pertinent to our subject that we cannot omit it :—

"Louis XIV. having sent seven French battalions to Ireland in the beginning of the year 1690, whether that he required the same number of Irish troops in return, or that James II., who was at that time in the country, thought proper to send them, three Irish regiments arrived at Brest in the beginning of May, on board French ships, under command of Justin McCarthy, Viscount Mountcashel, a lieutenant-general in England, and who still retained his rank in France. The regiments composing this brigade were Mountcashel's— an old regiment of long standing—O'Brien's and Dillon's, each consisting of two battalions, containing one thousand six hundred men, divided into sixteen companies. On their arrival in France, Mountcashel entered into an arrangement for this corps, by which the officers were to be paid as they are at present (1754): and the soldiers a penny a day more than the

French. This corps was sent to Savoy, where they distinguished themselves under Marshal de Catenat in the reduction of that province; particularly at the battle of Marseilles, gained by the French on the 4th of November 1693. Daniel O'Brien, colonel of the regiment that bore his name, having inherited his father's title, who had lately died, called it the Clare regiment. He died at Pignerol: Captain Murrough O'Brien served in Hamilton's regiment, Greder's, a German, and the Clare regiment. Lord Mountcashel having died at Barege, from a wound in the chest which he received in Savoy the year he went to France, his regiment was given to De Lee, and afterwards called Bulkley's regiment, Talbot, brigadier-colonel of the Limerick regiment, was appointed to the one De Lee had left. Talbot was the son of the duke of Tirconnel; he had served in France from his youth, and was deemed an able officer. He was succeeded by Charles O'Brien, Viscount Clare, brother to him who died at Pignerol after the battle of Marseilles.

Charles O'Brien went to France in 1691, after the surrender of Limerick, as captain of James II.'s bodyguard. It is probable that his regiment of dragoons, which he commanded at the battle of the Boyne, had been disbanded in Ireland. After the battle of Marseilles, he was appointed to the queen of England's regiment of dragoons; O'Carrol, the colonel having been killed. He revived the name of the *Clare regiment;* he was killed in 1706, at the battle of Ramillies, and his regiment given to Lieutenant-colonel Murrough O'Brien, who was descended from the house of Carrigogoiniol, a branch of the O'Brien family. When lieutenant-colonel, he distinguished himself at the battle of Ramillies by taking two stand of colors from the enemy, which were deposited in the house of the Irish Benedictines at Ypres. His skilful manoeuvre at Pallue, by which he saved Combray, is still greater proof of his talents; after it he received the rank of field-marshal of the king's army. 'If the Marshal de Montesquieu had done him the justice due to him for the affair at Pallue,' says Thuomond, 'he would have had a greater share in the king's favor than he possessed.' Murrough O'Brien retained the command of this regiment, under the name of O'Brien's regiment, till his death, which took place in 1720. He left a son called Daniel, a colonel of foot in the service of king Louis, who was created a knight of St. Lazarus in 1716, a peer of Ireland, under the title of Earl of Lismore, in 1747, and received the grand cross of the royal and military order of St. Louis in 1750. He died at Rome in 1759.

Dillon's was the only regiment of Lord Mountcashel's brigade that retained its name. It was raised in Ireland by Lord Dillon's grandfather, and commanded by Arthur Dillon, his second son, lieutenant-general of the king's army. He died at St. Germaine-en-Laie, 1734. This nobleman added to his illustrious birth superior skill in the art of war, and his exploits have been celebrated in the annals of France. He left several sons, the eldest of whom succeeded his uncle, Lord Dillon. Two were killed at the head of their regiments, at the battles of Fontenoy and Lawfeld ; and the last has been lately translated from the archbishopic of Toulouse to that of Narbonne.

Irish regiments were known as Dorington's, Rothe's, Burke's, Albemarle's, Fitzgerald's, Berwick's and Galmoy's. The regiments of Burke and Dillon were engaged at the battle of Cremona, February 1702, in which they particularly distinguished themselves, and contributed mainly to the defeat of the enemy. As a mark of the king's satisfaction he raised their pay.

Sheldon's regiment of cavalry distinguished themselves at the battle of Spire, on the 24th of November 1703. In 1708, the king of Spain began to raise two regiments of dragoons, and three Irish battalions, consisting of the prisoners taken from the English army in the battle of Almanza. These corps were officered by the half-pay officers who had served with the Irish regiments in France.

Burke applied for and obtained permission for his regiment, which had often served in Spain (in order to avoid shifting) to offer its services to the king of Spain. This being granted, he proceeded to that country, and subsequently served with distinction in Sicily, Africa and Italy, during the war of 1733, under the king of the two Sicilies, to whom his father, the king of Spain, had sent him in 1758. Burke's regiment remained in Naples ; it was called the king's corps, and received an addition of two battalions.

Through the changes which took place among the Irish troops in France, the king of Spain was enabled to increase his three Irish regiments of foot by a battalion each, so that he had six made up of the supernumary men who remained unemployed in France. They served at Oran in Sicily, and in Italy in 1733, 1734, with the highest distinction—four of these battalions, with the Waloon guards, were successful in 1713, in repulsing the enemy at Veletry, and in saving Don Philip, who was in danger of being taken prisoner."

Many Irish soldiers held high positions in the Netherlands. The archdukes, Albert and Isabella, promoted Henry O'Neill, the son of the great Hugh, to the command of an Irish regiment then in their service. They honored also with high rank in their armies, Rory O'Dougherty, the brother of the chivalrous, but ill-fated Sir Cahir, and Daniel O'Cahan, afterwards lieutenant-general to Owen Roe O'Neill. An Irish officer named O'Rorke was distinguished for his valor in the Italian campaign, and fell at the battle of Luzzara.

The following eloquent and interesting passage will give our readers an idea of how the Irish Chaplains excited their countrymen to deeds of martial valor, and cheered them on to glory :—

"Your ancestors have not disappointed the hopes that France built on them. Nervinde, Marseilles, Barcelona, Cremona, Luzzara, Spire, Castiglione, Almanza, Villa Viciosa, and many other places, witnesses of their immortal valor, consecrated their devotedness for the new country which had adopted them. France applauded their zeal, and the greatest of monarchs raised their praise to the highest pitch by honoring them with the flattering title of 'his brave Irishmen.'

The examples of their chiefs animated their courage: the Viscounts Mountcashel and Clare, the Count of Lucan, the Dillons, Lees, Rothes, O'Donnels, Fitzgeralds, Nugents and Galmoys, opened to them on the borders of the Meuse, the Rhine and Po, the career of glory, while the O'Mahonys, MacDonnels, Lawlesses, the Lacys, the Burks, O'Carrols, Craftons, Comerford, Gardner and O'Conner, crowned themselves with laurels on the shores of the Tagus.

The neighboring powers wished to have in their service the children of these great men; Spain retained some of you near her throne. Naples invited you to her fertile country; Germany called you to the defence of her eagles. The Taffs, the Hamiltons, O'Dwyers, Browns, Wallaces and O'Neills, supported the majesty of the empire, and were intrusted with its most important posts. The ashes of Mareschal Brown are every day watered with the tears of the soldiers to whom he was so dear, while the O'Donnels Maguires, Lacys, and others, endeavored to form themselves after the example of that great man.

Russia, that vast and powerful empire, an empire which has passed suddenly from obscurity to so much glory, wished to learn the military discipline from your corps. Peter, the Great, that penetrating genius and hero, the creator of a nation which is now triumphant, thought he could not do better than confide that essential part of the art of war to the Field Mareschal de

Lacy; and the worthy daughter of that great emperor, always intrusted to that warior the principal defence of the august throne which she filled with so much glory. Finally the Viscount Fermoy, general officer in the service of Sardinia, has merited all the confidence of that crown.

But why recall those times that are so long past? Why do I seek your heroes in those distant regions? Permit me, gentlemen, to bring to your recollection that great day, forever memorable in the annals of France ; let me remind you of the plains of Fontenoy, so precious to your glory; those plains where in concert with chosen French troops, the valiant Count of Thomond being at your head, you charged with so much valor an enemy so formidable ; animated by the presence of the august sovereign who rules over you, you contributed to the gaining of a victory, which, till then, appeared doubtful. Lawfeld beheld you, two years afterwards, in concert with one of the most illustrious corps of France, force intrenchments which appeared to be impregnable. Menin, Ypres, Tournay, saw you crown yourselves with glory under their walls, while your countrymen, under the standards of Spain, performed prodigies of valor at Campo Sancto and at Veletri.

But while I am addressing you, a part of your corps is flying to the defence of the allies of Louis ; another is sailing over the seas to seek amidst the waves of another hemisphere, the eternal enemies of his empire.

Behold, gentlemen, what all Europe contemplates in

you; behold herein the qualities which have gained esteem for you, even from your most unjust enemies."

With regard to distinguished Irishmen abroad Thomas D'Arcy McGee has the following :—"Of general officers, it would be hard to muster the lists. The Irish governors of important posts are more easily enumerated. One Browne was Governor of Deva, for Austria; another, Governor-General of Livonia for Russia; Count Thomond was Commander at Languedoc; Lally was Governor of Pondicherry; one Kavanagh was Governor of Prague; another, of Buda; O'Dwyer was Commander of Belgrade; Lacy, of Riga; and Lawless, Governor of Majorca."

Sutton, Count of Clonard, was Governor of the Dauphin, in France; Nugent was Minister of Austria at Berlin; Clarke, Duke de Feltre, was Minister of War in France.

"In Spanish America," says the author just quoted, "the Captains General O'Higgins of Chili, O'Donoju of Mexico, and O'Donnell of Cuba; the Supreme Director O'Higgins; the Generals O'Reilly, O'Brien and Devereux; the Colonels McKenna, O'Leary, O'Connor and O'Carroll, were all men of one generation—all Irishmen by birth or parentage." "To North America, within seventy years, we have contributed ten major generals, five commodores, a president, two vice-presidents, six authors of the Constitution, nine signers of the Declaration, upwards of twenty generals of brigade, and an immense amount of minor officers, and rank and file to the army."

It is now nearly forty years since McGee thus spoke. What a glorious number, if he still lived, he could now add to those given. Who can count the hosts of gallant Irishmen who distinguished themselves in the late war? The names of many of them shine upon the brightest pages in the history of the struggle for the Union. America can never forget what she owes to those devoted sons of Ireland who lavishly poured out their blood for her cause; she can never forget those bold and chivalrous men whose military genius, whose unflagging zeal, whose fiery valor, on every battle-field of the Rebellion, helped to preserve her from being torn to pieces, from having her limbs scattered like the branches of the lightning-riven tree. It does not come within the scope of this work to speak at any length of the great Protestant Irishmen who reflected credit on their country, or who helped to make her known to the nations. Many of their names are as familiar to the students of English literature as those of Milton or Byron. In many cases their whole inspiration was Irish, and their work made beautiful and solid by principles and ideas borrowed from their Catholic ancestors, or countrymen. "From the inner essence of Irish character," says Henry Giles, "came to birth, voice and might the turbid power of Flood, the deep thinking of Plunket, the Shakespearean sweep of Burke, with all the other men of flaming tongues, in whose burning hearts the fire of a generous nationality was kindled. If Irish genius gave nothing to the world but the eloquence of such men, in that alone it has given to the world an immortal contribution." It is not necessary for us to allude to Sheridan, Curran, Grattan, and a host of other great Irish Protestants whose fame is world-wide. Charles Phillips, after depicting in his own beautiful, though somewhat florid language, the virtues which characterize the Irish Catholic people, thus speaks: "Look to Protestant Ireland, shooting over the empire those rays of genius, and those thunderbolts of war, that have at once embellished and preserved it. I speak not of a former era. I refer not for my example to the day just passed when our Burkes, our Barrys, and our Goldsmiths, exiled by this system from their native shore, wreathed the 'immortal shamrock,' round the brow of painting, poetry and eloquence! But now, even while I speak, who leads the British senate? A Protestant Irishman! Who guides the British arms? A Protestant Irishman! In his speech at Dublin, early in this century, Mr. Phillips argues very correctly and eloquently that a great loss to the world was sustained through the Penal laws against Catholic education in Ireland. How many a *genius* was born in Ireland during the Penal Times, who for want of education lived and died without showing even a spark of the immortal fire that burned in his breast; "If we argue," he says, "from the services of Protestant Ireland, to the losses sustained by the bondage of Catholic Ireland, and I do not see why we should not, the state which continues such a system is guilty of little less than political suicide. It matters little where the Protestant Irishman has been employed; whether with Burke wielding the senate with his eloquence, with Castlereagh guiding the cabinet by his counsels, with Barry enriching the arts with his pencil, with Swift adorning literature by his genius, with Goldsmith softening the heart by his melody, or with Wellington chaining victory at his car, he may boldly challenge the competition of the world. Oppressed and impoverished as our country is, every muse has cheered, and every art adorned, and every conquest crowned her. Plundered, she was not poor, for her character enriched; attainted, she was not titleless, for her services ennobled; literally outlawed into eminence and fettered into fame, the fields of her exile were immortalized by her deeds, and the links of her chain became decorated by her laurels. Is this fancy? Or is it fact? Is there a department in the state in which Irish genius does not possess a preponderance? Is there a conquest which it does not achieve, or a dignity which it does not adorn? At this instant, is there a country in the world to which England has not deputed an Irishman as her representative? She has sent Lord Moira to India, Sir Gore Ouseley to Ispahan, Lord Stuart to Vienna, Lord Castlereagh to Congress, Sir Henry Wellesly to Madrid. Mr. Canning to Lisbon, Lord Strangford to the Brazils, Lord Clancarty to Holland, Lord Wellington to Paris — all Irishmen!"

Can it be that the land that has produced so many brilliant men as we have referred to in the course of this book is not worthy of self-government, of Home Rule? It certainly must be blind and stupid prejudice that tells us that though Irish genius can rule the world, aye, and a thousand worlds like this, it cannot rule the country God gave it as its inheritance. The glory of Irish talent, and the virtue of the Irish race the world over, is the strongest argument for me of the fitness of the Irish Nation to rule itself wisely and well. What tact has England shown in ruling Ireland? Where is her wisdom? Has she succeeded in making Ireland a land of peace, of plenty, of prosperity? Has she encouraged the fine arts, has she aided commerce, has she recompensed agriculture, has she done anything for the fisheries? Has she advanced civilization, or the spirit of religion in Ireland? Who can point out one good and lasting service rendered to Ireland during the last seven hundred years by England? She has banned education, she has burned abbeys, she has robbed and torn down churches, she has ground the peasant and the chief and sent them into exile, she has desolated whole villages and beggared cities, she has trampled upon every right human and divine, she has shipped tens of thousands of gentle Irish maidens to the Barbadoes to be sold as slaves in the market-place, she has butchered holy and learned bishops, she has strangled our princes in her prison-towers,—but yesterday she silenced our members of Parliament and cast them into gaol—while I write three Irish priests are confined in infamous cells —and the English Government, the Tory Government, has declared that *Coercion, Coercion, the Eternal Coercion* must be used to heal Ireland's wounds, to feed her hungry, to dry up her tears, to pacify her sons, to console her exiled children, to put her on the road to happiness and prosperity. Oh, the blindness and the folly of tyrants—of English tyrants. Oh, the madness of English statesmen. Gladstone, forever honored be his name, came between England and Ireland with the palm-branch in his hand, he came with a balm for all Ireland's woes, he came with a wand to charm out of Ireland's heart the memory of past wrongs, he came with light from heaven around his head, he came to lead England out of shame, and danger, and trouble, and to lead Ireland into peace, and joy, and glory—but he was rejected, he was cast down, he was all but stoned by his own bigoted fellow-rulers. Woe, woe, to England, the day she wholly rejects the saving, I may say the *holy*, policy which the greatest of English statesmen at present proposes.

"Give Ireland Home Rule, and she will leap from her bed in the sea, and draw nearer to the sun." And Home Rule she must have. It is not in the power of England, it is not in the power of the whole world to keep it much longer from her. But the world does not wish to keep it from her. The voice of the Nations has thundered forth that Irishmen alone have a right, or are fit, to govern Ireland. And so, my countrymen, in the cheering and hopeful words of one of Ireland's gifted sons: "Let us turn from the blight and ruin of this wintry day to the fond anticipation of a happier period, when our prostrate land shall stand erect among the nations, fearless and unfettered; her brow blooming with the wreath of science, and her path strewed with the offerings of art; the breath of heaven blessing her flag, the extremities of earth acknowledging her name, her fields waving with the fruits of agriculture, her ports alive with the contributions of commerce, and her tempels vocal with unrestricted piety." The following passage from Richard Lalor Shiel, probably the most eloquent appeal ever made in the British Parliament, while it shows us that the martial spirit of Ireland was not extinct in the beginning of this century, is a proof, a strong and powerful proof, of what England owes Ireland, and at the same time shows us the might and fire of Irish eloquence: "The Duke of Wellington is not a man of an excitable temperament. His mind is of a cast too martial to be easily moved; but, notwithstanding his habitual inflexibility, I cannot help thinking that, when he heard his Roman Catholic countrymen (for we are his countrymen) designated by a phrase as offensive as the abundant vocabulary of his eloquent confederate could supply,*—I cannot help thinking that he ought to have recollected the many fields of fight in which we have been contributors to his renown. The battles, sieges, fortunes that he has passed, ought to have come back on him. He ought to have remembered that, from the earliest achievement in which he displayed that military genius which has placed him foremost in the annals of modern warfare, down to that last and surpassing combat which has made his name imperishable,—from Assaye to Waterloo,

---

* Lord Lyndhurst had a short time before referred, in the House of Commons, to the Irish as "aliens, in blood and religion."

the Irish soldiers with whom your armies are filled, were
the inseparable auxiliaries to the glory with which
his unparalleled successes have been crowned. Whose
were the arms that drove your bayonets at Vimiéra
through the phalanxes that never reeled in the shock
of war before? What desparate valor climbed the steeps
and filed the moats of Badajos? All his victories should
have rushed and crowed back upon his memory,—
Vimiéra, Badajos, Salamanca, Albuéra, Toulouse, and
last of all, the greatest.—Tell me,—for you were
there,—I appeal to the gallant soldier before me (Sir
Henry Hardinge), from whose opinions I differ but who
bears, I know, a generous heart in an interpid breast;
—tell me,—for you must needs remember,—on that day
when the destinies of mankind were trembling in the
balance, while death fell in showers, when the artillery
of France was levelled with a precision of the most
deadly science,—when her legions, incited by the voice
and inspired by the example of her mighty leader,
rushed again and again to the onset,—tell me if, for
an instant, when to hesitate for an instant was to be
lost, the "aliens" blenched? And when, at length, the
moment for the last and decided movement had arrived,
and the valor which had so long been wisely checked
was, at last, let loose,—when, with words familiar, but
immortal, the great captain commanded the great as-
sault,—tell me if Catholic Ireland with less heroic valor
than the natives of this your own glorious country pre-
cipitated herself upon the foe? The blood of England,
Scotland, and of Ireland, flowed in the same stream, and

drenched the same field. When the chill morning dawned, their dead lay cold and stark together;—in the same deep pit their bodies were deposited; the green corn of spring is now breaking from their commingled dust; the dew falls from Heaven upon their union in the grave. Partakers in every peril, in the glory shall we not be permitted to participate; and shall we be told as a requittal, that we are estranged from the noble country for whose salvation our life-blood was poured out?"

Though this chapter is already growing long, and assuming an eclectic form, I cannot help inserting here Thomas Francis Meagher's eloquent tribute to Irish bravery:—

"We, the children of the Irish race, have memories that point to the loftier regions of our history—memories, that penetrate and disturb the clouds which overcharge the present hour, revealing to us in the light that quivers from them, many a fragment and Monument of glory. There are laurels interwoven with the cypress upon that old ruin, the home of our fathers, the sanctuary of our faith, the fountain of our love. Desolate as it is, it reminds us of our descent and lineage. Of the soldiers, the scholars, and the statesmen, who constitute the bright and indestructable links of that decent and lineage, we have no reason to be ashamed. The nation that lifts its head the highest in the world, would vote them statues in her Pantheon. Names and exploits that are dear to the Irish soldier arise in quick succession and star the field of memory. The names of

O'Neill, O'Donnell, Mountcashel, Sarsfield, Dillon and De Lacy awake, like the echos of a trumpet from the rugged heights and recesses of the past. There is the defense of Cambray, the retreat of Altenheim, the battle of Maplaquet. The colors of the Irish Brigade moulder in the church of the Invalides. France cannot forget the noble contributions made to her glory by the regiments of Burke, Galmoy and Hamilton. She cannot forget that, at Cremona, where the activity and vigor of her own sons were relaxed by the fine climate, the wines, and the gayeties of Italy,—when not a soldier scoured the neighborhood, or paced the ramparts,—the Irish regiments alone retained the vigor of military discipline, they alone were found regularly under arms, on parade, or at the posts assigned them—that they alone fighting fiercely beat back the cavalry of Prince Eugene, and the grenadiers of De Merci. Neither can France forget, that on the Adige—up through the mountains, whose shadow darken the northern shores of the Lake of Garda,—up through the passes where the best of the Austrian engineers had cut their trenches, and a gallant peasantry stood guard—up the face of those steep precipices that seemed accessible only to the eagle and the chamois, the Irish sprang and clutched the Keys of Riva. But not to the memory of France alone do we appeal for the vindication of the courage of our fathers. Spain which received the remnant of Tyrone's army, Austria in whose ranks so many thousands of the exiles perished—Russia whose forces were organized by Lacy, will bear witness that poor old Ireland has given birth to men, whose chivalry and genius entitle their country to a noble fate. In South America, too, there, where the Andes tower and the Amazon rolls its mighty flood, the Irish Celt has left his footprints on many a field of triumph. Venezuela, Chacabuco, Valparaiso, have recollections of the fiery valor before which the flag of the Escurial went down. And when the great and good Pope Pius IX. stood in his beleaguered palace, protesting against the invasion of his ancient and illustrious domain, an Irish Brigade went forth from the Green Isle to fight his battles. The return of that Brigade from Rome flashed an awakening brightness across the Irish sky. It was headed by an O'Reilly, in every respect a worthy kinsman of Andrew of Ballinlough, whose splendid charge with his army of dragoons saved the wreck of the Austrians at Austerlitz, and moreover, well entitled him to wear the spurs of Myles the Slasher, who fell at the bridge of Finae, fighting against the Cromwellians, having with his own hand slain four and twenty of the foe. The steamship that conveys them to Cork is greeted by a swarm of boats and yachts dancing brightly upon the waters of the noblest harbors in in the world, and as they ascend the river of Gougane Barra, the bells of Shandon and St. Finbar strike in and make glorious music with the cheers and thunders that announce the safe return of the gallant lads, who, at Spoletto, where they were only three hundred and sixty strong stood their ground for fourteen hours against twenty-two thousand of the Piedmontese—stood their ground till the last cartridge was gone, and who, at Loretto, smashing through, and trampling down three times their number cleared a road for Lamoriciere to escape. At Thurles, eight thousand torches flash at midnight, their redeemed name over the broad plains of Tipperary. In Wexford their courage and devotion received the attestations of men whose fathers won for the Black Stairs, and the valleys of the Banna and the Boro, a fame not less effulgent than that which illuminates the forests of La Vendee and the crags of the Tyrol: while in Kilkenny, the ovation which greets them has not been equalled since the Confederates under Ormond met the Nuncio in the Cathedral of St. Canice."

AVE MARIA!

Oh, never yet was a music sweet,
As an *Ave* wispered low;
Oh, the Angels speed on pinions fleet,
To hear its sacred flow;
      Ave Maria.

How sweet it sounds at the vesper hour,
When the maiden, meek and lone,
Is blooming like a lovely flower,
At the foot of Mary's throne;
      Ave Maria.

How sweet it floats o'er the stormy wave,
When the mariners kneel to pray;
How sweet it flows o'er the new-made grave
Of a friend just passed away;
      Ave Maria.

How rich it breathes in the chapel dim,
How rich 'neath cathedral dome;
More rich a sound, or more grand a hymn,
Never cheered a christian home;
      Ave Maria.

Oh, sweet is an *Ave* at all times,
'Tis the sweetest sound on earth;
It hath the ring of sinless climes,
'Tis a note of heavenly birth;
      Ave Maria.

GRAVES OF IRISH EXILES ON THE CONTINENT OF EUROPE.

SCARCELY a cathedral bell is rung on the continent of Europe that does not sound above the remains of some Irish priest or Bishop. Seldom a flower fades in the cloistered cemeteries along the banks of the yellow Tiber, or the castled Rhine, that some of its leaves do not touch the lonely grave of some monk or student from the green banks of the Shannon or the Liffey. The names of Irish students are carved on the flagged floors of many an abbey chapel, and on the walls of many a famous shrine from the Tagus to the Garonne. St. Fridolin sleeps in his island-city of Seckingen, in the abbey he himself founded for the Benedictines; the holy remains of St. Fiacre centuries ago were removed from the oratory of Breuil, and may now be found near the mausoleum of Bossuet, behind the high altar in the Cathedral of Meaux; the noble martyrs, Kylian, Colman and Totnan are buried in the principal church of Würtzburg; St. Frigidian lies at rest in the church of "The Three Holy Levites," at Lucca, while Cataldus awaits the Resurrection not far from the blue waters of the fair bay of Tarentum. Often the twelve knights of St. Rupert may be seen kneeling by the tomb of St. Vigillius, in Salzburg. St. Caidoc and St. Fricor are interred in the abbey of Centule, in the territory of Ponthieu, Picardy. In the collegiate church of Lens, in the diocese of Arras, the body of St. Vulganus is honored. Marianus Scotus, the chronographer, was laid to pious rest in the Church of St. Martin, beyond the walls of the city of Mentz. St. Tressan calmly reposes at Avenay, in Champagne. In a church guarded by the Fort of St. Andrew, at Salins, the relics of St. Anatolius are pressed in a silver shrine. St. Maimbodus securely sleeps in the shade of the castle rock of the valiant city of Montbelliard. The magnificent Cathedral of Mechlin is the tomb and monument of St. Rumold—prince, Bishop, martyr.

But to come to a later period of Irish history. How many Irish students are laid to rest forever on the hill of St. Genevieve! How many of them sleep their long sleep in the Franciscan Convents of Louvain and Salamanca, in the Dominican garden of Madrid, and in the consecrated ground belonging to the Jesuits at Lisle, Antwerp, Tournay, St. Omer, Douay, and Pont-a-Mousson. Florence Conroy sleeps near the high altar in the Franciscan Church of St. Anthony of Padua at Louvain; Thomas Stapleton's ashes are mingled with the dust of Belgium's most gifted sons in the chapel of St. Charles Borromeo; Luke Wadding has been laid near Hugh O'Neil, on St. Peter's Mount. In the Cistercian monastery, at Alcala, in Spain, William Walsh, from Waterford, on the Suir, lies in peace. The grand-souled and patriotic Bishop of Ferns, Nicholas French, passed away from life's toils and troubles at Ghent, in Belgium. His venerated body was piously placed at the foot of the grand altar in the parish Church of St. Nicholas in that city. A slab of purest marble, decorated with the Cardinal's hat and armorial bearings, has a beautiful and truthful inscription in honor of his memory. Ambrose Wadding, brother to the famous Luke Wadding, calmly rests at Dillingen; Bishop Edmond O'Dwyer, who governed the See of Limerick, silently lies in the subterranean chapel, dedicated to the Blessed Virgin, beneath the Church of St. James, in the city of Brussels.

The pious pilgrim to Compostella will find in the world-renowned temple of St. James, Apostle of Spain, the holy remains of two Waterford Bishops—Thomas Strong, of the Diocese of Ossory, and his nephew, the firm friend of Rinuccini, Thomas Walsh. The relics of Patrick Fleming and Matthew Hoar, martyred by the cruel followers of the Elector of Saxony, are treasured in the Franciscan convent of Wotiz, near Prague, in Bohemia.

Ward, Colgan, Lombard, MacCaughwell, Edmund O'Reilly, and the Stanihursts, men whose names will ever live among the names of Ireland's most gifted and patriotic sons, are all in far foreign graves. The winds of Ireland never chant their mournful dirge around their tombs, the maids of Erin scatter no flowers over their graves, the faithful peasants never pray above their ashes. They fell where they had bravely fought with voice and pen for the land of their love. They died far away from the Isle of their birth, with the great shadow of Ireland's suffering upon their breaking hearts. They sank to rest in the calm of silent convents, and they tranquilly rest either in the dim shades of old cathedrals, or in the peaceful aisles of chapels whose silence is never broken except by the prayer of some pious monk or Nun. Ah, it is a sad thing to die in exile. It is a sad thing to sleep in the earth far, far away from one's native land. But oh, it is a thousand times better for our noble students to rest in holy ground, to lie beneath holy altars and sacred pulpits, to rest in chapels where the Office is daily chanted, to rest in shrines where pilgrims ever pray, than to have their burned ashes scattered to the four winds of heaven by the sacrilegious and bloody hands of the minions of Henry or Elizabeth, or of the vile troopers of Cromwell. Though our Irish monks would naturally wish to repose in death at holy Lismore, at Diseart Kellach, or in Arran of the Saints; though our Irish friars, when the shadows and dews of dissolution were upon them, would long for the holy earth of Multifernan or of Roserilly, where Maurice O'Fihiley, *Flos Mundi*, reposes; still, we may easily imagine that we hear them say in the light and strength of their grand and glorious Faith :

> Care not for that, and lay us where we fall,
> Everywhere heard will be the judgment call;
> But at God's altar, oh, remember us.

SHADOWS.

All the earth is full of shadows,—
Shadows 'neath the palace wall,
Shadows from the cottage fall,
Shadows by the stately tower,
Shadows by the lowly flower,
Shadows on the hill and plain,
Shadows on the lake and main,
Shadows in the lonely glen,
Shadows in the hearts of men,
Shadows on the maiden's brow,
Shadows come we know not how,—
But the earth is full of shadows.

MISCELLANEOUS ARTICLES.

PROSE AND VERSE.

By Rev. William P. Treacy.

A PROTESTANT CRITIC IN CATHOLIC COUNTRIES.

TOWARDS the end of June, 1880, I stood beside the Scheldt, at Antwerp, in Belgium. I was waiting for a ferry-boat to take me across the river, on the other side of which I was to enter a train on its way to Ghent. I had just visited the famous picture galleries, churches, and oratories of the quaint old Flemish city. My mind was all aglow with enthusiasm; my heart still beat with deep and sweet religious emotion. The paintings I had seen, and the altars before which I had lately knelt, and the mellow light that flowed in upon me through the oratories, had become a part of my very being, and I felt that they were destined to remain as a manna to my soul forever. I stood gazing out over the sluggish waters; but marble altars, and gemmed crosses, and whispering piety, and visions of beauty still warmed my imagination. I could not part with the glorious images revealed to me by the brush of the old masters of the Antwerp school of painting. I stood on the crowded wharf as one in a happy dream.

But my reverie was rudely disturbed by my Belgian friend, who whispered to me in French—"There is a Protestant minister." Indeed, the sight of a parson in Belgium was an event important enough to deserve attention. I had not seen even one during all the time I had passed in that country. The gentleman now standing near me was typical. He was large and ruddy, wore a high hat and high collar, a white neck-tie, and a glossy black *surtout*.

I soon bade an affectionate farewell to my Flemish friend, entered the ferry-boat, and after a few minutes found myself seated in a train that slowly wound its way for Ghent. The apartments in Belgian trains run crosswise and form oblong rooms. I had a seat by a window at one side of the train, and I very quickly perceived that the Protestant clergyman had taken his seat by a window on the opposite side of "the box." Our fellow passengers were some *Paysans* and *Paysannes;* the former class wearing caps and blue smock-frocks, and the latter attired in variegated and picturesque costumes. A dead silence reigned for some time. I began once more to revel in the luxury of thought. All at once I was startled by the parson's deep and solemn tones. I did not catch the meaning of his words, but the sound of his voice was awe-inspiring. What could he have said? I fancied that he had warned us of some impending evil. The sepulchral echoes of his tones rang in my ears.

"Do you talk English, madam?" This time I fully understood him. He was addressing himself to a *paysanne* who sat near him. I was somewhat amused by his measured tones, and I waited with no little curiosity to hear the response of the person he had addressed so solemnly. She looked very much puzzled. But he did not seem alarmed. "Do you talk English, madam?" he again gravely asked.

"*Non*," was the woman's laconic response. The parson's face grew dark with disappointment. He muttered something to himself about Belgian ignorance, and looked out on the richly cultivated fields along the line. I, too, looked out of my window and noted with pride the prosperous condition of the most Catholic country on the old continent. Not a foot of ground was left untilled by the thrifty Flemings. No broad hedge-rows devoured the land. A cord, or imaginary line, divided the fields and farms. We rolled on through neat and comfortable-looking villages that rose up in the midst of flourishing vegetable gardens. A panorama of crosses, and statuettes, and "banners of the Sacred Heart" passed before me. I saw in the distance the glittering spires of magnificent churches and cathedrals — the proud monuments of Catholic devotion. Here and there in the corners of the fields I noticed a piece of blessed palm which the pious peasants had religiously planted there the preceding Easter. "Do you talk English, sir?" The sombre accents of the parson were heard once more.

"*Non*," was the answer of one of the passengers.

As I did not care to enter into conversation just then, I kept looking out of the window. After a little time I happened to turn a glance towards the troubled parson. His eyes met mine. I felt that I was caught.

"Do you talk English, sir?" he said to me as if in despair. I replied in the affirmative. The light of joy passed over his countenance. He piously raised his eyes and hands, and devoutly thanked Heaven that he had at length found one who knew a little English. He arose from his seat and approached me with great cordiality. We shook hands warmly, and he seemed to regard me as an old and valued friend.

"I see at once, sir," said he, as he sat down beside me, "that you are returning from one of the German Universities. I am a good judge of things, and very rarely make a mistake. You have been studying law or medicine. I should say rather medicine. You need not tell me your profession. I saw it at a glance. My name is Oswald Dobson—the Rev. Oswald Dobson.* I have been sent to the Continent by the Bible Society of London to take notes on the corruptions and abominations of the Roman Church in these benighted countries. In my travels through France, Belgium, Spain, Austria and Italy, I have collected a vast amount of useful information concerning the evils of Popery. On my return to London I intend to give a course of lectures in which I shall expose the secrets of Continental Papists. I assure you, sir, that I shall have the honor of dealing Romanism a mortal blow.

"I feel sir," I ventured to say, "that it would be difficult for a thorough, observant linguist to pass through so many countries without acquiring a vast store of information. But, if I am not mistaken, your knowledge of tongues is limited to the English. How, then, did you

---

* This article is substantially true. For obvious reasons, I have not called the Protestant tourist by his real name.

manage to gather up such a fund of damaging testimony against Catholics? You will pardon my curiosity, as I cannot boast of much experience in such matters."

"My dear sir, I see you have been long confined to the laboratory and dissecting-room. Why, to study the corruptions of the Romans, it is not necessary to learn their language. Actions, sir, speak to the eyes. Frenchmen, Spaniards and Italians act. I kept my eyes open; yes, sir, wide open, and I noted all their crimes and idolatry."

"May I ask what crimes you noticed?"

"What crimes have I not noticed in these priest-ridden countries? Why, sir, would you believe it? I saw crosses and images of the Virgin in almost every place imaginable. I saw them stuck up in the trees in the most solitary regions, as well as high above the market-places in the populous cities. And I saw men, women and children kneeling down and adoring them as idols. It is truly horrible."

"My dear sir, if what you say be true, I am indeed shocked. But who told you that they were really adoring their crosses or statues as gods."

"Who told me? Why, no one told me. No one had need to tell me. I saw them with my own eyes."

"It seems to me that you ought to have asked them whether they gave divine worship to stocks and stones or not."

"But those I speak of were Italians, Frenchmen and Spaniards. They could not speak a word of English, and I do not know a word of their barbarous languages."

"Then, sir, you may be forming a rash judgment on Catholics. I have seen them in many countries, and I must say, in justice to them, that I never found even one of them guilty of idolatry. Their priests tell me that even crosses are not to be adored in the strict sense of the word, but only venerated as the symbols of salvation, as the wood on which the Saviour died."

"Their priests told you so! My dear young friend, beware of Popish priests. They are as crafty as serpents and as dangerous. All the evils of our times are fomented by the Jesuits. I may say that all the troubles of society for the past thousand years have been caused by the treacherous sons of Loyola."

"Is it not too much, sir, to accuse the Jesuits of all the crimes of the past thousand years?"

"No, sir; I solemnly aver that even for the past fifteen hundred years they have been at the bottom of every revolution and every social disorder. It is a fact that cannot be denied even by their best friends and warmest advocates."

"You forget, sir, that the Jesuits are not much above three centuries old. You will forgive me for calling your attention to an historical fact."

"My dear young friend," said the parson, and he looked mysteriously at all the passengers, " the *Jesuits have always existed either visibly or invisibly.* They are to be found everywhere. Perhaps even in this car we are under their watchful eyes. Why, sir, you may shake hands with one and not know it. You may speak for hours with one and not recognize in him a member of that dread Society. The Jesuits are truly diabolical, and endowed with almost more than human power."

"Have you ever seen one of those fearful men?" I carelessly asked.

"Not I, sir; I would not look at one. I know the history of their bloody plots too well. I am not wanting in courage, but I think I would tremble with fear if I was persuaded that there was one on this train. These are the men that teach the benighted people all kinds of evil-doing. These are the men that tell the people to pay undue honor to the bones of saints, and even to their old clothes."

I was beginning to feel tired of this conversation. I asked myself what must the Bible Society of London be if this is one of its accredited agents. I thought of the absurdity of sending a man to study the state of Catholicity on the European Continent who knows no language but the English. I no longer wondered at the ignorance of English Protestants in regard to the true doctrine and practice of Catholics, when all their information was gathered from men as blind and illiterate as the Rev. Oswald Dobson.

"Have you visited Waterloo?" I asked, as I was anxious to change the former topic of conversation.

"Oh, I could not leave Belgium without doing that. No true Englishman could come over here without visiting that glorious battlefield where British arms won such glory. I uncovered my head as I trod that ground that had drunk so much of our country's best blood. I gathered up some of the clay as a memento to be kept by me forever. I had even the good fortune to be able to purchase a nail that belonged to the shoe of the identical horse which Wellington himself rode."

I smiled as he spoke of purchasing a nail at Waterloo. I had visited the famous battle-ground, and had heard from most reliable authority that a forge was kept constantly going making counterfeit "Wellington nails" for English visitors.

"My dear sir," I said gravely, "what possessed you to take up some of that clay of Waterloo? What honor can you pay to a nail? If these Belgian Catholics see you honoring such things, may they not accuse you of idolatry?"

"They accuse me of idolatry! Why, how can they with reason accuse me of idolatry?"

"With the same reason that you accuse them of it. You cannot deny that you pay honor to nails, horseshoe nails, and even to the clay they trample on daily. On entering the plain of Waterloo you were incautious enough to take off your hat. Those who saw you must have cried out, 'Oh, see that English idolater.'"

"My dear sir, I know you are only jesting. I never said that I adored either the clay of Waterloo or the nail from Wellington's horse."

"Did the Catholics ever tell you that they adored their pictures or statues, or that they paid Divine worship to the cross?"

"No, sir, they never did. It was not necessary. I

saw them do it with my own eyes."

"Excuse me, my dear sir, but you do not seem to me to be altogether consistent."

"My young friend, I tremble for your condition. I am afraid that the Jesuits have fascinated you. I see in your conversation the germ of error. I wish that I could be with you some time, and I would pour into your soul a burning fire. I would tell you much of the artifices of Romish priests. I would put you out of danger. Beware, young man, beware of the deadly influence of the Jesuits."

"I promise you, sir, that I will do all I can to be on my guard against all who may lead me astray. I love justice, truth, and right, and hope never to abandon them. I would take the liberty of advising others to do the same. Before you speak of the Catholics to the London Bible Society, I would suggest that you would ask some Catholics whether they adore as idols pictures, crosses, and images."

"I may not meet a Catholic who speaks English before I begin my course of lectures."

"Then I will tell you, sir, on the part of the Catholics spread throughout the whole world—*Catholics do not adore pictures, or crosses, or any mere creature.* They pay divine homage to God alone. If you dare tell an audience in London that Catholics worship as God any graven thing, you will be guilty of a shameful crime, of the blackest kind of slander."

"Why this strong and exciting language, my dear young friend?"

"My parents are Catholics."

"And you are?"

"I am a Catholic, thank God, and, more over, I am one of those horrible Catholic priests."

"Oh! oh!" exclaimed the parson, as if in agony.

By this time our train arrived at Ghent. I invited my Protestant friend to call and see me at the Jesuit College, Rue Barbe. It is needless to say that he did not accept my invitation.

TO A SINGING BIRD BY THE SEA.

O! sing, O! sing, thou sweet-voiced bird,
   Sing for the restless sea ;
Sing for the waves that never sleep,
Sing for the sad heart of the deep,
   O! sing for my bark and me.

O! sing, O! sing, thou joyful bird,
   Sing for the troubled sea ;
Sing the bright isles of clustering shells,
Sing for green rocks and sea-mossed cells,
   O! sing for my bark and me.

O! sing, O! sing, thou happy bird,
   Sing for the moaning sea ;
Sing for the ships that leave our strand,
Sing for the fleets that guard our land,
   O! sing for my bark and me.

O! sing, O! sing, thou gladsome bird,
   Sing for the stormy sea ;
Sing for the maids that vigils keep
With throbbing hearts beside the deep,
   O! sing for my bark and me.

O! sing, O! sing, thou winsome bird,
   Sing for the sad-souled sea ;
Sing for the rocks on ocean's breast,
Sing for the dead in graves unblest,
   O! sing for my bark and me.

THE FISHERMEN'S SONG.

Our boats are filled with their silver freight,
   Our work on the deep is done;
The shadows fall, for the hour is late,
   We'll steer towards the setting sun;
We'll sail to our homes far in the west,
   We'll follow the golden light;
As the sea-birds seek, at eve, their nest,
   So we'll sail for home to-night.
        Row, fishers, row,
           Our work on the deep is done;
        Row, fishers, row,
           We'll sail for the setting sun.

The sea we love when its face is bright,
   It is the fishermen's mine;
We plough its vales and hills of light,
   While day-glories above us shine;
But now that the shadows around us creep,
   We'll steer to our western home,
We'll fly from the darkness and the deep,
   We'll fly from the blinding foam.
        Row, fishers, row,
           Our task on the deep is done:
        Row, fishers, row,
           We'll sail for the sinking sun.

All day we toiled in the heaving sea,
  Our prows to the west we turn ;
To-night we'll rest from all dangers free,
  See lights in each cottage burn ;
God bless our wives and our daughters brave,
  For our boats they've prayed all day,
And now we come from the stormy wave
  Their love and faith to repay.
     Row, fishers, row,
       Our toil on the sea is done ;
     Row, fishers, row,
       Row swift for the setting sun.

IRISH MONKS IN CORNWALL.

St. Kieran; St. Albeus; St. Benignus; St. Columba.

St. Kieran, by some writers called Piran, was born in the little Island of Cape Clear. His early years were passed amid the wild scenery of the northern coast of Ireland. As the son of Lugneus, a noble of Ossory, and Liadain a lady from Carberry, in the south of Munster, he had at his command every worldly pleasure and advantage that could please or seduce the youthful mind. But Kieran, though a pagan, was not content with the things of this earth; his noble soul yearned after something higher, holier, more divine. He longed for the possession of the true light that "enlighteneth every man that cometh into this world." God never rejects the soul that seeks Him constantly, lovingly, humbly. And so, we are told, that Kieran was converted to Christianity by the pious conversation of a Christian laic. Soon after, having heard that the Christian religion was most truly taught and faithfully practised at Rome, he left Ireland and travelled thither. "And there he remained," says Archbishop Usher, "twenty years, reading divine Scriptures, many books of which he gathered together, and learning ecclesiastical rules with all diligence." The same author asserts that Kieran was consecrated bishop in the Holy City.

We know from Irish writers that Piran was for some time the disciple of St. Finian, Bishop of Clonard. Of this great man the moderate Alban Butler thus writes: —"Among the primitive teachers of the Irish Church the name of St. Finian is one of the most famous next to that of St. Patrick. He was a native of Leinster, was instructed in the elements of Christian virtue by the disciples of St. Patrick, and out of an ardent desire of making greater progress passed over into Wales, where he conversed with St. David, St. Gildas, and St. Cathmael, three eminent British saints. After having remained thirty years in Britain, about the year 520 he returned into Ireland, excellently qualified by sanctity and sacred learning to restore the spirit of religion, which had begun to decay among his countrymen. Like a loud trumpet sounding from heaven, he roused the sloth and insensibility of the lukewarm, and softened the hearts that were most hardened, and had been long immersed in worldly business and pleasure. To propagate the work of God St. Finian established several monasteries and schools; the chief of which was Clonard in Meath, which was the saint's principal residence. Out of his shool came several of the principal saints and doctors of Ireland, as Kieran the Younger, Columbkille, Columba, the son of Crinthain, the two Brendans, Laserian, Canicus or Kenny, Ruadan and others.

"St. Finian was chosen and consecrated bishop of Clonard. The great monastery which he erected at Clonard was a famous seminary of sacred learning. St. Finian, in the love of his flock, and his zeal for their salvation, equalled the Basils and the Chrysostoms, was infirm with the infirm, and wept with those that wept. He healed the souls, and often the bodies of those that applied to him. His food was bread and herbs, his drink water, and his bed the ground, with a stone for his pillow." We may easily imagine, under such a master, and among so many saintly companions, what progress in virtue the fervent Kieran made. Of him it could be truly said that "he ran in the way of the commandments." Like a star among stars he shone. "Having spent many years under St. Finian, of Clonard," writes Walsh in his Ecclesiastical History, "he retired to a lonely spot, since called Saigir, in the territory of Ely O'Carrol, and there erected a monastery. In a few years Saigir became a city of distinction, on account of the number of students that resorted to this establishment. The people of Ossory, being attached to the ancient rites of their ancestors, were not easily withdrawn from the errors of their superstition. However, St. Kieran preached among them with great success."

Alban Butler, in a note to his life of St. Kieran, Abbot, says: "About a mile's distance from the parish church of Kilcrogan, near the river Blackwater in the county of Kerry, is a curious hermitage or cell, hewn out of the solid rock, situated on the top of a hill; this cell is named St. Croghan's, who is the patron saint of the parish. The intelligent among the antiquaries say, that in this place the celebrated St. Kieran Saigir.... composed his rule for monks; although others say it was in the adjacent grotto. Be this as it may, the stalactical exudations of the cell are held in great esteem by the country people, who carefully preserve them, as imagining them to have many virtues from the supposed sanctity of the place they grow in." "His first residence" the Protestant author of Perranzabulo says, "was in the heart of Ireland, in a place encompassed with woods and morasses, close to a lake called Fuaran; here he built himself a cell for his habitation, to which his sanctity attracted such multitudes that a town was at last built there, called Saigir now from the name of saint, commonly called Sierkeran. Here, he showed all concord, and subjection, and discipleship to St. Patrick, present or absent, and was very successful in converting that people." Among others he had the happiness of converting his mother, Liadain. The author of St. Piran's life in Capgrave, affirms that "by the example of St. Patrick, St. Piran and many others inflamed with the Divine love forsook all worldly things and lead an eremitical life." In an ancient life of our saint we read, that on every Christmas night he was accustomed to repair to the nunnery of St. Cocchea, "that there he might offer up the Body of Christ." St. Kieran having zealously labored among the martial Ossorians, and having sanctified himself by fasts and prayers in his cell, resolved to leave Ireland and pass over into Brittany. The author of his life in Capgrave says that "St. Piran, calling together his disciples and the rest of the people, thus spoke to them : 'My Brethren and beloved children, it is the Divine Will that I should forsake Ireland and go into Cornwall, in Brittany.'" Before Piran's time many distinguished Irish saints had been in Brittany. "The example of St. Patrick and St. Benignus," writes the pious author of the Church-History of Brittany, "was imitated by many other Irish saints, which to enjoy a perfect vacancy from wordly affairs retired into Brittany to consecrate themselves to God in a life of austerity and contemplation. And in Brittany the Province whither they most frequently partook themselves, was Cornwall: In so much as Camden had just ground to say.—*That the people of Cornwall have always borne such a veneration for the Irish saints, which retired thither, that almost all the towns in that Province have been consecrated to their memory.* There is St. Burian, dedicated to an Irish religious woman of that name; to the church whereof King Ethelstan in the year nine hundred and thirty-six gave the privilege of a sanctuary. There is the town of St. Ives, so called from St. Iia a woman of singular sanctity, who came thither from Ireland. There is St. Columb, named not from St. Columbanus, as some erroneously imagine, but from an Irish St. Columba. There is St. Mewan, St. Erben, St. Eval, St. Wenn, St. Endor, and many other places, all which took their names from Irish saints." "The first Cornish Apostle, of any note," writes the Rev. Collins Trelawny, "was Corantinus, (now called Curry), born in Brittany, who first preached to his own countrymen, and then to the Irish, till being violently expelled from that island, he passed over into Cornwall, and settled at last at the foot of a mountain, called Menehont, was consecrated bishop by St. Martin of Tours, and had the satisfaction of converting almost the whole of Cornwall before his death. Scarcely was Corantinus gathered to his fathers, when a more celebrated man than himself landed in Cornwall, and from his extraordinary sanctity, acquired the highest reputation amongst the people.

"This illustrious man was Piranus, ... In confirmation of his doctrine, and in testimony of his sanctity, his chroniclers assert that God was pleased to work great miracles at his hands; and so great was his renown, that his cell was daily thronged with visitors from all parts of Ireland, whose numbers and officiousness became at last so intolerable to the saint, that giving out that he had received a divine call, and was desirous of preparing himself for his latter end by a more perfect retirement from all worldly distractions, he passed over into Cornwall, taking with him his mother, and Breaca, Sininus, Germochus, Iia, and many others, who landing at St. Ives, dispersed themselves over the country, and acquired great veneration among the people. Piranus went to the east, and settled himself in a district near the sea, that is now known by the name of Perranzabuloe, or 'St. Piran in the Sand.'"

"Here the holy man fixed his abode close to a spring of water, that still bears his name, but which was anciently called Fenton Berran. While 'from this well he drew his beverage' he daily refreshed the multitudes who thronged around him with the living waters of eternal life,—instructed the ignorant, confirmed the weak and earnestly exhorted them to turn from their dumb idols and worship their spiritual God in spirit and in truth. But it was not only *that* 'knowledge which maketh wise unto salvation' that Piranus imparted to them from the pure word of God;—from the abundant stores of a highly cultivated mind he instructed them in many of those elements of knowledge that are adapted to the purposes of common life—more especially communicating to them the art and mystery of working and reducing from their oxides the metals which abound in that neighborhood. So that, with good reason, the Cornish miners have always regarded with peculiar veneration the name of Piranus, as their tutelary saint and benefactor. Even at this day his memory is cherished throughout Cornwall, where, on the 5th of March, the 'tinners keep his feast, and hold a fair on the same day near his Church,' 'being allowed money to make merry withal, in honor of St. Piranus, their benefactor.'"

The true apostle never thinks of his ease and comfort. He is carried away by the fire of zeal. He fears neither trials, nor persecutions, nor labors, nor sacrifices. The perils of the ocean cannot daunt him, the burning sands of the desert cannot frighten him. With bleeding feet he travels in search of wandering souls. St. Piran was a true apostle. After having left behind him his country, his friends, his home, he went into the wildest part of Cornwall to sanctify his soul, and to wage war upon the idols of the druids. The spot chosen by him is thus beautifully described by Trelawny:—"The stranger, who, in that joyous season, when all nature is bursting into life, traverses the lovely scenes of southern Devon, and with thoughts still glowing with the recollection of her soft and verdant valleys, her deeply-embowered lanes, her meadows enamelled with a thousand flowers, crosses the dark waters of the Tamar, and from its wooded and high-towering banks, bears with him the further remembrance of her more romantic and sterner beauties—Oh, let him say, in the warmth of his recollections, as he approaches the north-western coast of Cornwall, how wild and cheerless is that long bleak, barren belt of sand that gird's the shore of Perran's Bay. The intervening moors, through which he has reached that desolate district, are of themselves, uninviting to any of nature's more attractive scenery—and yet are they not altogether destitute of interest—the purple heather, and the gorse's saffron blossoms, and the busy hum of bees, as they collect their golden treasure from the fragrant thyme, give life and animation to the scene,—and many a relic of olden times, which still tells of Cornish prowess, or Cornish superstition, employs the thoughts, and serves to invest with a peculiar interest those uncultivated moorlands which on every side terminate the prospect and almost without the aid of poetic fiction :—

———'immeasurably spread,
Seem lengthening as you go.'

"Yet these moors, wild and interminable as they appear, stand out in striking relief to the sea-girt tract that now bounds the way. What is here to gladden the heart of the passing stranger? Not a tuft of verdure refreshes his wearied sight—not a tree lifts up its branches to offer him friendly shade—even the gorse and the heather, those children of the desert, refuse any longer to bear him company; he pursues his solitary way—waste after waste of undulating sand meets him at every step—and the hollow moan of the Atlantic waves, as they lash the distant Cligga, or suddenly retire from the adjacent shore, falls in sounds responsive to the wildness of the place. All nature wears a garment of sadness. The very birds of heaven avoid the spot, and the sea-mews, soaring on high, scream pitiously over their region of desolation, and with hasty wings betake themselves to the rocks and the waves, as less wild and less unfriendly. The stranger passes on —he quickens his steps—and with anxious gaze looks forward to the termination of this tedious way. But a tract, if possible still more forbidding, rises before him with increasing barrenness. A succession of sand hills, varying in their elevation, enclose him on every side, and by intercepting his view of the sea in some parts, casting their dark shadows on it in others, stamp on every quarter the character of more than ordinary lonlines and melancholy. Yet it is a spot full of the deepest interest—a solitude of the most heart-stirring recollections. Oh, stranger, whoever thou art, 'put off they shoes from thy feet—thou treadest on holy ground,'— thou standest over a sacred memorial of bygone days." Yes, stranger, thou standest on holy ground, for here hundreds of years ago St. Piran and his monks wept, and prayed, and fasted, and offered up the holiest of all sacrifices—the sacrifice of the Mass. History, "and popular tradition, confirmed by antiquarian research, has long pointed to Perranzabuloe, as the site and sepulchre of an ancient British Church, founded at a very remote period, flourishing for a succession of ages in the midst of a very fertile district, and dispensing to a rude but religious people the blessings of Christianity, in its simplest form of primitive purity. At that distant day, the northern boundary of the extensive Hundred of Pydar yielded to none other in Cornwall, either in the fertility of its soil, or the abundance of its produce. Alas, how has 'the fruitful place become a wilderness' and 'the pleasant portion a desolation.'" The burning zeal, the fervent charity, the humility, the meekness, and the life of perpetual sacrifice led by the holy monk Piran, helped to convert thousands of the druids, and endeared him to all. Nothing is so lovely or so lovable as virtue. No wonder that those adorned with it are so esteemed, and so venerated, even by the wicked themselves. After his death the Cornish people still cherished the pious memory of Piran, "and immediately erected, with their own hands, a church inscribed with his name, and dedicated to the service of that pure religion which he so faithfully taught...... There 'the incense' of prayer, and 'the pure offering' of praise, were daily lifted to that Name which already was great among the heathen ; and there the flame which Piran had enkindled in the hearts of the Cornishmen, burnt brightly and steadily for many successive generations.

"The church of St. Piran, thus erected .... became the resort of Christian worshippers from all parts of the world, and took a conspicuous lead in diffusing the light of pure religion, throughout the country. The Britons had already become as highly distinguished for the purity and simplicity of their faith as they had been before for their blind superstition and barbarous idolatry. 'How often in Britain,' says Chrysostom, who lived in the fourth century, 'did men eat the flesh of their own kind. Now they refresh their souls with fastings.' And St. Jerome, writing about the same time, with a more direct reference to Cornwall, 'the Britons who live apart from our world, if they go on a pilgrimage, will leave the *western parts*, and seek Jerusalem, known to them by fame only and by the Scriptures.'"

The church erected to the memory of St. Piran, at Perranzabuloe, like all the churches of that early period, was built in the simplest style. It was, however, in some respects superior to many of them; in this, at least, that in place of being formed of wattles, it was of solid stone. For centuries it was hidden away from human sight by the mountains of sand which were heaped over it by the wild winds that swept through Cornwall. It did not become plainly visible till as late as the year 1835.

Trelawny, speaking of the benefits St. Piran conferred upon the inhabitants, says: "A benefactor he was in truth to the souls and bodies of thousands whose ignorance he enlightened, whose faith he strengthened, and among whom he left a pure, simple, unadulterated form of Christian worship." Again he says justly that the venerable monk could, "in the decline of years, triumphantly point to the success of his missionary labours."

The author of St. Piran's life, in Capgrave, says that "he was one of the first twelve bishops that St. Patrick consecrated." Some authors tell us that he preached in Ireland before the arrival of its great apostle. We are assured by others that on his way from Rome he met St. Patrick, and that great was the joy of both. Camden calls Piran "a holy man, who came from Ireland."

Writers tell us that St. Piran, knowing that his end was drawing near, called around him his disciples, and having spoken beautifully to them of the things that are of God, he ordered his grave to be dug, and then "he went down into it on the third of the nones of May, and there rendered up his soul to God, which with great glory was received into heaven."

Even before the time that St. Kieran preached in Cornwall, St. Albeus and St. Benignus, with tongues of fire, called upon the people of Britany to tear down their idols, to turn away from the worship of the sun, to abandon their false belief in cataracts and storms, and rushing rivers, and to erect altars to the true God. St. Albeus was converted by some Britons, and in order to show his gratitude towards them used his great eloquence in preaching for some time, to their pagan countrymen. It is stated that he was in Rome before St. Patrick had set foot on the Irish shore. "After his return home," writes Butler, "he became the disciple and fellow-laborer of that great apostle of his country, and being ordained by him first Archbishop of Munster, fixed his seat at Emely which has been long since changed to Cashel. With such a commanding authority did this apostolic man deliver the dictates of eternal wisdom, to the people of Ireland; such was the force with which, both by words and example, he set forth the sanctity of the divine law, and so evident were the miracles with which he confirmed the heavenly truths which he preached, that the sacred doctrine easily made its way to the hearts of his hearers, and he not only brought over an incredible multitude to the faith of Christ, but infused into many the perfect spirit of the gospel, possessing a wonderful art of making them not only Christians but saints. King Engus having bestowed on him the isle of Arran, he founded in it a great monastery, which was so famous for the sanctity of its inhabitants, that from them the island was long called Arran of Saints. The rule which St. Albeus drew up for them is still extant in old Irish, as Usher testifies. Though zeal for the divine honor, and charity for the souls of others, fixed him in the world, he was always careful, by habitual recollection, and frequent retreats to nourish in his own soul the pure love of heavenly things, and to live always in a very familiar and intimate acquaintance with himself, and in the daily habitual practice of the most perfect interior virtues. In his old age it was his earnest desire to commit to others the care of his beloved flock, that he might be allowed to prepare himself in the exercises of holy solitude for his great change. For this purpose he begged that he might be suffered to retire to Thule, the remotest country toward the northern pole that was known to the ancients which seems to have been Shetland, or, according to some, Iceland, or some part of Greenland; but the king guarded the ports to prevent his flight, and the Saint died amidst the labors of his charge, in 525, as the Ulster and Innisfallen annals testify."

Though St. Albeus (Ailbe) was retained in Ireland by the pious king Engus, still twenty-two of his monks were allowed to continue their journey, in order to enlighten the unhappy children of the North. Oh, who can tell the greatness, or the length and depth of the trials and sufferings of that heroic band of missionaries while, far from their own mild climate, and the peaceful shades of their monastery, they labored in cold and hunger, among a cruel and barbarous people.

"St. Ailbe," writes Father Walsh, "lived under the pious king Engus, and having erected his cathedral on a convenient site, which that prince had presented, he soon after laid the foundation of a monastery and college, in which human and heavenly sciences were taught gratuitously, and to which students from all parts of Europe resorted. Among the number of eminent persons who received their education under Ailbe, are reckoned Colman of Dromore, and Nessan of Mungret. St. Ailbe justly revered for his piety and sanctity, was looked upon as another St. Patrick, and a second patron of Munster. He is deservedly ranked among the fathers of the Irish Church."

"During the incumbency of St. Ailbe," continues the

learned author just quoted, "a synod was held at Cashel, attended also by the king and chiefs of the Desii. St. Declan, of Ardmore, was present. Many valuable decrees regarding morals and ecclesiastical discipline were enacted."

The laborious Cressy, the Benedictine monk, after having spoken of Bachianus, who, though a Briton, was a disciple of St. Patrick, thus writes: "Another holy bishop and disciple of St. Patrick challenges once more a commemoration in this History (The Church-History of Brittany), to wit St. Albeus, in whose life extant in Bishop Usher we read, that when he heard that St. Patrick had converted to Our Lord, Engus king of Munster, and was with him in the royal city of Cashel, he came to salute them. Now the king and St. Patrick much rejoyced at the arrival of St. Albeus, whose joy to see them also was great. There the holy man reverently entertained his master, St. Patrick, for he was very humble. After this king Engus and St. Patrick ordained that the Archiepiscopall See of all Munster should for ever be placed in the Citty and chair of St. Albeus."

It is very probable that St. Albeus was baptized by the illustrious British saint, Kebius, who is said to have spent some time under St. Hilary. The following passage from the pen of the great Protestant Usher may be read with interest—it refers to the baptism of Ailbe: "Lachanus gave the Holy Child to certain Britains, who brought him upp with great care, giving him the name of Albeus, because he was found alive under a rock, and the Grace of God was with him. After these things there came thither a certain Brittish Priest, sent by the See Apostolick into Ireland, many years before St. Patrick, to sow the Faith of Christ there. But the Irishmen being pagans, would not receive him, nor believe his Doctrine, except a few. He came then to the inhabitants of Munster, where he found the Holy child Albeus praying in the open air with his eyes raised up to heaven, that the true Faith might be revealed to him and saying, My desire is to know the Creator of all things, and to believe in him who made heaven and earth and all creatures in them; For I know that the elements were not made without a skillfull Workman, neither could any man produce these things. When the holy child had thus prayed, the said Priest who overheard him, saluted him and according to his heart's desire instructed him in all things: which having done he baptised him, continuing the same name of Albeus to him."

Bishop Usher also tells us that St. Albeus, whi'e at Rome, "was instructed in the knowledge of the Holy Scriptures by St. Hilary," the famous Bishop of Poitiers.

The name of St. David, bishop of Menevia, is one of the most illustrious, is one of the most venerated, in the annals of Britany. Thirty years before his birth St. Patrick is said to have foretold David's coming, and his greatness in learning and sanctity. An Angel revealed to Ireland's Apostle the future glory of the famous British saint. In allusion to St. Patrick's prophesy we read in the *Collect* of the ancient church of Sarum the following words, which are repeated yearly on St. David's Feast: "O, God, who by an Angell didst foretell the Nativity of thy Blessed Confessor, Saint David, thirty years before he was born; Grant unto us, we beseech thee, that celebrating his memory, we may by his intercession attain to joyes everlasting."

Though Giraldus Cambrensis assures us that St. David was baptized by an Irish Bishop called Releveus still the author of "The Church-History Of Brittainy Under Brittish Kings," says that this undoubtedly is a mistake, and that the honor of having baptized David belongs to St. Albeus, Bishop of Munster.

St. Benignus, who also labored in Britany, was very much like the gentle St. Francis of Sales. He had a winning grace about him that gained the hearts of all who came in contact with him. There was nothing repulsive in his austerity, nothing disagreeable in his fervent piety. He moved like an angel among men and showed in his whole conduct how sweet and pleasant are the ways of sanctity, how beautiful and charming are those souls that are adorned with interior grace. Those who beheld him were forced to acknowledge that the yoke of the Lord was light and sweet. About the year 465 he succeeded St. Patrick in the See of Armagh. He was long the constant companion and the favorite disciple of that saint. "Benignus," writes Father Walsh, "was the son of Sesgnen, a chieftain of Meath. On his conversion and baptism he received from his kind preceptor the name Benignus, as it was expressive of his mild disposition and good qualities. Instructed by our apostle in learning and religion, he became eminent in piety and virtue, and though not yet a priest he was entrusted with the care of remote places, and so great were his services to religion that he was considered a second apostle. Like his master he foresaw the approach of his end. Having sent for Jarlath, he received the body of the Lord. His soul departed to eternal rest on the 9th November, A. D, 468."

The Church of Drumlias, in the barony of Drumahare, and bordering on Lake Gille is said to have been founded by St. Patrick, who placed Benignus over it. It is recorded that a pagan fortress was bestowed on St. Patrick and Benignus, by Lughaid, lord of the country near Tuam, Co. Galway. At this place a church was erected called Killbannon. In John Colgan's "Acts of the Irish Saints," we read of a church called Temple Benain, or the temple of St. Benignus.

"As for St. Patrick's Successor," writes Cressy, "he also after seven years spent in care of his province, thirsting after solitude, and willing to see again his most beloved Master, came to Glastonbury, desirous to receive from him a most perfect Rule of Monastical Profession. This he did, saith Malmsburiensis, by the admonition of an Angel. And being come thither he demanded of St. Patrick what place he should make choice of to live in Union with God alone, divided from human society. The Answer given him by St. Patrick, who encouraged him to persist in his present purpose, is thus recorded by Adam of Domerham: Benignus, saith he, discovered to St. Patrick the motives of his journey; who exhorted him to pursue happily his well begun purpose, saying, Goe, my beloved brother, taking only your staff with you. And when you shall be arrived at the place appointed by God for your repose, wheresoever having fix'd your staff in the ground, you shall see it flourish and grow green, there know that you must make your abode. Thus both of them being comforted in our Lord with mutuall discourses, Saint Benignus being accompanied only by a youth nam'd Pencius, begun his journey through woody and marish places. But as soon as he was arriv'd in an Island where he saw a solitary place, which he judg'd fit for his habitation, he presently fixed his staff in the ground, which without delay wonderfully grew green, and brought forth fresh leaves. There, therefore, Saint Benignus resolv'd to abide to his death in the service of God alone. And to this day the same Tree, the witness and sign of his Sanctity, remains flourishing with green boughs, near the Oratory of the blessed man."

"The same Authour (Adam of Domerham) further proceeds to declare how by another miracle God testified that the Holy man's watchings, fastings, and prayers with other austerityes were acceptable to him. Although, saith he, that solitary place separated from worldly conversation was very opportune and proper for attending to God and Divine things: Yet one incommodity it had, that there was no water near: So that young Pincius was compelled every day to fetch water almost three miles off, whence it came to passe that partly througe weariness, but principally through suggestion of malignant Spirits he grew disheartened, which the Holy man perceiving oftimes endeavoured to comfort and encourage him. At last taking compassion of his labours, he prostrating himself on the ground, humbly and heartily besought our Lord to open for his servant a spring of water, which might sufficiently supply his necessities. After which admonish'd by an Angelicall vision he gave his staff to young Pincius, commanding him to a certain place full of reeds, and there striking the ground with his staff, he should without doubt find water, so earnestly desired by them. The child obeyd, went to the place, and in the name of the Blessed Trinity he struck the ground three times, making three holes in it with the end of his staff; which he had no sooner done, but immediately a fountain gush'd forth; from whence to this day a brook, and that no small one, is supplied, which is both good for fishing, and healthfull likewise for many infirmities. The same narration is likewise to be found in John the Monk, and the summ of it in Capgrave; who calls the Island in which St. Benignus liv'd, by the name of Ferramere. Bishop Usher in confirmation of this revelation made by our Brittish Historians, touching St. Benignus' coming into Britany, collects likewise from ancient Irish Writers that the same Holy Bishop four years before his death relinquish'd his Archiepiscopall See of Armagh." Cressy also tells us that six hundred and thirty years after the death of our saint his sacred body was translated to Glastonbury, by the direction and care of

Thurstin, then Abbott, the ceremonies and solemnity of which Translation are to be read in the Antiquities of that famous Monastery.

We gather from the "Antiquities of Glastonbury and Malmsburiensis" that "the venerable Bishop St. Patrick preaching the Gospell through several provinces of Ireland came to a plain call'd Brey (or Berg:) which was very spacious and beautiful. With which being delighted, he determined there to celebrate the Feast of Easter then at hand. His first acquaintance and familiarity in that Province was with a certain man, who having heard his Doctrin presently believed, and receiving the Sacrament of Baptism was changed into a new man. With him St. Patrick lodged. This man had a young child call'd Beonna, who bore a tender affection to St. Patrick, so that he would oft play with him sometimes kissing his foot, which he would presse to his breast. Whereupon St. Patrick with a propheticall eye, perceiving the great Graces which the Divine bounty would confer upon the child, gave him the name of Benignus. A while after when the Holy Bishop was ready to take his journey, the child with pittifull cryes begd that he would not forsake him, saying that if he forsook him he would dye. He was therefore forc'd to receive him into his waggon, and withall prophecied that he should be his heyr and successor to the Bishoprick."

The meeting of St. Columkill and the famous St. Kintigern is thus described by Cressy; "Whilst St. Kintigern lived among the Picts, St. Columba (called by the English Columkill) hearing at his Monastery in the

Island of Hy the fame of this holy Bishop, came with a great troop of his disciples to visit him; and was mett by him with a like multitude, which they divided on both sides into three companies, the first of young men, the second such as were of perfect age, and the third venerable old men; all which in the way towards one another sung spirituall songs. And when St. Columba came in sight of the Bishop, turning himself to his Disciples he said, 'I see a pillar of fire as it were a golden crown in the third quire descending upon the Bishop and casting a celestial splendour about him.' Then the two Holy men approaching to one another with great fervor of affection gave and receiv'd mutuall kisses and embraces."

St. Columba who preferred the monk's cowl to the king's diadem, is justly regarded as one of the greatest of the patriarchs of the monastic oder in Ireland. He is also appropriately called the Apostle of the Picts. "To distinguish him from other saints of the same name," writes Butler, "he was surnamed Columkille, from the great number of monastic cells, called by the Irish, Killes, of which he was the founder. He was of most noble extraction from Neil, and was born at Gartan, in the county of Tyrconnel, in 521. He learned from his childhood that there is nothing great, nothing worth our esteem or pursuit which does not advance the divine love in our souls, to which he totally devoted himself with an entire disengagement of his heart from the world and in perfect purity of mind and body. He learned the divine scriptures, and the lessons of an ascetic life under the holy bishop St. Finian, in his great school of Cluain-iraird. Being advanced to the order of the priesthood in 546, he began to give admirable lessons of piety and sacred learning, and in a short time formed many disciples. He founded about the year 550, the great monastery of Dair-Magh, now called Durrogh, which original name signifies 'Field of Oaks,' and besides many smaller, those of Doire or Derry in Ulster, and of Sord or Swords, about six miles from Dublin. St. Columba composed a rule, which, as Usher, Tanner, and Sir James Ware inform us, is still extant in the old Irish. This rule he settled in the hundred monasteries which he founded in Ireland and Scotland. It was chiefly borrowed from the ancient oriental institutes, as the inquisitive Sir Roger Twisden notes of all the British and Irish monastic orders.

"King Dermot or Demetrius, being offended at the zeal of St. Columba, in reproving public vices, the holy man left his native country, and passed into North-Britain, now called Scotland. He took along with him twelve disciples and arrived there according to Bede, in the year of Christ 565, the ninth of the reign of Bridius, the son of Meilochon, the most powerful king of the Picts; which nation the saint converted from idolatry to the faith of Christ by his preaching, virtues and miracles. But this we are to understand of the Northern Picts and the Highlanders, separated from the others by Mount Grampus, the highest part of which is called Drum-Albin; for Bede tells us in the same place that the southern Picts had received the faith long before by the preaching of St. Ninyas, the first bishop of Whithern in Galloway; . . . .

"The Picts having embraced the faith, gave St. Columba the little island of Hy or Iona, called from him Y-colm-kille, twelve miles from the land, in which he built the great monastery which was for several ages the chief seminary of North-Britain, and continued long the burying place of the Kings of Scotland, with the bodies of innumerable Saints, which rested in that place. Out of this nursery St. Columba founded several other monasteries in Scotland. In the same school were educated the holy bishops Aidon, Finian and Colman, who converted to the faith, the English Northumbers. This great monastery several ages afterwards embraced the rule of St. Bennet.

"St. Columba's manner of living was always most austere. He lay on the bare floor, with a stone for his pillow, and never interrupted his fast. Yet his devotion was neither morose nor severe. His countenance always appeared wonderfully cheerful, and bespoke to all that beheld him, the constant interior serenity of his holy soul, and the unspeakable joy with which it overflowed from the presence of the Holy Ghost. Such was his fervour, that in whatever he did, he seemed to exceed the strength of man; and as much as in him lay, he strove to suffer no moment of his precious time, to pass without employing it for the honor of God, principally either in praying, reading, writing or preaching. His incomparable mildness and charity towards all men, and on all occasions, won the hearts of all who conversed with him, and his virtues, miracles, and extraordinary gift of prophecy, commanded the veneration of all ranks of men. He was of such authority, that neither king or people did anything without his consent. When King Aedham, or Aidanus, succeeded to his cousin Conall in the throne of British Scotland, in 574, he received the royal insignia from St. Columba. Four years before he died, St. Columba was favoured with a vision of angels which left him in many tears, because he learned from those heavenly messengers, that God, moved by the prayers of the British and Scottish churches, would prolong his exile on earth yet four years. Having continued his labours in Scotland thirty-four years, he clearly and openly foretold his death, and on Saturday, the ninth of June, said to his disciple Diermit: 'This day is called the Sabbath, that is day of rest, and such will it truly be to me; for it will put an end to my labours.' He was the first in the church at Matins at midnight; but knelt before the altar, received the Viaticum, and having given his blessing to his spiritual children, sweetly slept in the Lord, in the year 597, the seventy-seventh of his age. His body was buried in this island, but some ages after removed to Down in Ulster, and laid in one vault with the remains of St. Patrick and St. Brigit. The great monastery of Durrogh in King's County, afterwards embraced the rule of the Canons Regular, as did also the houses founded by St. Brendan, St. Comgal, etc. He was honoured both in Ireland and Scotland, among the principal patrons of those countries, and is commemorated in the Roman martyrology on the ninth of June, but in some calendars on the seventh, which seems to have been the day of his death."

"Columba," writes the Duke of Argyll, "was little inclined to melancholy as soon as he had once surmounted the great sorrow of his life, which was his exile: little disposed even, save towards the end, to contemplation or solitude, but trained by prayer and austerities to triumphs of self-sacrifice; despising rest, untiring in mental and manual toil; born for eloquence, and gifted with a voice so penetrating and sonorous that it was thought of afterwards as one of the most miraculous gifts that he had received of God; frank and loyal, original and powerful in his words as in his actions—in cloister and mission and parliament, on land and on sea, in Ireland as in Scotland, always swayed by the love of God and of his neighbor, whom it was his will and pleasure to serve with an impassioned uprightness. Such was Columba. Besides the monk and missionary there was in him the makings of a sailor, soldier, poet and orator. To us, looking back, he appears a personage as singular as he is lovable; in whom, through all the mists of the past and all the crosslights of legend, the man may still be recognized under the saint—a man capable and worthy of the supreme honour of holiness, since he knew how to subdue his inclinations, his weakness, his instincts, and his passions, and to transform them into docile and invincible weapons for the salvation of souls and the glory of God."

LINES ON FINDING A SINGING BIRD DEAD IN THE SNOW.

What a fount of joy, of rapture,
    Was this wood-born child of song!
Like a smile or ray of sunshine,
    Through the air he passed along;
All the Summer he was making
    Verses wild, yet sweet of flow;
Ah! how sad to see his plumage
    Flying with the flakes of snow.

Priest and bard would come to listen
    To his thrilling matin lay,
And the bard would sit all dreamy,
    And the priest kneel down to pray;
Hear the winds above him sighing!
    Do they whisper of his woe?
Like a bunch of bleeding roses
    Now he lies upon the snow.

Ah! no more we'll see him building
    Happy homes of down and moss;
Ah! no more we'll hear him chanting
    On the chapel's golden cross;
In the earth rich seeds are hidden,
    Flowers will come in Summer's glow;
But our garden will be lonely,
    For its bard sleeps in the snow.

KIND HEARTS.

Kind hearts are found in every land,
   And noble souls in court and cot,
Our race is one fraternal band,
   Though strange our fortunes and our lot;
A pilgrim's life my life has been,
   I've met stout Teutons and gay Franks,
And friendship true I've always seen
   Upon the Rhine and fair Seine's banks.

Beneath Canadian pines I've slept,
   When winter came in robes of snow,
And though for home I nightly wept,
   Kind words oft came to chase my woe;
The woodmen welcomed me with joy,
   And made me share their frugal fare;
They bade me be once more a boy,
   And cast away my look of care.

The Belgians sang for me their songs,
   They heard my songs with tearful eyes;
The brave Poles told me of their wrongs,
   And Romans told me of their skies:
For every land true love I feel,
   Oh, every land was kind to me;
Hear Nature speak—a thunder-peal—
   "True men are men where'er they be."

AN ODE TO ST. ISIDORE.

(St. Isidore, Patron of Madrid, was an humble laborer who sanctified himself in the midst of his daily toils. While his hand guided the plough, his heart communed with God and His holy Angels. The various aspects of nature gave him continual food for divine contemplation.)

Wake not the golden stringed lyres,
   Let their rich music sleep ;
Be still, be still, ye human choirs,
   Ye lutes a silence keep ;
For birds of snowy wing and breast,
   And scented winds among the trees,
And wells that in deep valleys rest,
   And sunlit streams that gild the leas,
Will claim their right for evermore
To sing of pure-soul'd Isidore.

There comes a voice from hidden lakes,
   Softer than Summer's breeze,
There swells a hum by lonely brakes,
   Like music on the seas.
The tempest-breath shakes mountain-peak,
   And 'mong the rocks makes melody ;
The birds through all the forests speak
   In tones of richest harmony ;
And all in measured numbers pour
The praises of St. Isidore.

Teach us, meek Saint, we humbly pray,
    The Lord in all to view,
His steps to trace in meadows gay,
    And in the heavens blue ;
To read His Beauty in each flower
    That we espy in cultured dell,
To know what is the awful power
    That bound the vale by rocky fell ;
May all in Nature we explore
Lead us to God and Isidore.

I ROAM A LAND OF GOLDEN DREAMS.

I.

I roam a land of golden dreams,
By soft, green groves, and waterfalls;
I roam through meads, by soundless streams,
And see far-off fair city walls;
Dear Land of Sleep, how calm art thou,
How peaceful are thy silent dells—
But hark, what sounds are coming now?
They are! they are! the matin bells.
     O! matin bells,
     No sound excels
Your music sweet in waking dells.

II.

I kneel with saints for ages dead,
The angels play for me their lyres,
In Paradise I seem to tread,
Around me stand celestial choirs;
Mute Isle of Sleep, how still art thou,
How tranquil are thy voiceless dells--
But hark, what sounds come rushing now?
They are! they are! the matin bells.
     O! matin bells,
     No sound excels
Your music sweet in waking dells.

III.

The stars have faded from the sky ;
Ah! with the stars my dreams must part ;
With night my fairest visions fly,
With day will come old pain of heart.
Yet welcome be the hour of light,
With Light young Truth forever dwells ;
Grim darkness fears the morning's sight—
Ring in loved scenes, glad matin bells!
      Sweet matin bells,
      No sound excels
Your music rich in waking dells.

I'LL TELL MY BEADS.

I'll tell my beads when my heart is sad,
And my sorrows will fly away;
Full well I know that each bead has power
All the floods of woe to stay.

For it lifts me up, and bears me far
O'er the highest hills men see,
It lifts me above the farthest star,
To the Throne of Queen Mary.

'Tis a golden link that binds my heart
To the heart of my fair Queen ;
'Tis a precious gem I would not part
For all that the eye hath seen.

BE NOT AFRAID.

Sad soul, sad soul,
  Be not afraid;
Thy cross was made,
  Thy burden weighed,
By Hands that bled for thee;
  Sad soul, sad soul,
    Be not afraid.

Poor soul, poor soul,
  Be not afraid;
Sweet Jesus knows
  Thy ills and woes,
And deeply pities thee;
  Poor soul, poor soul,
    Be not afraid.

Faint heart, faint heart,
  Be not afraid;
Lo, angels come
  To lead thee Home,
And take thy load from thee;
  Faint heart, faint heart,
    Be not afraid.

HOLY SPIRIT, COME AND GUIDE ME.

I.

Holy Spirit, come and guide me,
    For Thy Light I daily pine ;
All around is dark and gloomy,
    Let Thy Rays upon me shine.

II.

From my soul dispel all shadows,
    From my heart now banish care ;
Teach me how to bear my crosses,
    Give me sweetness in my prayer.

III.

Speak to me of Heaven's beauties,
    Tell me of Thy Sinless Land ;
Lead me up that Holy Mountain
    Where but Purified may stand.

IV.

Lead me o'er the paths of virtue,
    Keep me far from shame and sin ;
Give me peace in holy actions,
    Drive from me all strife and din.

V.

Show the vainness of false pleasures,
    Show how fleeting are man's days,
Show that Thou alone canst give me
    Force to walk through stainless ways.

THE LAST VICTIM OF ELIZABETH'S REIGN IN IRELAND.

BR. DOMINICK COLLINS, S. J.

Now therefore, O my sons, be ye zealous for the law, and give your lives for the covenant of your fathers. 1 *Mac.*, Chap. II, v. I.

ON a bright summer's evening, a young noble, gaily attired, attended by a large number of friends and servants, rode up to the gates of the Jesuit Novitiate at Compostella, the capital of Gallicia, in Spain. He had just made a pilgrimage to the tomb of St. James, in that city, and now came to seek admittance among the lay-Brother novices of the Society of Jesus. After bidding farewell to his friends and retinue, he dismounted and entered the Novitiate.

The Rector and a few of the Fathers came to the parlor to see him, and welcome him. They little dreamed that he was coming to ask for a place among the humblest of their novices. They all well knew that the gay young officer before them was born of noble and illustrious parents in Ireland, that he had served with distinction in fighting against the heretical enemies of the Most Christian King, and that he was now high in the favor of King Philip, in whose army he had held, during eight years, a rank suitable to his birth and services. When he had made known his determination to enter religion, the Rector frankly said to him: "I fear, sir, that you are not a fit subject for our poor Novitiate. Here you will have to cast aside all earthly pomp and pride. Here you will have to lead a life of mortification, obedience, and humiliation."

"Fear not to receive me, Rev. Father. I am prepared to suffer all things for the love of Jesus Christ, my Captain and my King. As a soldier I am accustomed to obey, and to feel the want of many things. In the past I have sought for empty glory; let me now learn to humble myself." The earnestness of the young officer prevailed on the Rector to receive him into his house.

O'Callan, for this was the young man's name, was placed among the lay-Brothers as his humility had desired. Before he had yet received the habit of the Society a violent infectious disorder broke out in the College. He immediately proved his courage and zeal in attending the sick, and showed by the performance of the most humiliating offices, that he was worthy of a place among the sons of St. Ignatius. After he had made his novitiate, and taken his religious vows he was given as a companion to Father John Archer, who was to accompany the Spanish fleet, which was about to be sent by Philip to aid the Irish Catholics in freeing themselves from slavery and persecution. The tyranny of Elizabeth, and the barbarity and insolence of her brutal soldiers and servants in Ireland, had roused the Irish chiefs to action. Hugh O'Neill and Hugh O'Donel had kept the Red Hand and the Banner of Tyrconnel proudly flying in defiance of the hosts that England could send to tear them down. After O'Neill's splendid victory over Bagnal at the fort of Blackwater, in Tyrone, a thrill of joy went through the heart of not only every Irishman at home, but also through the heart of every true Irishman on the Continent, whether his place was in the professorial chair at Salamanca, in a convent in Italy, or in a gay camp in France.

Nothing was more agreeable to the patriotic heart of O'Callan—in the future we will call him *Collins*, the name he assumed on entering religion—than to go and give spiritual aid and consolation to the kerns who were fighting under the banners of Ireland for their country, their altars, their homes, their lives.

With all the generous feelings of a soldier, and all the zeal of a fervent religious, Dominick Collins went on board one of the Spanish ships. During the voyage he faithfully attended the sick sailors day and night. All the time he could spare from his arduous duties he spent in prayer and meditation. As he drew near the Irish coast how his heart throbbed, as he thought of once again beholding the hills and vales of his dear native shore. He watched with an anxious eye to catch the first glimpse of the land of his love, the Isle of his dreams, the cherished home of his forefathers. He looked over the blue waters, he looked far off into the distance,—

"'Till a faint grey line
Rose in the Northern sky ; so faint, so pale,
Only the heart that loves her would divine
In her dim welcome all that fancy paints
Of the green glory on the Isle of saints."

Soon after his arrival in Ireland, Dominick was taken prisoner by the heretics, in the fort of Beerhaven. "Contrary to the law of nations, and in violation of their pledges, he alone was put in chains; for the besiegers had guaranteed the safety of all the besieged on condition of the castle being surrendered to them, and had given the most solemn pledges to this effect to Dominick himself, who had been the pacificator and the messenger of the besieged. But they seemed to consider that to have seized a Jesuit was a vindication of every breach of faith and perjury. His hands were tied behind his back, and he was brought to Cork by a troop of soldiers, where he was thrown into the common prison. He lay here three months, till the time of the assizes for the trial of all criminals, when he was tried."

On the day of his trial Brother Collins appeared in court dressed in the habit and mantle of the Spanish sons of St. Ignatius. Mountjoy, Viceroy of Ireland, grew angry at the sight of the clerical dress, and demanded why he dared appear before him in that most odious costume.

"I have dared to come before you in this habit, because I have no reason to be ashamed of it. It is the habit of St. Ignatius, of St. Francis Borgia, and of St. Francis Xavier. I glory in it in life, and I hope it will be my only winding sheet in death."

"You seem," said Mountjoy, "to have a good deal of courage. If you will only renounce your vain religion and enter into the army of our good Queen, Elizabeth,

I will obtain for you both rank and fortune, and I promise you my unchanging friendship."

"I have fought," said Brother Dominick with warmth, "under the glorious banners of the kings of France and Spain; I now fight under the banner of Ignatius, and think you, that I would dishonor my name, insult my country, deny my religion, and humble my Order, by apostacy from the Faith, by drawing the sword in the cause of the cruel, heartless irreligious Elizabeth? Away with your fortune, your rank, your false friendship. From my soul I scorn them."

Mountjoy grew enraged at these noble words. He ordered the Brother to undergo all kinds of the most cruel torture. For several days preceding his execution he was left to the mercy of brutal soldiers, who did all they could to make him suffer. But all they could do could not shake his constancy, disturb his patience, or destroy the holy joy and peace of his soul. The heretics, being, at length, provoked by his great serenity and courage, hastened the day of his death.

"On the last day of October, 1602," says Tanner, "at the dawn, having no respect for the day, which was Sunday, they led him out to execution, with his hands tied behind his back and a halter round his neck. He walked calmly along, with his eyes raised to heaven and his mind fixed on God, reflecting on Christ bearing His cross. When he arrived at the foot of the gallows, he fell on his knees and kissed it, commending his passage to God."

He then prayed for his poor bleeding country, and for his enemies. After that he mounted the ladder with as proud and happy a mean as ever he wore in climbing up the side of a conquered fortification in the Netherlands. What a picture of heroism, of grandeur, of fervor, is that of Dominick Collins, standing on the topmost step of the dread ladder, robed in his religious habit, and addressing burning words to his Catholic countrymen. O, how precious is the Faith for which Collins is about to die. Listen, O, listen, children of Ireland, to the dying words of this hero, and treasure them up in your heart of hearts: "Look up," he said, "to heaven, and, worthy descendants of your ancestors, who ever constantly professed it, hold fast to that Faith for which I am about to die."

There was a stir among the crowd. The heart of the multitude was touched. Many eyes were wet with tears as men and women thought of the high birth, the rank, the fortune, the fame, the piety, the courage, the zeal of the speaker. The mass began to heave to and fro. There were murmurs, and looks that foretold the strong rising of an indignant populace. "The officers, perceiving this," continues Tanner, "to prevent any further effect on the crowd, ordered him to be thrown off the ladder. Nor was he allowed to hang long on the gallows; for, while yet breathing, and palpitating, the executioner, in punishment of his constant profession of his religion, cut open his breast, and, taking out his heart, held it up to the people, uttering the usual 'God save the Queen.' Thus this last victim to God in Ireland in her reign preceded the queen, guilty of so much innocent blood, to the Judgment seat of God. On the following night, the Catholics collected his mangled limbs with great pity, and consigned them to the earth in a chapel not far from where he suffered."

ROME.

"But Rome in all her glory is a grave."
Schiller.

With Rome The Spirit dwells forever,
Her soul is Truth—that's life and light;
Against God's Arm is man's endeavor
To sink her deep in death and night.
No more are pagan splendors burning,
No Caesar sits upon her throne,
No more her ships with slaves returning
By all the winds of heaven are blown.
But Papal Rome with life is gleaming,
She is Earth's Lamp amid its gloom,
Who styles her *grave* is idly dreaming,—
She'll light the Nations to their tomb.

THE HOLY VIATICUM.

In Catholic countries on the Continent the Holy Viaticum is carried to the sick under a rich canopy in solemn procession. The bells of the church give notice to the public ; the priest vested in his holy robes, is accompanied by acolytes bearing lighted torches ; one rings constantly a little bell to admonish the people that Jesus is passing by, and crowds of the faithful, especially members of the confraternity of the Blessed Sacrament, join the procession and carry lights.—*The Dove of the Tabernacle.*

Waves of holy sound are floating
Through the vesper, Belgian dell :
"See ! the Priest is bearing Jesus,"
Sweetly sings the silver bell.

Rays of gold fall down from heaven,
Crowning acolytes and Priest ;
Wells of lillies pure are springing
Up to cheer the Last, Grand Feast.

Roses line the pathway, sighing
As the Saviour passes by ;
'Neath the grass the violets humble
Strive to meet their Maker's Eye.

Peasants kneel, with burning tapers,
Burning hearts, and loving eyes ;
"Mercy, Jesus, on the dying—
Mercy Thou dost highly prize !"

Lo! the cot, so poor and lowly,
　Where a parting child doth dwell;
"Comfort, dear one, here is Jesus,"
　Softly sings the silver bell.

Jesus loves the simple cottage,
　Where no pride can ever be;
There He thinks of His dear Mother,
　And his home in Galilee!

"Welcome, Jesus! Welcome, Master!
Cleanse my heart," the sick boy sighs,
"Jesus, Jesus, I adore Thee,"—
　Breathes the child in Paradise!

OUR LADY OF SORROW.

Dense the gloom of all creation—
  On the blackest spot of all
Is a lonely Virgin's station,
  Weeping o'er man's deepest fall.

Dead is Jesus, and His Mother
  Is abandoned on the Hill;
Men have slain their God, their Brother,
  Now their mother's cup they fill.

In the city Jews are boasting
  Of the crime that stains to-day,
Horror, they are vainly toasting;—
  "Pilate," "Herod," "great are they!"

Dead is Jesus, thou art sighing,
  Mother of the Tender Heart,
Thou art weary, thou art dying,
  Sad is now thy doleful part.

Mother dearest, Virgin tearful,
  Will no mortals watch with thee?
Are the sons of Adam fearful
  Of the Cross—their Saving Tree?

In the darkness, full of sadness,
  May I on the Hill be seen;
There I'll hate all sinful madness—
  There I'll love my King and Queen.

Mary weeping, Jesus bleeding,
  Ever will be dear to me;
Sighing, moaning, warmly pleading,
  May I stand on Calvary!

THE WORLD.

'Tis vain to seek for bliss below—
   The ancient curse will ever burn;
Our earth is but the nurse of woe—
   Who seeks true joys, to God must turn.

Our gardens bear each hateful weed,
   While all around the briers bloom;
From Paradise no blissful seed
   Was blown afar to Adam's tomb.

There is no stone on earth to build
   A house where drossless joys abide;
There is no gold with power to gild
   A peaceful home for human pride.

The world is but a stagnant lake,
   Reflecting lovely shores and skies;
Its dazzling stillness dare to break,
   And lo! what foulness in it lies.

COME, AND SEE THE CAPITOL.

Oh, come and see the Capitol,
   'Tis white as daisies an the lea ;
Oh, come and see the Capitol,
   'Tis white as foam upon the sea :
'Tis like a dream-built palace,
   All beautiful and bright :
'Tis like a gleaming iceberg
   Crowned with the stars of night.

Oh, come and see the Capitol,
   'Tis like a hill of snow,
Oh, come and see the Capitol
   With the moonlight all aglow ;
'Tis like a magic castle
   Or a lilly centuries old,
'Tis like a fairy mansion
   With its windows lit with gold

Oh, come and see the Capitol,
   And its goddess—Liberty ;
Oh, come and see the Capitol,
   And remember thou art free,
And thank the God of Battles,
   Whose right arm blessed the brave,
And pray the God of Nations,
   Our Fatherland to save.

TO AUBREY DE VERE.

Thou art, chaste bard, like that sweet bird —
By heavenly longings strongly stirred—
That soars to be the better heard
    By watchers on the tower and hill.

Thou singest not for groveling men,
For those who walk life's lowly glen,
For dwellers on the plain or fen,
    But watchers on the tower and hill.

Thy hand's a wand of light and fire
That touches not thy lofty lyre,
Save to awake some grand desire
    In watchers on the tower and hill.

We daily hear thy noble song,
Which heaven and earth love to prolong,
Not from the base, inglorious throng,
    But watchers on the tower and hill.

Chaste as the stars of chastest flame
Is the chaste light of thy chaste fame;
Thy songs have souls; they'll keep thy name
    'Mid watchers on the tower and hill.

A SOUL IN SIN.

It was God's temple years ago,—
   Behold it now ;
With love and faith it once did glow,—
   Behold it now ;
Its altar was the Spirit's throne,
Its incense rose to Him alone,
With praises rang its every stone,—
   Behold it now.

In ruin lies this temple fair,—
   A thing of shame ;
It breathes no more of holy prayer,—
   This place of shame ;
Its hymn of love is heard no more,
No angels flock here to adore,
The serpent's slime is on its floor,—
   Dark place of shame

THE BARD.

I.

The bard is like a timid bird
That's seldom seen but ofttimes heard
    Singing sweet and gladsome strains;
  Singing in the pines and briers,
  Kindling Nature's bardic fires,
  Waking all the woodland choirs,
    And the songs upon the plains.

II.

The bard is like a linnet gray
That sings his time and life away,
    Cheering lonely hours and days;
  Cheering with his fount of song
  Pilgrims as they pass along,
  Cheering e'en the heedless throng
    Passing o'er life's busy ways.

III.

The bard is like an angel bright
That speaks to man, both day and night,
    Calling him to higher things;
  Calling him from mart and street,
  Where a thousand passions meet,
  Calling him to God's own Feet,
    And the board of kingly kings.

DOMINICUS DE ROSARIO.

HIS ACCOUNT OF THE SIEGE OF CASHEL, AND THE DEATH OF FATHER BARRY.

ON a certain day, in the year 1656, a Dominican priest was walking up and down his little cell, in his humble and poor convent in the street Rua Nova de Almada, Lisbon, telling his long black beads. He was a fine picture to look upon, with his noble and venerable figure, his immaculate white robe, and his fair and pleasant face. He did not look like a prisoner in his narrow room, but like a man on a mountain-peak breathing fresh, pure air, and surrounded with the glories of skies not far above his head. And so he was on a mountain-top, for was he not on "the bright mountain of Prayer."

This Dominican who was telling his beads, was a true religious, a great literary man, and honored by kings and queens; at the time of which we write he was one of the confessors of the queen of Portugal. He was an humble man, as may be proved from the fact that he refused the archbishoprics of Braga and Goa.

Not far from the Dominican convent stood the palace of the duke of Braganza, John IV, of Portugal. While Father Dominicus was praying, the king and his advisers were consulting together concerning the fittest man to be sent as ambassador to the court of Louis XIV. Portugal had then many distinguished and noble statesmen and diplomatists. Who shall be chosen from among them? The king and council unanimously agreed that Father Dominicus de Rosario should represent Portugal at the court of France. The humble Dominican on learning the extraordinary honor conferred upon him, and the great responsibility of the office, endeavored to have some one else chosen in his place. But the king would not yield to his entreaties, and so he had to leave the peaceful little convent of Lisbon and depart for the French Court.

The court of Louis XIV. is famous in history as the model of "politesse," of good taste, and of magnificence. Louis himself was an able, prudent king, and has been justly styled—The Great. His place in the world's estimation is with Charlemagne and Clovis. He was "great in peace and war." He had the happy faculty of discerning talent, and the better gift of rewarding it. He exalted himself, strengthened his throne, and glorified his reign and his country, by the favor he showed men of genius. He had in his army a Condé, a Turenne, a Luxembourg, a Créqui, a Catinat, and a Villars; he had in his cabinet a Colbert, and a Louvois; Boileau and Racine wrote his history; Bossuet and Fenelon instructed his children; Flechier, Bourdaloue and Massillon instructed himself. To such a king and to such a court was Father Dominicus sent. But he was well qualified to appear before any king or any court. He had long been the intimate of nobles, and of Philip IV., of Spain. He had associated with profound and brilliant scholars and ecclesiastics in Lugo, in Gallicia, at Burgos in old Castile, in Louvain, and in Lisbon.

Dominicus was received by the king and his court in a manner suitable to the representative of a sovereign. Louis was soon charmed with the modesty, prudence, learning, and piety of the gifted son of St. Dominic. And the Dominican agreed with the opinion of all that Louis was the greatest and most amiable monarch of his time. A sympathy soon sprang up between them which helped to render the monk's embassy an entire success. Life at court was distasteful to Father Dominicus, and, as it is also to us, we will not here dwell upon his receptions by Louis, nor his negotiations in the king's cabinet, but will follow him to the Dominican Convent, Saint Jacques, at Paris, and steal in upon him during the hours of recreation so that we may hear some of his conversation.

As the convent of Saint Jaques was a "House of General Studies" for the Dominicans, it had students from different countries of Europe. Ireland, then forbidden the advantages of education, had several of her devoted sons studying in this venerable establishment.

Soon after the arrival of Father Dominicus the Irish students requested their superior to grant them permission to pass some time in recreation with him. The superior kindly consented to their request.

Without permission, dear reader, I will lead you into the presence of the illustrious Portuguese ambassador and introduce you to him. Perhaps, you are afraid that he speaks only the French of Louis XIV., or the strange tongue of Portugal. Be not alarmed, Father Dominicus de Rosario, or Daniel O'Daly, has a sweet Kerry accent, and was a pupil of the Convent of the Holy Cross, Tralee. He is gifted with a royal Irish heart and head. Neither in the convent, nor in the court, has he lost the warmth and generosity that belong to the sons of Ireland. He is still the same Daniel O'Daly as when he chased the red deer on his native hills of Kerry.

"Welcome, welcome, a thousand welcomes," the old priest exclaimed, as the young Irish Dominicans entered the recreation-room. "Come to my heart, children of Erin, children of the sorrowful, yet ever glorious Isle. How it gladdens my heart to meet you, future apostles, future martyrs, for the land and faith that I love."

The old man wept as he embraced his young brethren in the Lord.

After all had been seated for some time, and had rejoiced and sorrowed, and sorrowed and rejoiced over the news from Ireland, one of the students, a fit representative of old Tipperary, asked Father O'Daly to give himself and his companions a full account of the glorious martyrdom of Father Richard Barry.

"Ah, poor Father Barry," said Father O'Daly in a low and tender voice, as he heard the name of his martyred brother-priest mentioned, "it was my part to write an account of his sad but sublime death. Oh, cruel laws that command the deaths of holy priests, and the desecration of sacred things. Ah, my brothers, pray day and night for our afflicted country. Pray that God may raise us up a Moses who will lead our unhappy people out of the darkness of slavery and persecution into the light of freedom and peace. *You* cannot now carry a sword to smite our country's oppressors, but you have a beads by your side which has more virtue than a thousand swords. But do you all wish me to read for you an account of the sufferings and death of the prior of Cashel."

All wished to hear the story of Father Barry's death. Did they not all wish to die like him? Did not all these white-robed youths long to shed their blood for the glory of their country and their God. How martyrs died was a subject near and dear to them.

Father O'Daly had to go to his cell for his manuscripts, but he soon returned to the recreation-room, which was now as solemn as a tomb.

"It is necessary, my dear brothers," began Father O'Daly, "to give you a short sketch of some events which preceded the mardyrdom of Father Barry.

"The apostate Earl of Inchiquin, in 1647, made an attack upon 'Cashel of the King.' The old town, badly fortified, was easily taken, and its streets soon ran red with the blood of its Catholic inhabitants. The garrison, with the priests and religious, and many of the citizens retired to the Cathedral Church, which was seated on the summit of the famous Rock of Cashel. Nobly did the little band of soldiers repel the assault of the infuriated enemy. In vain did the apostate followers of Inchiquin strive to force their way into the Cathedral; back they were driven, and many a one of them rolled down the side of the Rock, leaving tracks of blood along his way.

"At length Inchiquin suspended the deadly fight, and sent an officer to treat with the bold leader of the garrison. 'The Earl of Inchiquin,' began the enemy's officer, as he stood face to face with the heroic defender of the Rock, 'has sent me to treat with you, and to demand a surrender.' 'What are the conditions upon which Inchiquin demands a surrender?' asked the Catholic soldier, proudly.

'He grants you, and your fellow-soldiers, permission to depart with your arms, ammunition, and all the honors of war.'

'Are these all the conditions?'

'No, he demands that you abandon the citizens and clergy to his mercy.'

'Enough, enough,' cried the generous Catholic Captain, 'you have come here to insult me, and my garrison. Go back to the renegade Inchiquin, and tell him that we, true Irishmen and soldiers, can never listen to such base terms. Tell him, moreover, that we would sooner, a thousand times sooner, consecrate our lives to God on this glorious Rock of St. Patrick, than see its holy sanctuary profaned by dogs.'

"Back the officer went to Inchiquin, and the assault was immediately renewed with redoubled ferocity.

"My brothers, it is useless to dwell upon the devotedness and heroism of the garrison; the enemy being 7000, and the defenders of the seat of the Monarchs of Munster, the defenders of the temple of the Living God, being only 300, the Rock was taken and desecrated, and the altar-steps were empurpled with the blood of children and women, of gallant soldiers and holy religious. So great was the slaughter that the aisles of the Cathedral were blocked up with the corpses of the slain.

"Among the martyred was Father Boyton, a fervent religious of the Society of Jesus. This brave priest during the fierce combat thought only of saving souls. The enemy finding him in the act of administering the last Sacraments to a dying soldier slew him with the Adorable Host in his hand.

"The cruel heretics slew the women who clung to the statue of St. Patrick. They beheaded, as for treason, the great crucifix which stood at the entrance of the choir, and hewed off its hands and feet. Then were torn in shreds the pictures of the saintly monks, and kings of Ireland. The sacred vessels were broken, the precious vestments were cast on the floor for carpeting, or worn by drunken soldiers in the streets of the town; the altars were overturned and the Puritan leader with the archiepiscopal mitre on his head, and the crozier of the great Saint-King, Cormac, in his hand, had the folly and the audacity to boast that he was not only governor and lieutenant of Munster, but also Archbishop of Cashel."

Here Father O'Daly paused to wipe away a tear that dimmed his eye. The eyes of his hearers were also dimmed by tears, and their hearts beat wildly as they thought of the wrongs of their country, and the insults heaped upon their holy religion

"My dear brothers," continued Father O'Daly, "I am now come to the sad, but glorious death of Father Barry.

"When the Puritans gained possession of the Rock, they found Father Barry robed in his Dominican habit, and holding a sword in his hand. The colonel, who led the assault, was favorably struck by the grave and noble appearance of the Father, and said to him:—'I see you are a brave man, and I promise you safety if you will cast off that dress which we hate.'

'My dress,' said Father Barry, firmly, 'is the emblem of Christ and His passion, and the banner of my warfare. I have borne it from my youth, and will not put it off in death.'

'Monk, be more careful of yourself,' said the colonel, sternly. 'If you fear not to die, you shall soon have your way; but if you desire to live, cast away that traitor's dress.' 'Never,' said the father, warmly, 'shall I cast aside my holy habit. And here to your face, I tell you, that this habit is not the dress of traitors, or cowards, but of true men, and good, who know how to die for their country and creed.'

'Hold sir,' cried the enraged colonel, 'if you foolishly look for martyrdom, we will soon satisfy your desire.'

'Since so excellent an occasion is offered me,' said Father Barry, 'of showing my love for Him who suffered on the Cross for me, I must not lose it. To suffer for my devotion to my country is my joy, and to die for my holy religion is my gain. I fear neither you, nor Inchiquin, nor your band of Puritan vipers.'

"This answer provoked the colonel so much, that he immediately handed the brave Father over to his brutal soldiers, who struck him, and spat upon him. They then tied him to a chair and applied a slow fire for about two hours, from the soles of his feet to his thighs. At length the blood bubbled forth from all his pores. Throughout this cruel torture the Father showed the courage and patience of a Christian hero. The officer, growing weary of the heroic, though sad spectacle, ordered an end to be put to the sufferer's life by a thrust of the sword. Father Barry died with his gaze fixed on heaven.

"After the heretics had evacuated Cashel and its Cathedral, the vicar-general called together the few surviving priests and people, who, together with the notary apostolic, Henry O'Cullenan, formed a procession, and carried the body of the glorious Dominican to a convent of his order, where, having sung the *Te Deum*, they laid it down to holy rest."

Just as Father O'Daly had finished the last sentence, the bells of the convent tolled, and all the young Dominicans retired to their different cells in silence.

Father O'Daly, who never lost his first religious fervor, also instantly retired to his little cell, full of sadness at the thought that as cruel a fate as Father Barry's awaited many of his young Irish brethren who were to sleep happily that night under the roof of Saint Jacques.

SWEET NIGHT.

Sweet night thy calm is on my soul,
    I feel thee on my spirit grow;
Thy stars, like visions, o'er me roll,
    Thy dews, like grace, around me flow.

So fair is darkness in thy train,
    That she can soothe the babe to sleep;
O! why should sorrow, guilt, or pain,
    With thy soft shadows ever creep?

Ah! why shouldst thou the mother be
    Of crimes that fear the light of day?
Thou bringest thoughts of God to me,
    Thy grandeur helps my heart to pray.

UP, UP, AND MOUNT FOR EVERMORE.

I.

The birds that leave the clear blue skies
      To feed upon
      Earth's carrion,
Though plumed like angels, I despise.

II.

A burning star I would not be,
      If in my glow
      Base thoughts should flow
To earth, and its impurity.

III.

I am not made of common clay;
      Man's clay was found
      In Eden's ground,
And not upon the king's highway.

IV.

Proud soul, spread out they wings, and soar;
      Thou art no clod,
      Fair type of God,
Up, up, and mount for evermore.

I AM WEARY OF THE CITY.

I.

I am weary of the city,
Weary of its strife and din,
Weary of its pains and pleasures,
Weary of its works of sin,
And I sigh for deep, green meadows
In whose depths the skylarks nest,
And I bless that dear, good valley
Where in youth I found sweet rest.

II.

I am weary of the city—
Though I came bright fame to win—
And my heart is dark with sorrow,
And my soul grows sick within ;
How I long for singing woodlands,
And for homesteads free from care,
How I long for that old hamlet
Where we hailed the Night by prayer.

III.

I am weary of the city,
'Tis the selfish work of man,
And a dark cloud hangs above it,
Like a dismal pall, or ban ;
So I pace its streets full weary,
And I weep amid its blaze,
And I grieve that I am severed
From loved Nature's dew-bright ways.

IN THE COUNTRY.

Once more in the green, wavy meadows,
Once more 'neath a sky, broad,--blue,
Once more by the gold-sanded streamlets,
And hedge-rows of flowers and dew;
Once more I sit 'mid snow daisies,
With hearts of the purest gold,
Once more and I leave life's shadows
To live in the days of old.

Again I am fanned by the breezes
That rifle the sweet, wild flowers,
Again I am drinking the music
That flows from the bird-loved bowers;
Again I kneel down in our chapel
And join with our village choir,
And my heart grows warm and tender,
And my soul soars higher and higher.

How grand are Thy Works, dear Master,—
The dark green chain of high hills,
How fair are Thy Works, loved Father,—
The vales, and the lakes, and rills;
O! vain are the world's false sages
Who tell us Thou art not near,
O! blind are the foolish dreamers,
Who see not Thy foot-prints here.

MATER INVIOLATA.

I stood in thought beside a circling sea,
Whose waters were more clear than morning light ;
More calm than those that first met Adam's sight,
More beautiful than those of earth can be ;
No slimy weed, nor jagged stone nor tree,
Was ever mirrored in those waters bright ;
But there I saw deep golden rays that might
Shine in the court of the Divinity ;
'Twas thy pure soul, O Mary, kind and sweet,
That came to cheer my heart and glad mine eyes—
For in thy soul so calm, so pure, so mild,
The piercing gaze of God could never meet —
As there, alone, the Sun of Justice lies—
A thing of earth, or aught by earth defiled.

OH, THUS THE BARDS.

Enthroned among the dark-green pines
By no one seen, the linnet sings ;
Enthroned among the lone, dark pines
The linnet's voice now clearly rings ;
He recks not who may hear his songs ;
He recks not though they be not heard,
He sings of loves, and joys, and wrongs,
He sings for self, the happy bird.

The shepherd on the lonely hills,
At eventide pours forth his strains ;
He pipes of meads, and flocks, and rills
And hamlets on the flowery plains ;
He dreams not, that deep in the vale,
The toilers pause to hear his voice,
He dreams not that his sweet notes sail
Far off, to make sad hearts rejoice.

Oh, thus the bards in their charmed cells,
Think of their lyres and not of men ;
Oh, thus the bards in their hidden cells
Forget the workers in life's glen ;
They sing their songs to please themselves,
And not to please the world's dull ear ;
They sing their songs to soothe their souls,
Not dreaming of the listeners near.

ON SMILES.

A smile is the light from our souls,
   'Tis the sunshine that leaps from our hearts,
O'er the sea of the world it shines,
   And the calmness of heaven imparts.

Oh, keep the old smiles fair and bright,
   They can cheer thy sad brothers in woe;
We heed not the darkness of night,
   While we see thy red lips all aglow.

A smile is a fountain of bliss,
   'Tis a gem in our Innocence set;
Oh, 'twere sweet, in a world like this,
   If our smiles we should never forget.

WHAT IS LOVE?

Love is an angel, my child,
    With pinions of golden light;
Love is an angel, my child,
    Beautiful, pure, and bright;
And she dwells with God in the skies,
    And she dwells in the hearts of men,
And she shines in each maiden's eyes—
    You'll meet her, but I know not when.

Love is an angel, my child,
    Tender, and kind, and fair;
Love is an angel, my child,
    Sweet as our garden air;
And she leads us the Passion Way,
    The Way that Our Lord hath trod,
And she helps us to watch and pray—
    For Love is the Spirit of God.

YEA, LORD, THOU KNOWEST THAT I LOVE THEE.

(ST. JOHN, XXI. 15.)

I.

Thou knowest, Master, that my heart is Thine,
Proud, weak, and sinful, though it be;
Thy Sacred Heart forever must be mine—
I'll live in Thee, and Thou in me.

II.

My chosen One art Thou, O! Spotless Dove;
For Thee I've longed, and wept, and sighed;
When can I meet Thee, Whom my soul doth love?
Why from mine eyes Thy beauty hide?

III.

O! haste, sweet Lord, possess my throbbing heart,
Or give me wings to seek Thy sky;
It seems to me that I have Mary's part,
I burn with love, of love I die.

IV.

Thou art my paradise, O! purest Lord,
Thy name brings peace and joy to me;
In loving Thee I find a sweet reward,
O! what a bliss Thy fair face to see.

V.

Thy sorrows flood my heart with bitter grief,
Thy tears to me seem never dry ;
In weeping o'er my sins I find relief,
If tears come not, I know I'd die.

VI.

No more I'll waste my love on fading flowers,
No more I'll love earth's cup of dross ;
In thoughts of Thee alone I'll spend my hours,
Sole treasure now for me—Thy Cross.

VII.

Kind Master, Thou canst read my inmost soul—
Look far beyond my selfish love,
Look not upon my passions outward roll,
And Thou wilt see in Whom I move.

VIII.

How sad it is to love, and still not show
That love is master in the heart ;
How sad it is to wander to and fro,
And from one's Love still live apart.

IX.

Through all my life I've loved my Holy Love,
Yet from His side how oft I stray ;
O! how I sigh for that fair land above,
Where on His Breast I'll rest alway.

OUR LADY OF MONTAIGU.

A FAITHFUL HISTORY OF THE CELEBRATED SHRINE OF OUR LADY AT MONTAIGU, BELGIUM.

I take occasion now to declare, in obedience to the decree of Pope Urban VIII. that all I am about to narrate rests upon merely human authority. I am far from proposing any of the wonders that I may recount as articles of our holy and divine faith.

MONTAIGU—THE EARLY HISTORY OF THE MIRACULOUS STATUE.

Montaigu is a pleasant little Flemish village, which crowns the summit of a small round hill in Brabant. It is situated at a distance of about one mile from Sichem, three from Diest, fifteen from Louvain, and thirty from Brussels. The sight of its ponderous old sign-posts, with their grotesque figures and high sounding inscriptions, is well calculated to produce an agreeable impression upon the weary traveller. The grandeur of its noble Church, the solidity of its ancient buildings, and the ample dimensions of its chimney-stacks, lend it an air of comfort not found in many of our more modern and delicately framed hamlets. To a visitor altogether ignorant of its history, Montaigu would be a difficult riddle. He could never account for the relatively vast number of its hotels; he could never dream why almost half the town is engaged in selling crosses, rosaries and religious engravings. The thousands of men and women from Germany, Holland and Belgium that would pass around him with slow pace and solemn looks would perplex him.

"Why," he would ask, "this prayerful throng? Why are the very children in the streets so silent and recollected? What is this deep mystery that surrounds me? I really never saw anything like this before. Am I at Lourdes or Loretto?"

"No," he would be kindly answered, "you are not at Lourdes, nor Loretto; you are at the celebrated shrine of Our Lady of Montaigu."

Montaigu is very different now from what it was four centuries ago. At that time it shared with all Belgium the horrors of cruel war. To add to its misery, the forests that surrounded it were infested by robbers and lawless men of every description. Its poor inhabitants passed their days in laborious toil and constant fears. Their nights were often so many lonely hours of vigil. The cross never comes without accompanying grace. Sorrow is a gift of Heaven. So in their utter distress the afflicted villagers turned their eyes towards God. But, feeling their own unworthiness, they wished for a powerful intercessor. To whom should they turn if not to the Mother of the afflicted, to Mary the Refuge of sinners? They turned to Mary, and humbly besought her to pray to her divine Son for them. "Show forth thy power, O Mary," they cried; "bring us peace and consolation."

In order that they might be the more entitled to her guardianship, one of them placed a little statue in her honor upon the trunk of a wide-spreading oak which stood near the middle of the village. Henceforth Mary's power and goodness were felt in Montaigu. The great Queen of Heaven seemed to have set her throne of mercy upon the humble Flemish hill. Wonderful favors were bestowed upon all who prayed in the shadow of the oak. The blind came, and the light of heaven beamed before their eyes; the lame were carried thither, and they went away leaping for joy; hearts wounded with grief were healed after the recital of one Hail Mary: souls steeped in sin passed by and they repented of their crimes. At these wonders the inhabitants of Diest, Sichem, and all the neighboring towns flocked with enthusiasm around the miraculous image. Thus the pilgrimage was begun.

A SHEPHERD ATTEMPTS TO STEAL THE STATUE.

A simple shepherd who tended his master's flocks upon the wooded slopes around Montaigu resolved to take the wonderful image to his cabin and there to honor it it in private. With this intent he one day approached the oak, and, seizing the statue, quickly hid it in his bosom. Immediately the poor fellow lost the power of his limbs. To his horror, he found his feet fastened to the ground. The Immaculate Virgin, who had chosen the precise spot in which she should be honored, thus plainly showed her desires. Hour after hour passed slowly away, and still the unfortunate herdsman felt himself tied to the earth. As night was coming on, his master became uneasy about him, and determined to go in search of him. After much trouble, to his astonishment, he found the wretch at the foot of the old oak. The shepherd, with great simplicity, told his master all that had passed. They both replaced the statue on the tree, and went their way talking of the miracle which had happened.

THE STATUE MIRACULOUSLY SWEATS BLOOD.

Mary's life on earth was a sorrowful one. The long red sword of Simeon was never fully drawn from her heart. But now her sufferings are over. The Queen of Martyrs is now the Queen of Angels. If Mary could suffer, the sins that are daily committed would change in a moment all her joys to sorrow. A single mortal sin would again place her at the foot of the Cross. This is what she makes known to us by her tears at Lourdes, by her sweat of blood at Montaigu. It is the sad vision of sin, it is the awful chalice of the world's iniquity, which forces her to give miraculous signs of sorrow Oh! if we love Mary we must hate sin. But, to come to the fact. According to grave and learned authors, the statue, on one occasion, sweated large drops of blood. Five magistrates, all gentlemen worthy of faith, were present when the miracle occurred. They saw the blood with their own eyes, and touched it with their own hands. After a diligent examination of everything in the chapel, they remained fully convinced that a great miracle had been wrought in their presence. The next day they still found the drops of blood around the base of the statue. One of them, Walter Vuckelenus, gathered up the blood with a white piece of linen. This cloth was long preserved as a precious relic.

THE STATUE DISAPPEARS.

We must here frankly confess that, about the year 1580, the statue suddenly disappeared. How it vanished is altogether unknown. Many suspected a sacriligious robbery. The number of pilgrims, however, in no way diminished, as Mary still seemed to favor the chosen spot. Now, more than ever, the broad arms of the oak seemed to bend with the weight of blessings; its every leaf seemed to possess a supernatural power; its deep shadow fell like heavenly balm upon the sad and afflicted. A gentleman from Sichem, who had received some special graces from Our Lady of Montaigu replaced the lost statue by a new one.

In 1587, many Jesuits, at the request of the Duke of Parma, inaugurated camp-missions among the Spanish soldiers at that time stationed in Belgium. Father Thomas Sailly, S. J., was named director of these apostolic labors. This zealous missionary soon became one of the chief promoters of devotion to our Lady of Montaigu. He was, at the time of which we write, stationed at the garrison of Sichem. He loved to direct his steps, while reciting his office, towards the hill on which Mary was so lavish of her gifts. Each time he approached the venerable oak he felt his heart filled with ineffable joy. Not satisfied with visiting the shrine himself, he wished also that the soldiers should, from time to time, honor the Queen of Montaigu. He soon had the happiness to see many of them wending their way towards Mary's favorite spot. It not unfrequently happened that a poor soldier went there sick, and returned to the barrack in full vigor.

In 1602 Godefroi Van Thienwinkel, the good parish priest of Sichem, caused a little wooden chapel to be built at Montaigu. As this was not capacious enough to hold the pilgrims that flocked thither, it soon became necessary to built a larger one. This second church was consecrated in 1604, on the feast of the Holy Trinity, by Matthew Van Hove, Archbishop of Malines. The Virgin of Montaigu showed her signal love for Rev. Father Sailly by suddenly freeing him from a malady which the doctors had declared incurable. This took place in 1606. Father Sailly died on the 8th of March, 1623.

About three months after the consecration of the Church, it was endangered by the enemies of Belgium and of the Catholic religion. The Dutch heretics were furious against the Louvain Jesuits, who had been appointed by the Archbishop to hear confessions in the new sanctuary. The publication of indulgences on the Feast of the Assumption, August 15th, 1604, had especially stirred up their hatred. They sought, therefore, the means to extinguish the devotion to our sweet Lady of Montaigu. The plot was prepared for the 8th of September following, the day on which the Church celebrates the Feast of the Nativity of Mary. An immense crowd of pilgrims were to gather around the shrine on that day. This offered an excellent occasion for striking a bold and successful blow. The heretics were confident of success, as the Spanish regiments were just then engaged at Ostend, a considerable distance off. That same day the Provincial of the Belgian Jesuits, Very Rev. Bernard Oliverius, and the learned Father Cornelius a Lapide, with two other members of the Society, were present at Montaigu. The pious pilprims from an early hour attended at the sacred offices in the Church. In the midst of their devotions they were terrified to learn that a large body of Dutch horsemen from Brida and Berg-Op-Zoom had entered the village. Most of the poor people fled on all sides in dismay. The Jesuits, forgetful of their personal safety, thought only of saving the most sacred and precious objects of the sanctuary from the rapacious and sacrilegious hands of the enemy. Father Oliverius had the happiness of placing the miraculous image in security. Father a Lapide made a vow to Mary, and then seized the Blessed Sacrament. This good Father at once hid himself and his Divine Treasure among the bushes. The other two religious also saved different objects of value.

The soldiers, however, came to the threshold of the temple. Their fury was boundless when they found it deserted and despoiled of its treasures. One of them, Anthony Laenen, who was mounted upon a blind horse, rode into the sanctuary, and sneeringly cried : " If thou art she who givest sight to the blind, make my horse see."

These impious words had scarcely been pronounced, when the horse was indeed cured, but his wicked rider was struck blind. Even this miracle did not touch the enraged enemies of Catholicity. They smashed in pieces everything they had found in the sanctuary, and tried several times to set the Church on fire. Happily their efforts were vain, for Mary guarded carefully her own dear shrine. At length, tired of their fruitless labors, the soldiers rushed again upon the village, and having sacked it, set it on fire. They then departed with ferocious joy. They treated with great barbarity the few peasants they took with them. As they passed the wood they almost trampled upon the concealed a Lapide. But, thanks to our Saviour, this great and learned Father was not discovered by his merciless enemies. When all danger had passed away, the Jesuits hurried to replace Our Lord in His tabernacle. Our Sweet Lady, too, was placed upon her throne. Since then she has never failed to pour abundant graces, consolations and gifts of all kinds upon all the pious pilgrims who visit her favorite shrine of Montaigu.

It is well to remark here that the superb Church which we now admire at Montaigu was erected in 1609 by the pious Prince and Princess, Albert and Isabella. On account of the constant wars which troubled Belgium, this noble sanctuary was not dedicated before the month of June, 1627.

THE OLD OAK.

So great was the veneration for the venerable oak upon which the statue had been originally placed that visitors felt happy if they could take away with them one of its leaves or acorns. Many, however, desired to have something more, and the consequence was that entire branches had soon been cut off. There was even danger of the whole trunk's disappearance. In 1602, therefore, the whole tree was cut down by public authority, and divided into three parts. One of the parts was joyfully received by the Archduke Albert. The other two pieces were transferred to the Church of Sichem. Statues and crosses carved out of fragments of the oak were eagerly sought after in all parts of Europe. His Holiness, Pope Urban VIII., the Queen of Spain and France, the Archduke Leopold, and hundreds of other illustrious personages received some of them with veneration and gratitude from the virtuous Isabella. The ladies of the different Catholic Courts of Europe wore them on their necks. Most of the little crosses were encased in silver and gold, and ornamented with precious stones. Several miracles, according to Sanderus, were wrought in favor of those who honored Our Lady of Montaigu by wearing a cross from her chosen oak.

PILGRIMS AT MONTAIGU.

WE have it on excellent authority that over 20,000 pilgrims have sometimes assembled on the same day at Montaigu. Among these may be counted Cardinals, princes, distinguished warriors and men of letters. For the edification of our readers, we shall now speak of some of Montaigu's pilgrims.

THE IRISH SOLDIERS VISIT MONTAIGU.

The Irish soldiers on the continent of Europe were as pious as they were brave and generous. In France and Spain, in Austria and Belgium, they practised the virtues that they had learned in childhood in their dear old native isle. The O'Neills and O'Donnells, the McMahons and Maguires, remained faithful to the last to Ireland and their adopted countries, to God and the Virgin Mother.

Numan (Hist. des miracles de N. D. de Montaigu, 4 edit., 1613) tells us that an Irish Jesuit, Father Walter Talbot, Chaplain to Colonel William Stanley in 1598, with his fellow countrymen, frequently made pilgrimages to Montaigu. The sweet Queen of Montaigu always received the poor exiles kindly. She healed their wounds, consoled their hearts, and sent them away loaded with graces. Wherever they went the Irish soldiers spoke with enthusiasm of the admirable Lady of Montaigu. We may be sure that they often prayed to her for their "own loved Island of sorrow."

ALBERT AND ISABELLA.

Every year, for nine successive days, the illustrious Prince and Princess, Albert and Isabella, were accustomed to make a pilgrimage on foot from Diest to Montaigu. It was a touching sight to see these royal pilgrims accompanied with their whole court, march slowly and piously along the road leading to Mary's shrine. Pomp and pride and worldly respect were trampled under foot as the illustrious band approached Mantaigu. All hearts bowed freely and lovingly before the great Queen of Heaven. No sooner was the sanctuary entered than all souls melted away in a sweetness that was not of earth. Albert and Isabella, together with their suite, prostrated themselves before Mary, and offered her their most sincere and respectful homage. The sweet Lady of Montaigu was pleased with their devotion, and in return she poured upon them graces rich and abundant. Albert and Isabella were blessed in life and death by her. At this day the name and fame of these royal and pious souls are the joy and consolation of the Belgian people.

BLESSED JOHN BERCHMANS, S. J.

Blessed John Berchmans, a young Scholastic of the Society of Jesus, was a special servant of the Most

Blessed Virgin. At a very early hour she won all the affections of his pure heart. Her name was ever ready to flow from his lips, her sinless soul was a beautiful vision that never faded from his eye. Happy youth, generous youth, who trampling upon earthly love, rose up into close union with the Queen of Angels.

The shrine of Our Lady of Montaigu was very dear to young Berchmans. His consolation was great whenever he could make a pilgrimage to it. His home, in the little town of Diest, was about three miles from Mantaigu. I see from an old map that at this time woods lined the route on both sides. At present it is not thus. The road, however, is still well shaded by four fine rows of trees. Little John was accustomed to make his pilgrimage in silence and prayer. As I lately walked along this same route, I fancied that I beheld this dear child with his little rosary in his hands; I thought I saw his lips move fast; I saw the big tears of devotion roll down his glowing cheeks; I accompanied him in spirit to the House of Mary; I saw him fasten his tearful eyes upon the statue of his sweet Mother. The light of faith and innocence shone round about him: I heard him breathe out the secret throbbings of his heart; I gazed upon him until my own soul melted away within me. Oh! who can tell the sweetness of the hours passed by Blessed Berchmans in the sanctuary of Montaigu? Who can describe the holy intercourse of his pure soul with the Immaculate Virgin in her favorite dwelling place? If at Montaigu the poor sinner is raised so far from earth, if the hardest and most ungrateful hearts are there so softened and inflamed, what shall we say of the devotion, the ecstacy, of our saintly youth? According to several authors, it was there he consecrated himself irrevocably to the Blessed Virgin by a vow of chastity.

May Blessed Berchmans obtain for us all a great purity of soul and body, and a special devotion to our dear Lady of Montaigu.

THE STUDENTS OF THE LOUVAIN CATHOLIC UNIVERSITY.

About a month ago, at midnight, the university students commenced their march from Louvain for Montaigu. The night was calm and clear. A dead silence rested upon the old classic city by the Dyle. It was a time favorable to prayer and contemplation. All at once the silence was broken, and five hundred manly voices chanted forth the Litany of the Blessed Virgin. It was a grand thing to hear these five hundred young men, the pride and hope of a dozen countries, sing with enthusiasm of the Queen of all nations. Surely the age of devotion is not gone. The Church is ever young and beautiful. Her children in every age and clime give us rare examples of piety and faith. In the midst of the infidelity and indifference that surround us, have we not here a striking example of Christian fervor? For nearly five hours our pilgrims trod their pious way. They changed, from time to time, the order of their spiritual exercises. Now they poured out hymns in Mary's honor ; now, as they passed through the sleeping villages, they softly recited the rosary.

The morning light was reflected from the star-covered roof of Mary's Sanctuary when the pilgrims came in sight of it. Oh! that first glimpse of the old far-famed shrine! It thrills the heart through and through with delight. The students could not control their joyous emotions on seeing it, so they burst out into a song of triumph. Their swelling "Magnificat" filled the air far and near. It was a pleasant sound. The peasants, with heads uncovered, rested in the fields to hear it. The last of our generous youths had stood at the entrance of Montaigu's Sanctuary before the echoes of their voices died away upon the outer air. All received Holy Communion with great love and devotion.

All honor to the students of the Catholic University of Louvain.

It would be an injustice to the devotedness of the Jesuit Fathers if we did not add here that it is they who have organized this yearly pilgrimage of the University students. On the above-mentioned night the Rev. Father Castelein, S. J., the able Director of their Sodality, with two other pious and learned Jesuits, conducted the pilgrims to Montaigu.

MY VISIT TO MONTAIGU.

I shall never forget my first visit to Montaigu. As I entered the village I seemed to go into a new atmosphere. A feeling of wonderful calm came over me. I seemed to have left far behind me the din and strife of this world.

I entered the venerated Sanctuary while a Solemn High Mass was being sung. The vested priests looked grand. Sweet music from the choir filled the Church. Thousands of pilgrims piously knelt before the altar. If in the village streets I enjoyed such a calm, what was my peace when I prostrated myself before the statue of the fair Queen of Montaigu? You who have knelt at Lourdes or Loretto can tell; you who have felt the sweet influence of Mary's presence understand it. Beside me knelt an old soldier who had fought under Napoleon. I saw the medal on his breast, and his eyes were wet with tears. In the shadow of a pillar I noticed a few nuns. They had left the solitude of their holy cells to come and taste the peace and sweetness of Mary's home. I saw hands firmly clasped that shone with precious stones. I also saw hands that had been made brown by the summer sun. The rich and poor alike shared the bounty of the Mother of all. Everything in the sanctuary helped to inspire devotion. The trophies of Mary's power and goodness that hung against the walls, the sighs, the tears, the half-whispered prayers, told of hearts deeply touched by interior grace. The very faces of the pilgrims seemed to glow, so great was their devotion, I never before beheld a whole congregation so profoundly absorbed in prayer and contemplation. Mary is, indeed, the Queen of Montaigu. There she is felt by the sweetness of the place; there she is seen by the greatness of her works. Faith must be dead, and charity cold, in the soul that visits Montaigu without feeling deep religious emotions.

After Mass had been said, a young peasant, holding a large cross in his hands, came out of the Sacristy and placed himself in front of the main altar, over which is seen the miraculous statue. In a few minutes a large body of peasants stood beside him. They all knelt down together. Their venerable Curé gave them a benediction. After that they commenced a hymn in honor of the Most Blessed Virgin, and wound slowly out of the Church.

Three other bands of pilgrims went through the same ceremonies during my stay in the Church. God bless the Belgian people. May He aid them in their struggle for justice.

MIRACLES WROUGHT AT MONTAIGU.

The miracles that have been wrought at Montaigu are countless. All Belgium has witnessed them for upwards of four hundred years. The heaps of crutches and exvotes that crowd Mary's Sanctuary fully attest them. Let us hear what De Feller says in his *Dictionaire Historique:* Justus Lipsius was neither credulous nor enthusiastic. In a little work of his, written with as much candor as good sense, we find mention made of one hundred and thirty-seven miraculous cures which took place at Montaigu. These have been attested by the civil authorities of different places, examined by the wise and judicious Miraeus, Bishop of Antwerp, and approved by the grave and prudent Hovius, Archbishop of Malines. There are many of these miracles, the details of which cannot be read without producing full conviction as to their veracity. But, if of these one hundred and thirty-seven miraculous facts, only one is true, the incredulity of the impious is as much confounded as if all were true.

WORLD-MUSIC.

There lies sweet music in dead strings,
And melody in pine and reed,
Low songs are heard in streams and springs,
And harmonies in every mead.

The world is one vast Organ,—made
To yield all voices and rich notes;
Through air and sky, through lane and glade,
A wondrous song forever floats.

THE BEAUTY OF CHILDHOOD.

Childhood is the sinless garden
Where men walk before they fall;
Childhood is the blissful Eden
Where Man knows not passion's thrall.

Childhood is the flower-bound haven
We must leave to cross life's sea;
Childhood is the morning's glory
Shining o'er Man's misery.

Long I've sought for sinless faces,
And for hearts all free from care,
Yet I've found but wasted graces,
And black sorrow everywhere.

Let me gaze upon that child now,
Its pure robe is undefiled,
Not a stain upon its white brow,—
O! what bliss to be a child.

OCEAN WAVES.

Where did we meet, blue waves, blue waves?
  Out on the lone, wild seas?
On Chile's coast? By Thor Mor's caves?
  Or by the Hebrides?

When did we meet, blue waves, blue waves?
  When storms were raging high?
When gallant ships went down to graves
  To sleep where rich pearls lie?

White waves, white waves, I know we met
  'Neath heavens that did not smile;
The time, the place, ah! why forget—
  But welcome to our Isle.

You bring me back old memories
  Of loved and flowery lands;
You fill my soul with melodies
  Heard on far distant strands.

You've traveled far to meet me here,
  You come with many a wile
To give me joy, to give me cheer,
  Upon this fairy Isle.

Oh, welcome is your voice once more,
  You bring new life to me;
Thrice welcome to our cottaged shore—
  Glad children of the sea!

APOSTLES LOVE THE RACE OF MAN.

I.

Apostles love the race of man,
   Their land is where they work for God;
They view each spot from Pole to Pole,
   And love it as their native sod.

II.

They set no bounds to their wide prayer,
   Their hands are lifted high for all;
On friend and foe, on bond and free,
   They make God's saving graces fall.

III.

They seek no earthly wealth to gain,
   They work for that which never dies,
God's glory and Man's glory too—
   These are the only things they prize.

IV.

Pour down, O Lord, thy sacred fire
   Upon this frozen heart of mine;
Enlarge my heart, enlarge my love,
   'Till I embrace all hearts in Thine.

ON SEEING THE CAPITOL.

I.

O! Vision chaste, white Capitol,
   O! Freedom's Home, lift up thy head;
How beats my heart, how swells my soul,
   Beneath thy glorious dome to tread.

II.

Here Freedom lives and wears a crown,
   And Speech is free to plead for Right;
Here tyrants wear no boding frown,
   Here Justice has more force than might.

III.

Our land is free, thou art its heart,
   Thy blood is flowing through its veins,
Our land is free, we'll never part
   With thee, for gaudy courts and chains.

IV.

O! Vision chaste, loved Capitol,
   O! Freedom's Tower, lift up thy head;
How throbs my heart, how glows my soul,
   Beneath thy glorious dome to tread.

NO UNALLOYED HAPPINESS ON EARTH.

I.

You will not find on our banned earth
   A home of peace and rest,
A spot secure from sin and woe,
   An isle where all are blessed;
A land where sunshine ever falls,
   And shadows never lie,
A city filled with festal halls,
   Yet free from Sorrow's sigh.

II.

You will not find on our sad earth
   A way unwet by tears,
A garden where sweet roses blow,
   But ne'er a thorn appears;
A clime where bloom unfading flowers,
   Where death is all unknown,
A man that never felt lone hours
   Though master of a throne.

III.

The land we tread is not for us,
   We are but pilgrims here,
O'er moor and barren hills we'll roam
   Before our Homes appear;
Our feet must bleed on thorny ways,
   Our grief must pass in sighs,
Our brows must brown 'neath burning rays
   Before we reach the skies!

IV.

The Virgin—purest of her race—
  The gentlest Maid e'er seen,
Upon this hapless land of ours
  Was crowned "The Martyr Queen ;"
And Jesus—King and Lord of all—
  The Dearest, Greatest, Best—
Knew Herod's Court, and Pilate's Hall,
  And on a Cross bought rest.

TO A PRIEST.

I.

When Jesus' grace is flowing,
When Jesus' heart is glowing
Before thy ravished eyes,
    Oh then remember me.

II.

When on the altar lying
He hears thy heart's deep sighing
And makes sweet joys arise,
    Oh then remember me.

III.

When death is o'er me stealing,
And the abbey's bell's sad pealing
Tells that my spirit flies,
    Oh then remember me.

NO MORE WE'LL SAIL O'ER A TROUBLED SEA.

No more we'll sail o'er a troubled sea,
    No more we'll gaze on a frozen lake,
No more we'll tread o'er a scentless lea,
    No more we'll sigh by a songless brake.

Thou art now free from this land of sin,
    And free from it countless scars and ills;
Thy throne is built, far from earthly din,
    Amid the calm of eternal hills.

My home is lone, for I miss thy face,
    For I hear no more thy step or voice,
But, praised be God, and His strong, pure grace,
    The thought of thee makes my heart rejoice.

I see thee, friend, with a palm in hand,
    While the saints and stars around thee shine;
I watch thee walk through the blessed land,
    Till I wish thy blissful lot were mine.

We'll meet again on that heavenly shore,
    Which no sullied soul can touch or see;
We'll meet where angelic hosts adore
    Their Lord and God—the Holy Trinity.

THE OLD YEAR IS NOT DYING.

Toll ye the church-bell sad and slow,
And tread softly, and speak low,
For the Old Year lies a-dying.
                    LORD TENNYSON.

The Old Year is not dying,
        Sad dreamer,
His banners still are flying,
        False dreamer,
Though dark the night and chill,
He fills his bumper still,
And laughs with right good-will,
        Poor dreamer.

He scorns to hear thee crying,
        Thou dreamer,
"The Old Year lies a-dying,"
        Thou dreamer,—
No Hour has ever died,
No Day from Man can glide,
Old Years fore'er abide,
        Wild dreamer.

MOTHER'S BEADS.

Bright birds and butterflies I chase,
Or play with flowers and polished seeds,—
How sweet and mild is mother's face,
She tells for me her Blessed Beads.

We go and kneel beside a tomb,
Her eyes are wet, her sad heart bleeds;
My father's dead and in the gloom,
She tells for him her Blessed Beads.

My brother, Tom, was lost at sea,
He sleeps his sleep 'mid shells and weeds;
When thunders roar, and winds blow free,
She tells for Tom her Blessed Beads.

Our darling Joe, young, noble, brave,
Received red scars for noble deeds,
When mother sees bright banners wave,
She tells for Joe her Blessed Beads.

In every pain, in every grief
In all her hourly woes and needs,
A mother's heart can find relief
In counting o'er her Blessed Beads.

IF THOU WERT NOT MY LOVE, O! GOD.

I.

If Thou wert not my Love, O! God,
  How dark and sad my heart would be;
If Thou wert not my Hope, O! God,
  How could I bear earth's misery?

II.

A weary pilgrim I have been
  Since morning dawned upon my way,
A weary pilgrim I must be
  'Till night her star-gemmed flags display.

III.

A few kind friends to-day I met,
  I had to pass before their door;
They greeted me—they wept for me—
  But now they dream of me no more.

IV.

I fain would sit upon this rock,
  And take that rest so long denied;
But no, ah, no, I must move on
  'Till I have crossed Life's Desert wide.

V.

The sands are hot, the sands are red
  With blood that fired my heart and brain;
How can I stand the simoon's breath?
  My God, forgive, if I complain.

VI.

If Thou wert not my Light, O! God,
  How dark my brightest day would be,
If Thou wert not my Strength, O! God,
  How could I bear Life's misery?

THERE IS ALWAYS LIGHT IN HEAVEN.

I.

There is always light in Heaven—
  Not the light we see afar
When the West with gold is flowing,
  Nor the light of moon or star.

II.

Not the light the royal Poet
  Saw around his music thought,
Nor the light the favored Moses
  From the mountain summit brought.

III.

There is always light in Heaven,
  Light the Just alone can see
When the day of life is ended,
  And the soul from earth is free.

ST. MARY MAGDALEN.

I.

Now bind thy tear-wet hair,
    O mournful Magdalen!
And dry thy blue eyes fair,
    O sad-faced Magdalen!
Heed not Jerusalem's sneers—
Cleansed in thy love and tears
Is the red guilt of years—
    O favored Magdalen!

II.

Now to the desert fly,
    O thrice-blessed Magdalen!
And watch, and pray, and sigh,
    O holy Magdalen!
And sanctify thy days
With hymns of love and praise,
Stern Penance guard thy ways,
    O loving Magdalen!

III.

Thy course will soon be run,
    O lovely Magdalen!
Thy crown will soon be won,
    O fading Magdalen!
A bark by billows cast,
A flower in winter's blast,
This hour may be thy last
    O blissful Magdalen!

FAIR SPOUSE OF CHRIST.

(TO THE CHURCH.)

Fair Spouse of Christ, thy glory 'round me shed,
    Cast on my soul the poet's purest fire;
Give to my songs new life when I am dead,
    For I have loved thee and thy lyre.

I long to praise thy sons—the bard and saint,
    I long to sing sweet songs of my loved Queen,
But my weak soul, a wearied bird, grows faint
    Ere heaven's beauty it hath reached or seen.

I long to tell the world how deep and strong
    My love for thee is—Bride of Life and Truth;
I long to sing for thee one burning song
    Ere pass away the loving days of youth.

Chaste Spouse of Christ, all beautiful and fair,
    My soul is kindled with bright thoughts of thee;
For thee I'll sing, for thee shall rise my prayer,—
    My only One, forever dear to me.

TO THE QUEEN OF MAY.

Oh, sweetly swell celestial lyres
   Upon each Christmas Day,
But sweeter, richer, softer sounds
   Thy voice, fair Queen of May;
Oh, may we hear thy voice so sweet
When God, our Judge, we rise to meet.

Oh brightly waves the censers pure,
   When heavenly spirits pray,
But brighter still when for us pleads
   Thy voice, sweet Queen of May;
Oh, may we hear thy voice so sweet,
When God, our Judge, we rise to meet.

A martyr's love is dear to God,
   And dear a hermit's lay,
But dearer far than either is
   Thy voice, mild Queen of May;
Oh, may we hear thy voice so sweet,
When God, our Judge, we rise to meet.

Then, Virgin dear, e'er be our guard,
   Our love, our hope, our stay,
And grant, oh grant, at death we'll hear
   Thy voice, kind Queen of May;
Oh, may we hear thy voice so sweet,
When God, our Judge, we rise to meet.

DARK OF EYE, AND DARK OF SKIN.

Dark of eye, and dark of skin,—
   But her soul was glowing;
Her pure heart was free from sin,
   All her beauty was within,
Graces 'round her path were flowing.

Faith and Love—her richest store;
   Fairest angels glowing;
Entered through her cabin door,
   Knelt upon her earthen floor,
Watched her soul in beauty growing.

All despised the dark-skinned maid,—
   Yet her soul was glowing;
'Neath that veil of darkest shade
   They knew not a heart was laid
Fairer than the rose-tree blowing.

A PEOPLE'S PRAYER.

What future ours? Ah, none can say;
　The Nations fall, as leaves now fade,
The hills themselves must melt away,
　Stern death is never long delayed;
But God is kind, and Him we trust,
　To Him we send a People's prayer;--
Oh, Source of Love, oh, King Most Just,
　We place our land beneath Thy care;
Save her from shame, and crime, and wrong,
　Give her the light to do Thy will,
Her days of greatness, oh, prolong,
　And guide her steps up Virtue's hill.
On all the land look down, dread God,
　On all our deeds, oh, kindly gaze,
Ah, rule us with a Father's rod,
　And, oh, forgive our erring ways.
By black Missouri's hasty wave,
　By shelled Patuxent's friendly side,
In home and school, in field and cave,
　May Thy rich blessing e'er abide.
Oh keep our swords fore'er at rest,
　And make our ploughs like sabres shine,
Bless North, and South, and East, and West,
　Oh bless them with a love divine.

FAITH, HOPE, AND LOVE.

I.

Yes, take my harp and break its strings,
    Destroy for aye its tuneful voice,
Take from me all that nature brings
    To make my lonely heart rejoice.

II.

Hush songs of birds, hush songs of streams!
    In darkness hide each green-boughed tree;
Stay, stay the summer's cheering beams,
    Let all earth's beauties fly from me.

III.

But leave me Faith, and Hope, and Love—
    Three lamps to light my awful gloom—
But let me cling to God above—
    Then welcome be the martyr's doom.

MY SOUL IS LIKE YON GLOWING FIRE.

My soul is like yon glowing fire,
Burning with a fond desire,
    To ascend on high.

My life is like yon taper bright,
Wasting fast its measured light,
    Soon, oh, bliss, to die.

My steps are like the dew at morn,
Passing from the rose and thorn,
    Passing from earth's joys and woes.

My heart is like the tiny bark
That flies the waves, when they grow dark,
    And seeks in port a sweet repose.

LINES TO SISTER ANGELINE.

(*A Sister of Charity.*)

I.

Only the Spirit of Wisdom,
   Only the Spirit of Love,
Only the Spirit of Jesus,
   Only the Heart of the Dove,
Could teach thee to fly from earth's pleasures
   And sigh for the Far, and Unseen,
To toil for the sick and the lowly,
   To toil for the poor,—Angeline.

II.

Only the Solace of Virgins,
   Only the Spirit of Love,
Only the Spirit of sweetness,
   Only the Voice of the Dove,
Could breathe in thy soul the sweet warning
   To follow the Virgin's pure Queen,
To think of the Lamb and His Beauty,
   To long for His Face,—Angeline.

III.

Only the Spirit of Courage,
   Only the Spirit of Love,
Only the Spirit of Goodness,
   Only the Heart of the Dove,
Could give thee the bliss and the sweetness,
   The changeless and holy serene,
That light up thy soul with pure sunshine,
   That brighten thy heart,—Angeline.

A HYMN TO THE QUEEN OF MAY.

Had I the mind of the poet king,
   And the voice of St. Dunstan's lyre,*
I could not write—I could not sing,
   As my heart and my soul desire;
No human power can frame the sound,
   No earthly choir can chime the lay
Worthy of thee - forever crowned—
   Our loved and loving Queen of May.

The hermit in his rocky cell,
   The virgin from her still retreat,
The woodman in his piny dell—
   Ay, thousands in the noisy street:
The poor and rich, the wise and great,
   Where'er our Pontiff holds his sway,
To thee their hearts now elevate,
   O loved and loving Queen of May.

Within the winding catacomb,
   When burning Christians lit the night,†
What song was heard 'neath Pagan Rome,
   So pure, so pleasing in God's sight?
What song rolls down St. Peter's aisles?
   What music does its organ play?
What song can win dear Jesus' smiles?
   Thy hymn, O loving Queen of May!

Let maidens bring thee wreaths of snow,
   Let youthful bards sing sweet of thee,
Let all Life's veterans to thee go,
   And bend their hearts when bends their knee,
But, like St. John, O! let me love
   Thee as my Mother and my stay;
And grant, O grant, I'll see above,
   My loved, my loving Queen of May!

---

* An angel played one day on the harp of St. Dunstan.
† Nero caused many of the early Christians to be braced in tunics steeped in pitch, and then placed at certain distances, then set on fire to light the streets at night.

SACRED IS THE GLORIOUS BANNER.

Sacred is the glorious banner
   Reddened with a patriot's gore ;
Blessed is the noble banner
   That a Christian soldier bore.
Though its folds are torn and gory,
Bards will sing its deathless glory,
Chiefs will tell its thrilling story,
And if e'er it be unfurled,
Brave hearts will shield it 'gainst the world;
Tyrants well may crouch and fear
When that banner's folds appear ;
Trampled slaves may freely rise
When it meets their timid eyes ;
Maids will kiss it in their dreaming,
Priests will bless it proudly streaming,
Swords will guard it brightly gleaming ;
Men will hang it in some temple
   Where nuns pass their lives in prayer ;
Maids will place around it burning
   Lamps of gold and tapers fair ;
And the shadows nightly falling,
   When the Sisters chant their hymns,
Ne'er will touch its folds of glory,
   Ne'er will make its brightness dim.

THE BELL IS THE VOICE OF GOD.

Golden dreams through my mind are gliding,
  Bright scenes of home before me roll,
Child on my father's knee I'm riding—
  When lo, on my ear the toll, toll, toll;
From the matin bell rings to my soul—
  I am the Voice of God.

Up from my couch, while quickly leaping,
  I raise my soul to God on high,
Soon from books I am gaily reaping,
  The golden crops that in them lie ;
And the noon-day bell whispers right well—
  I am the Voice of God.

The sable clouds of night are falling,
  Their shades upon my thoughts are now,
My actions of the day recalling,
  I kneel to pray with sober brow ;
Then the vesper bell chimes out so well—
  I am the Voice of God.

Thus my life I am calmly spending,
  Within St. Mary's peaceful walls,
To pray'rs and games, to studies tending,
  As each of them to my lot falls ;
And I hear the swell of the college bell—
  As if the Voice of God.

ON DUST, ON CLAY, WE DAILY TREAD.

On dust, on clay, we daily tread,
   Yet in the dust what treasures lie,—
There sleep the bravest, noblest dead;
   There sleep the saints of yonder sky.

The young will come, the old will go,
   And all must tread o'er dust and clay,
And most must sleep in dust 'till blow
   The trumpets of the Judgment Day.

The virgin, fair as early morn,
   The hero, that for justice bleeds,
The Prince, to crowns and kingdoms born,
   Must sleep in dust like trampled weeds.

On dust, on clay, we daily tread,
   Yet in the dust we all shall lie;
The dust shall be our humble bed,
   E'en while our souls are crowned on high.

The young will come, the old will go,
   And all must tread o'er dust and clay—
And most must sleep in dust 'till blow
   The trumpets of the Judgment Day.

A VOICE IN THE SOUL.

On the silence of my soul
Falls a voice like falling snow:—
"Keep thy passions in control,—
Sin is mother of earth's woe ;
Earth and earthly things despise—
Be thy goal Fair Paradise."

Day and night I hear this Voice,
Through my soul it gently flows,
In its music I rejoice,—
How it cheers me in my woes!
Spirit, Lover, to mine ear
Thy soft Voice is sweet and clear.

LINES ON THE DEATH OF AN IRISH MAIDEN IN EXILE.

I.

She came from a green vale in Erin,
　With sunshine in heart and in eye ;
Oh, little they thought when they blest her,
Oh, little they thought when they prest her,
　She left them to pine and to die.

II

The brightest of maidens in Erin,
　Her laugh was more gay than a song ;
Oh, little they thought when she started,
Oh, little they dreamed when she parted,
　Her heart would be broken ere long.

III.

The bravest of maidens in sorrow,
　Her soul was all lovely with grace ;
Oh, well did they know from her childhood
That Mary, "the flower" of the wildwood,
　Would ever prove true to her race.

MY LAST HYMN.

I.

Lord, let me see Thy Lovely Face,
And let me fly to Thee;
O! Source of Life! O! Light, O! Grace,
Look kindly now on me.

II.

Through weary ways I've sought Thy Will,
Though weak and frail was I;
But let me praise Thee, love Thee still,
Then gladly will I die.

III.

My sins are countless as the waves
That yonder rise and fall,
But they are buried in deep graves—
I've wept above them all.

IV.

Sweet Jesus of the Sacred Heart,
My God, my Lord, my King,
From Thy fair Throne I'll never part,
To Thee I'll ever cling.

V.

Ye Angels, strike your sweetest lyres!
Ye Virgins, chant your songs!
Ye holy Saints, light incense-fires!
Rich music, float along!

VI.

A pilgrim from a far-off shore,
A brother seeking rest,
Now comes to dwell forever more
Upon his Saviour's breast.

ROME, THE MOTHER OF ALL CHURCHES.

TO PROTESTANT ENGLAND.

I.

Come back to me, my Fallen child,
Thou art the fruit of Heavenly Love;
I grieve to see thee thus defiled:
Come back, come back, my Fallen dove.

II.

A mother's heart in me thou'lt find,
I'll think not of thy sinful days;
My Daughter, come,—speak not unkind
To her who weeps thy dark, sad ways.

III.

The holy font is near at hand,
I've laved in tears a robe for thee;
Thou art a dear though fallen land:
Come back, come back, my child to me.

MY SECRETS.

Thou hast not read half my secrets yet,
A garden sealed is my inmost soul,
Thou seest the foam on the high, loud waves,
But not the depths of the great sea's roll.

Thou seest the rays on the rolling tide,
They come from above and not below,
My thoughts from thee and the world I hide—
The light of Outside I freely show.

Read not from my smiles, nor from my tears,
The hermit thoughts that I love to keep,
The birds that start from the stormy main
Tell naught of the Ocean's secret deep.

The waves roll back from the sandy shore
And leave to our view its pearls and shells,
But no waves will roll from my soul and show
The Secret Thought that within me dwells.

Ofttimes a wreck on the sea is found
That tells a tale of mad Ocean's strife,
But naught you'll find on the tide of time
To tell a tale of my inner life.

'Round rocks and caves the sad sea is heard
Murmuring, at dead of night, its wrongs,
But none shall hear from my long-locked lips
The thoughts that flow through my soul's low songs.

My secret thoughts, to my God all known,
I love to keep from a world too cold,
No man shall delve in my secret mine—
The thoughts I hold are more pure than gold.

I'll keep them all as the miser keeps
The shining ore he has worked to win,
I'll keep them all, and no man will know
From my outward deeds, my thoughts within.

I must not reveal the sweet, sweet thoughts
That I feast on oft when I'm alone,
I must not reveal the glorious thoughts
That I have crowned on my hearts high throne.

HOPE ON.

The night is dark,
And thy frail bark
Was never made for sailing
Across a sea
Where winds blow free,
And frighted birds are wailing;
But, O! fear not,
God's brightest smile
Will light thee upon thy way;
Thy bark will reach a Blessed Isle
By the break of the Coming Day.

TO A BEACH BIRD.

Pour out thy song, thou, little bird,
    And dread not storm or sea,
Thou hast a native right to join
    Earth's choir of melody.

If I could chant thy thrilling lay,
    How often would I sing ;
I'd make the valleys, and the woods,
    With my sweet music ring.

I'd sing beside the bed of pain,
    In palace and in cot,
I'd sing beside the prison-gate,
    And soothe the prisoner's lot.

I'd sing upon the city's walls,
    And o'er its dusty ways,
My harp would yield for evermore
    A hymn of love and praise.

But I am neither bird, nor bard,
    No font of song is mine,
I listen to thy witching song,
    And hoard its notes divine.

MY GOD, I'M TIRED OF WORLDLY THOUGHTS.

I.

My God, I'm tired of worldly thoughts,
   I long to think of Thee,
I long to think of all Thou art,
   Of all Thou art to me.
Thou art my Source of life and light,
   My Brother and my Friend,
Thou art my Lord, my God, my all,
   My Joy, my Hope, my End.

II.

When shadows fall upon my path,
   And tears bedew my eyes,
Thou flingest stars from Thy right hand
   To light and cheer my skies :
When man forsakes my bed of pain,
   And leaves me pine alone,
I feel Thy aid, I hear Thy voice,
   I see Thy blessed throne.

III.

Dear Master of my heart and soul,
   Now give me thoughts divine,
And make my mind hence forward be
   Thy pure and sacred shrine ;
Oh, lift me from this world of sin,
   Oh, lift me to the sky ;
Oh, bid me scorn the things of earth,
   For Thee, oh, let me die.

THE BIRD AT STEINBERG CHAPEL.

Old Steinberg's lonely chapel stood
Beside a lake, half in a wood;
Swans daily swam the lake's smooth blue,
And round the wood fair flowerets grew,
The tall pines seldom moved or stirred,
But songs of birds were often heard
By pilgrim-students who drew near
The chapel, filled with love and fear;
But ah, how sad to think, alas!
No choir was there to chant at Mass;
The holy priest did all he could
To teach the children of the wood
Some simple hymns and melodies,
Some songs to move, if not to please;
But all in vain, they could not learn
His simplest tunes to fitly turn;
One morn, at Mass, the people heard
The clear, sweet singing of a bird—
Not on the trees in open air,
But in God's House, God's House of Prayer;
Not 'mong the pines of the dark wood,
But in the shrine the songster stood;
All through the Mass the sweet bird poured
His songs of praise, while all adored
The Tender God, the Gracious King,
Who taught the wild birds how to sing;
And after Mass the peasants spoke
Of the sweet thoughts the bird awoke
Within each mind, within each heart,
When into music he did start;
And some there were who said, and thought,
The bird from Heaven his music brought;

Now, all the Sunday service o'er,
The sexton locked and barred the door;
But, sad to think, he did forget
The bird was in the chapel yet;
The bird was there, and there alone—
One worshiper before God's Throne;
All day and night the little thing
Sang songs of praise before his King.
A week has past; the bells are rung,
And back the chapel-gate is swung;
Through all the woods the peasants pass—
They come once more to Holy Mass;
They speak in love of that sweet bird
Who all their noblest feelings stirred;
They wonder if he'll come to-day
To sing again his wondrous lay;
They wonder if he'll come and sing
Before their Sacramental King;
But, ah! their grief when they behold
The lovely songster dead and cold;
Upon the altar's linen white
His little body met their sight;
He died, not on the seats or floor,
But by the Tabernacle door;
Tears dimmed each hardy woodman's eyes,
And maidens filled the church with sighs,
And children wept more bitter tears
Than children weep in tender years;
The gentle priest interred the bird,
And all the trees with music stirred,
For all the birds in Steinberg's grove
Sang o'er their dead a song of love;
For every bird and every pine
Sang o'er the Bard of Steinberg's Shrine.

WEARY PILGRIMS.

All earth's pathways lead to Heaven,
  O! youthful pilgrims journey on;
The ways you tread lead up to Sion,
  O! happy pilgrims travel on.

The gleaming gates now stand before you,
The shining streets now lie before you,
The golden City glows before you,
  O! weary pilgrims travel on.

Pause not, nor look behind,
    But journey on;
Sweet rest you soon will find,
    So journey on;
The longest road at last will end,—
E'en now fair angels on you tend,
    So journey on.

So journey on, O! pilgrim band,
You soon will reach God's Blessed Land,
Before God's Throne you soon will stand;—
Seek not the roses on your way,
Earth's beauties soon must fade, decay,
    So travel on.

Through brake and wood,
And solitude,
    O! journey on;
O'er hill and plain,
In joy and pain,
    Still travel on;
With hope-lit eyes,
'Neath darkened skies,
    O! travel on.

Hear! hear! those songs of joy and love,—
They are but echoes from above;
    Hasten, pilgrims, on.

'GAINST WINDS AND TIDES.

'Gainst winds and tides my bark I'll steer,
Gold beacon-lights must soon appear,
The breath of flowers now fills the air—
'Neath yonder clouds lie gardens fair,
The storm is loud, and fierce, and strong,
Yet still I hear the beach-bird's song;
A land-breeze whispers to my sails,
I feel the peace of peaceful vales.
The waves that round me rise and roar
Now rush to kiss my native shore.
Speed on, brave bark, the lights appear,
The sea grows still, the port comes near;
O! God, my God, now clasp Thy son,
His sea is sailed, his race is won,
O! God, my God, I've longed for Thee,
And could not rest on land or sea ;
Away from Thee no heart can sleep,
Away from Thee all eyes must weep,
Sad bells of sorrow in us toll,
Wide seas of grief around us roll,
Sharp thorns are springing on our way,
Dark clouds are floating o'er our day,
The stars that come at night to glow
Reveal our deepest floods of woe ;
The morn oft brings us new-born pains,
And friends oft forge our hardest chains ;
Our hearts, sweet Lord, must seek in Thee,
Their peace, their bliss, their liberty.

THE DYING CHILD TO HIS MOTHER.

Mother, place me in the garden
  Where my little sisters sleep;
Place me 'mong the marble crosses
  Where the kneeling people weep;
Place me where the lonely cypress
  Waves, at eve, its dark green head;
Place me where the timid willows
  Tremble o'er each flower-decked bed.

Shadows fall on lake and river;
  All the woods are void of glee;
Winter comes with clouds and tempests—
  Summer ne'er will come for me;
I am tired of ever straying
  Through this cold and cheerless land;
I am tired of nightly roaming
  Up and down life's dreary strand.

Mother, place me in the starlight
  Flowing through the broken tower;
Place me where the bells of silver
  Daily ring the vesper hour;
Place me where my friends and kindred
  Oft will come to weep and pray;
Place me where my sainted fathers
  Calmly wait the Judgment Day.

Brightly now the moon is shining
  On the hill, and plain, and town ;
Heaven's golden gates now open—
  Lo ! an angel with a crown ;
He is coming like the morning,
  With a radiant face and mild ;
Now a sweetness fills my chamber
  As from florets fresh and wild !

Welcome angel, welcome guardian,
  Stay a little while with me ;
Tell me of God's lovely mansions—
  What fair land is this I see?
Mother, mother, I am going—
  Life, for me, is at its close ;
Bear me to the Blessed Garden,
  'Neath the Cross let me repose.

POETIC INSPIRATION.

I cannot hear the red-breast's lay
But I am moved to seek my lyre,
I cannot see a daisied way
But comes again the same desire.

Oft in the city's living tide
I see some faded, wasted flower,—
I hasten on, or turn aside,
To strike my harp for one sad hour.

I hear a tale of woe and pain,
Or learn some tidings sweet to me,
I seize the lyre, I must again
Pour out my soul in melody.

TO THE REV. ABRAM J. RYAN.

Loved Priest, loved Bard, how like my native Isle,
   My heart hath found those sweet sad songs of thine;
Bright beaming through their mist of tears—the smile
   Of Holy Faith is seen, a peace-lit, rainbow sign.

Like pure and holy wells, to light their spring
   From sacred cells, deep, deep, within thy breast;
To darken hearts bright cups of joy they bring,
   To wearied souls they waft the balm of rest.

The star of hope sleeps on their floods of woe,
   And on their waves forever floats a prayer;
The Cross is shining in their depths below,
   And o'er them glows the arch of heavens fair.

Along their shores is heard the surge of war,
   A nation's soul is in their sorrowed tone,
A people's wail they carry near and far;
   "The field is lost, tho' with our dead 'tis strewn."

"The field is lost!" Oh, no, not lost! Not lost,
   Since one great master-hand was found to thrill
The earth with pity for the blood it cost,
   And love for generous hearts forever still.

"The Conquered Banner" shall forever wave
   In pride above the dark, green towers of time,
And bright shall gleam the stainless Southern glave,
   Now glorified in deathless songs sublime.

The lost, lost cause in noble song is won,
   Its dead still live, led on by Robert Lee,
As long as mountains stand, or rivers run,
   Thy songs will give the shout of "Victory!"

TO AMERICA.

All hail! thou bride of Liberty!
   No fetters now thy fair limbs own;
Thou sittest by the lake and sea,
   With toilers standing round thy throne
No thirsting swords around thee gleam,
   No guns look forth to guard thy sway;
Thou rulest o'er the field and stream,
   Without an army's red array;
In every home thy soldiers dwell,
   Calm-seated by their peaceful fires;
But let thy trumpet blasts once swell,
   And they will rise as rose their sires!
What empire thine, oh, youthful Queen—
   Proud, noble hearts, and hills of gold;
Bays, where ten thousand ships are seen,
   And virgin fields of wealth untold.
Kind Nature toiled to make thee grand:
   Brave men have bled to make thee *One*.
Oh, sun-lit land! oh, glorious land,
   The glad earth cries to thee, "Well done!"
By Hudson's wave, Elias' crest,
   Thou rulest over laboring kings;
In North and South, in East and West,
   The anvil's heard, the toiler sings;
Thy cities grow by sea and lake,
   Like rushing willows by a stream;
New homes arise in mead and brake;
   Thy woods with stout-built hewers teem;
O'er all the seas tired pilgrims come;
   They saw thy star—its light they seek;

They come to build in thee a home,
   On some far plain or lonely peak ;
Oh, welcome them—brave, sterling men—
   They've fled from tyrant laws and chains ;
Give them the peace of wood and glen ;
   Give them the freedom of thy plains ;
Their toil will turn thy clay to gold ;
   Their brain will think and plan with thee ;
Their hands will keep thy flag unrolled ;
   Th ir strength will ever keep thee free ;
America, forever wield
   Thy power for good and not for ill ;
True Science and Religion shield
   From dark Oppression's hand and will ;
On Truth and Justice, Heaven smiles,
   And loves the land to both allied ;
God is the foe of all man's wiles,
   The enemy of pomp and pride ;
Oh, land of lakes and boundless fields ;
   Oh, last retreat of Freedom now,
To thee a freeman homage yields ;
   Before thy face he bends his brow ;
"Land of the free," "home of the brave,"
   May recreants never touch thy shore ;
May thy starred banner proudly wave,
   O'er States United evermore ;
The hour is past that saw thee weak,
   A child among the nations great ;
A babe without a voice to speak,
   A slave enchained by force and fate ;
No Nation now more free than thou ;
   Thy ships are ploughing every sea,
Honor and glory crown thy brow ;
   All hail ! fair Bride of Liberty !

LOVE OF IRELAND.

Can it be wrong to love the Land
Our brave sires died to free?
Can it be wrong to prize the shore
That saints have yearned to see?
   No, Oh, no!
 The saints in heaven cry,—"No!"

Can it be wrong to love the fields
Where sainted men are laid?
Can it be wrong to hail with joy
The fairest Isle God made?
   No, Oh, no!
 The saints in heaven cry,—"No!"

IRISH BARDS.

Where have they found their melodies?—
Those melodies that melt the soul—
Deep in lone woods, or by sad seas,
Or on broad meads where deep floods roll?

Where have they caught the wondrous strains
That wet with tears the long-dried eyes?—
On Winter hills, on misty plains,
Or in the clouded, mournful skies?

Oh, tell me, Davis? Moore say where
You found the music of your lyres?
Speak, speak, Mac Carthy, and De Vere—
What Muse your noble Song inspires?

Does Music haunt old Erin's cells,
Where long ago her hermits prayed?
Are there kind angels in her dells,
Who teach how sweetest songs are made?

A HOME RULE SONG.

Now let us claim our ancient right,
The tyrant band must fall, or yield;
Our foes divided—ours is might
To force them from the battle-field.
    Hurra! Hurra!
  For Ireland's Parliament! Hurra!

Too long divided we have been,
Now One in aim and heart we stand;
Spread out our Banner's folds of green,
And give one cheer for Fatherland!
    Hurra! Hurra!
  For Ireland's Parliament! Hurra!

We claim a right to make our laws,
We now demand our Parliament,
We trust in God, and our good cause,—
The time we wait is time misspent.
    Hurra! Hurra!
  For Ireland's Parliament! Hurra!

THIS IS MY NATIVE LAND.

Land of the lovely shrines!
Fount of the sacred wells!
Ward of the mystic towers!
Church of the blessed bells!—
      This is my Native Land!

Child of the greenest waves!
Harp of the sweetest lays!
Lamp of the deathless flame!
Star of the brightest rays!—
      This is my Native Land!

Isle of the richest vales!
Nurse of the fairest flowers!
Love of the bravest men!
Bride of the brightest hours! –
      This is my Native Land!

Home of the chastest maids!
Love of Redemption's Sign!
Nun of the sainted fame!
Casket of jewels divine!—
      This is my Native Land!

SWEET LYRE, ADIEU.

Sweet lyre, adieu, adieu forever!
I lay thee by the lone, green sea,
Its troubled heart shall never, never,
Grow weary of thy melody.

Its winds and waves shall touch thy strings,
And saddest harmonies awake,
Its storms shall sweep thy music-springs,
While ships go down, and brave hearts break.

Sweet lyre, adieu, adieu forever!
The World cares not for songs from me,
I'll sing no more; but Earth shall never
Be left without sweet sounds from thee!

THE END

www.ingramcontent.com/pod-product-compliance
Lightning Source LLC
Chambersburg PA
CBHW021623250426
43672CB00037B/367